I AM GOD
AND SO ARE YOU

I Am God and So Are You-Discovering the Power of Your True Self is a story about looking for something. It is about a search powered by the certainty that when that something is found, there will be no doubt. It is the story of the universe in search of itself – a search for meaning and for answers.

So tell me who I am, tell me where I come from, and why have I come here? Where will I go when it comes time for me to leave? And, most of all, please tell me why I ask these questions. Because I ask them, the answers must make a difference in my life, and if they make a difference in my life, they make a difference in everyone's life.

I Am God and So Are You brings you on the journey of self-discovery that answered these questions for me over the course of a forty-year inquiry into the nature of humanity's true self. This book presents a straightforward path to the experience of the inner peace that is your true self and that lives within you and is available to you now. Experiencing this peace generates an energy that extends into space and connects you with everyone in the world. Indeed, we are more than connected; we are One, sharing together this experience we call life on earth.

The experience of inner peace is a wealth-producing experience meaning that inner peace increases your personal experience of well-being in all areas of your life. *I Am God and So Are You* shows you how you can experience your life in any way you choose.

PRAISE FOR

I AM GOD
AND SO ARE YOU

DISCOVERING THE POWER OF YOUR TRUE SELF

"*I Am God and So Are You* helps reconcile the ancient conflict between organized religion and spiritual reality."

- THE REVEREND TIM VIVIAN, PhD, VICAR,
GRACE EPISCOPAL CHURCH, BAKERSFIELD, CALIFORNIA
ASSOCIATE PROFESSOR OF RELIGIOUS STUDIES, AUTHOR OF 14 BOOKS
CO-DIRECTOR, INSTITUTE FOR RELIGION, EDUCATION, & PUBLIC POLICY (IREPP)

• • •

"*I Am God and So Are You* is a compelling story and philosophy. Upon integration of James Wilhelm's flawless logic into my daily life, I have enjoyed fulfillment, tranquility, and meaningful relationships."

- MAUREEN M. O'ROURKE, MD

• • •

"James Wilhelm's personal journey can guide you to the awareness that you are a spiritual being having a human experience and you can live as large as you dare to dream."

- MARIE L. YORK, LIFE COACH & ARTIST

• • •

"The first words that came to my mind after reading *I Am God And so Are You* were: 'Mind blowing! Life changing!' Jim's life journey of scientific and spiritual research offers a simple to follow plan that transformed my thinking and my life."

- EILEEN ENNIS, LEGAL ASSISTANT

"I Am God And so Are You is riveting, amazing, and inspiring. I like the author's amazing encounter with his teacher who patiently guided him in his path and his amazing experiments witnessed by others. This book is the author's transformational story from a young age of 13 to right now. Read this book and you will experience powerful life transformation."

- ALMA APOSTAL, MOTIVATIONAL SPEAKER

● ● ●

Every word in this book resonated with my heart. I read it over the weekend because I could not put it down. That was two weeks ago and already I am experiencing a new level of peace and confidence, my bonds with family and friends are strengthening, and new business opportunities have presented themselves.

- ALETHEA GROSSMAN, MARKETING CONSULTANT

I AM GOD
AND SO ARE YOU

DISCOVERING THE POWER
OF YOUR TRUE SELF
. . .
JAMES C. WILHELM

I AM GOD AND SO ARE YOU: DISCOVERING THE POWER
OF YOUR TRUE SELF
By James C. Wilhelm

Published by Clear Purpose Press, Inc, Boynton Beach, FL

Hardcover ISBN 978-0-9857545-0-1
Perfectbound ISBN 978-0-9857545-1-8
eBook ISBN 978-0-9857545-2-5

Library of Congress Control Number: 2012942686

DEDICATION

With love and appreciation to my parents, James Wilhelm and Agnes Wilhelm, my loving wife, Patti, my children, and siblings.

Special thanks and gratitude to those who assisted with review and critique including Maureen O'Rourke, Marie York, Dennis Connell, Carl Foster, Richard Craig and all of you who have supported me through the years.

With loving memory to my friend, John Gradoni who inspired the title and transitioned to infinity on November 5, 1975.

CONTENTS

INTRODUCTION

I had a long conversation recently with one of my old friends. This conversation was completely different from most of the other conversations we have had during the past seventeen years. Generally, when we talk, he tells me how amazing his life is. My friend enjoys a wonderful relationship with his wife and two children, has a job he loves, makes a lot of money and lives in a big, expensive home. When he initiated this most recent conversation with me, however, he had just returned from a vacation in South America, during which he had no phone service, no Internet access, and also spent a lot of time with people living in severe poverty. This gave him plenty of time to evaluate his life, which resulted in his sudden realization that all the things he had always valued might not be the most important things in life.

He especially questioned his job and his large home, stating that what he did for a living was exciting and challenging but ultimately meaningless, and his home had so many rooms that his family seldom entered most of them. He was in a state of general malaise, looking to me to help him find a way out. He had always viewed himself as a happy and fulfilled person; now, he wasn't so sure. This is something I have heard many times from many different people.

We may have different definitions of success, but most of us agree that we want to be happy. It is in this search for happiness that many of us lose our way. We may concur that happiness is the result of having a satisfying job, a certain amount of money, a comfortable home, and a healthy family. Each of these is important, but once we acquire that satisfying, high-paying job, many of us discover that the job is not so satisfying and the pay is not that high. We may grow tired of that beautiful home or our fine automobile. If any of these things happens, we may suddenly find ourselves less happy. So maybe there is something else to this happiness thing.

What is truly valuable? All that is alive wants to continue living. Even insects try to evade death by avoiding threatening situations and struggling against predators. We all choose to feel secure, comfortable, and at peace, even if we never verbalize these choices in this way. We may experience temporary happiness, but to know genuine and lasting happiness, we must be at peace with ourselves and our world. While happiness may require us to be situated in certain circumstances, lasting peace requires no specific conditions for its realization. Peace is available to each of us right now, regardless of our circumstances. Best of all, the universe itself has provided us all with a simple way to experience lasting inner peace right now. I call this pathway self-understanding. That is what this book is about.

Introduction

Self-understanding is about knowing who you really are. Self-understanding connects you with your true identity, your highest self; it makes available to you the power to create your life in any way you choose. *I Am God and So Are You – Discovering the Power of Your True Self* illuminates the process of self-understanding and explains in simple terms how you can access and activate the creative power that lives within you.

This book is the story of my lifelong investigation of the process of self-understanding. This story is fact; it comes directly from selected memories that are, in many cases, supported by my journals and, in all cases, confirmed by witnesses who were present when the events took place. The life events chosen for inclusion in this book were selected from thousands of others in order to reveal something about the connection between one's transient human personality and one's eternal, highest self. This highest self is your God self, and it is found only within you.

In this book, I explain and analyze the events I recount so we can see why these events took place and how they contribute to the process of self-understanding. All of the people in this story are real; they all participated in the story as described, and no names have been changed. In some cases, the words used in quoted dialogue are exactly those used at the time. In cases where I do not remember the exact words, the dialogue has been re-created with words that preserve the original meaning and intent of the conversation.

I did not wake up one morning with a process that I thought could transform my life. Instead, the process was revealed one step at a time over many years of experimentation and observation.

I ultimately called this process self-understanding because as I practiced the process I gained an understanding of my true self, which I later confirmed through further investigation and experimentation. Self-understanding opens the door to the peace that lives within you. Anything is possible in the presence of this peace; it is the key to a life of happiness and fulfillment.

The process of self-understanding comprises five elements I call universal creative drivers. I became aware of the universal creative drivers by reverse engineering and analyzing thousands of my life experiences, observing the relationship between my thoughts and actions and the experiences that resulted from them. These relationships formed larger patterns, and those patterns revealed the five drivers that can help one connect their individual, conscious mind to the wisdom and power of their highest self.

I Am God and So Are You – Discovering the Power of Your True Self defines these five universal creative drivers and describes how you can practice them to create anything you can imagine. The creative drivers are the motivating force of the universe, and they impact your life universally.

Above all, *I Am God and So Are You – Discovering the Power of Your True Self* is about living peacefully. Peace begins with a feeling inside. That feeling generates an energy that extends into space and finds a way to connect with everyone in the world. Everything that has existed in the past, all that now exists, and all that ever will exist, including God, is one. We are more than connected. We are one, and that is why your feelings are perceived by people all over the world.

There is infinite value in knowing your truth. Self-understanding can lead you to this truth. You have the means to experience self-understanding – which is God knowledge – and it is available to you right now. It is no further away than your next breath.

Your breath is your interface with your God self. You can feel your breath moving when you pay attention to it. When you feel the air fill your lungs and listen to the silence inside of you, you will know peace. Once you know it, no one and nothing can take it from you.

> Then said a teacher,
> Speak to us of teaching.
> And he said:
> No man can reveal to you
> aught but that which
> already lies half asleep
> in the dawning of your knowledge.
>
> *The Prophet* – Khalil Gibran

You have walked this path before and you know it well. Because you knew you would forget having walked this path, you placed clues along the path to guide you. This book is one of those clues.

Self-understanding is a pathway to your true self and a way to rediscover your connection with your God self. This connection opens new vistas of possibility for you and for humanity and provides you with new ways of looking at the world that make the previously unimagined commonplace.

I Am God and So Are You

Chapter 1

THE QUESTION

Most of us have wondered where we come from and why we are here. I was about four or five years old when I started thinking about God and the origin of life. My parents and my maternal grandmother spoke often of God in the context of their religion and I was influenced by what they said.

My dad told me that Roman Catholicism was the world's one true religion, the only pathway to heaven, and at the time, I believed him. His name was James, the only son of two Irish Catholics. He was the driving force behind my practice of Roman Catholicism. I did not know at the time that my dad and my maternal grandmother, who I called Nanny, were teaching me a belief system created by people. That's how it is for all humans. We start out with a fairly clear, unclouded vision of the world and before we know it we're viewing everything through colored sunglasses that prevent us from seeing what is real. The whole process begins before we are born and happens so slowly that we fail to notice the transition from a clear view to colored glasses.

Many of us live and die without waking up to the fact that we have based all of our life decisions upon unverified information told to us by other people who may never have verified it for themselves. I was flabbergasted to see that my mom and dad, apparently intelligent people, never questioned the way they had been taught to view God. I began wondering why I should believe anything I had been told about God – or about anything else. I was only a child, but I thought that my opinion about God was just as valid as anyone else's, even as valid as those inspired writers who were responsible for creating the Bible, the Gospel, the Good News. I traced it back in my mind, and it was clear that somebody had told something to somebody else and long before that message ever got to me it became accepted as fact and law and was incorporated directly into people's everyday lives. Perhaps it was time for somebody to say something different about these facts and laws that we all seemed to accept so blindly.

My grandmother was not a storyteller; she told me only two stories about her personal life and they were all I needed. She did not tell me about the rules of Catholic practice nor did she tell me that I would go to heaven if I followed them or hell if I did not. Her name was Maureen McCormack. She lived her first ten years in a Roman Catholic orphanage in County Westmeath, Ireland. After that, her uncle brought her to his farm where she lived, worked, and broke her left leg when she was about thirteen. Because she was never taken to a doctor for treatment, her thigh bone knitted together with her foot pointing directly backward. Her leg atrophied until it was almost nothing but skin covering bone, usable only as a balancing stick that she dragged behind her when she walked.

Nanny came to New York to live with her aunt in 1919. Shortly after arriving in New York she saw a doctor about her leg for the first time in her life. The doctor told her there was nothing that could be done. She made up her mind that God would heal her and began praying for healing every day. After several years of prayer, her foot spontaneously healed as she stepped from a bus in front of the church where she prayed each day. She felt a sharp pain when she put her foot on the ground, and when she looked down her toes were pointing forward. Her leg began to gain muscle and with time she was able to walk normally. She called this a miracle. Though I had never seen my grandmother's atrophied leg with the toes pointing backward, I believe she experienced what many people call a miracle. If Nanny prayed and her leg healed, then, I thought, perhaps it is possible for similar things to happen for others. My belief in her story and in the possibility of instant healing helped inspire me to learn more about what is possible for a human being.

Nanny told the second story on a summer day in 1958 when Gary, my younger brother, and I were visiting her. She told us that late one night Jesus appeared to her at the foot of her bed. She said Jesus spoke comforting words to her and told her she was loved and had nothing to fear.

"What did Jesus look like?" I asked.

Nanny had a beautiful statue of Jesus on the night table next to her bed and she gestured in that direction, saying, "He looked like that statue. He was dressed in a red robe with a white tunic underneath. When he spoke I felt peaceful." What stood out for me was that Nanny said she felt peace and love surrounding her as if it were being transmitted from Jesus. I looked past the living room through the open door of Nanny's bedroom about twenty feet away and pictured Jesus standing there at the foot of her bed. After that, meeting God became my primary goal.

That night before going to bed I prayed to God, asking him to come to me. I told God I wanted to see him so I could know for sure if he was real. I wanted certainty of God's existence. I wanted to know what God looked like, how he communicated, and how he made things happen. I concluded my prayer by saying, "It's okay if Jesus comes to me but I really want to see you in person."

Back home in Massapequa the following week, I lay down in the grass in front of the house, my hands folded behind my head, looking for God in the clouds. I had seen pictures in my Missal of God sitting on clouds, and I looked for him every day for several weeks. God did not come to me that year. I soon stopped looking for him in the clouds but did not stop asking him to visit me.

Chapter 2

A ROLL OF THE DICE

My exploration of the God connection did not stop but I took it in a different, more practical direction. In 1959, while practicing prestidigitation with a deck of playing cards in the family room, I decided to try an experiment. I wanted to see if I could discern the suit and rank of the cards without looking at them. If I named enough of them correctly then I would prove to myself that information was somehow being exchanged between me and the cards, or maybe even between me and God.

I shuffled the deck and held it in my left hand. Looking at the back of the top card, I said its name then turned it over with my right hand. When I saw that I had named it correctly, I felt excited anticipation. I named the next card and turned it over; again, I was correct. Wow! I continued through the deck, keeping track of my success rate. After going through the entire deck I had named the card correctly about forty times. I reshuffled and did it again with similar results. I decided to try a variation of the experiment with my pair of dice. I held them in my closed left hand for a few seconds and then named the number I thought would come up when I rolled them. I rolled the dice onto the card table and when they came to a stop, the number I named was the number on the dice. I rolled the dice again and again, selecting the numbers correctly about eight out of ten times.

I wondered about this process. I already had a sense that information could come directly into our minds from some unknown place. I was pretty sure it was not necessary to see, hear, smell, taste, or feel an object or an event in order to know something about it. At eleven years old, I confirmed that some kind of connection existed between my mind and the cards and dice and it was not an accident or a coincidence. I didn't have to struggle to know; I didn't have to peer into some other world or perform a ritual. I simply knew. I wondered if I could do it, and when I attempted it, the information seemed to pop right into my mind. I heard it in my mind like I would hear any other thought. Another question loomed large for me: was I predicting the cards and numbers, was I causing them, or was it some combination of both?

I ran upstairs to the kitchen to show my mother what I was doing with the cards and dice. I thought she would be impressed with my ability to predict those cards one after the other. Instead, after a few minutes of watching me name the cards and the numbers on the dice, she seemed to accept it as a naturally occurring event and said, "You have ESP." I asked her what that meant and she told me that I might have a talent for extrasensory perception. "Everybody has ESP," she said. "Some people, like Aunt Louise, and apparently you, seem to have a natural understanding that there is more going on in life than meets the eye." If that was the case, I suspected that most people must ignore their natural ability or maybe they did not even believe ESP was possible.

"But mom, how can the information travel from the card to my brain without a wire and why can't we see it or measure it?" I asked.

"You don't need a wire and there is no meter that can measure it," mom told me. "We just saw it happen; we just don't know how it happened." With that, she turned around and walked out of the kitchen and down the hall toward her bedroom. She returned a moment later with a small paperback book in her hand and handed it to me. It said *ESP* in large letters at the top of the cover and, below that, *Extrasensory Perception* in smaller letters. The pages were brown; the cover was worn and wrinkled. I had not seen this book before. I looked up at my mom, feeling like I was holding the Golden Fleece. She said, "If you practice this you can get better at it, just like practicing your trumpet makes you a better trumpet player." I began reading it right away.

In addition to mind experiments, I pursued other things. I read books about alchemy, physics, various mystical arts, and other scientific and spiritual books written for children my age. I built rockets in my basement laboratory and launched them in my backyard. I built small airplanes with white mice inside and flew them at the baseball field. My brothers, sisters, and friends and I also pursued other kinds of games and experiments.

When I had received no communication from God by spring of 1961, I began to doubt whether God would ever make himself known to me. At that time our family of practicing Roman

Catholics consisted of four boys and two girls: I was the oldest, then came Gary, Kathleen, Gerard, Thomas, and Eileen. A seventh baby, to be named Maureen, was expected in December, then Patrick was born in 1963 and Linnea in 1965. After three years of asking God to show himself, I had to be practical. I was just a kid; why would God take his precious time to visit me? I imagined that if God did appear to me, he would be a superhuman being dressed in white robes, with a large white beard and long white hair, speaking English with a deep voice. For me, this was not to be.

Chapter 3

A DIFFERENT WAY TO SEE

I rode the bus to school as usual on a beautiful morning in May 1961. My thoughts were occupied with the fast approaching last day of school at Plainedge High School in Massapequa, New York. After ten minutes in homeroom, I went to the boys' locker room to dress for gym. The physical education class was held outside to take advantage of the warm weather, so with my gym uniform on I went out to the sports field to wait for class to begin. Suddenly the locker room door flew open and Mr. Drego stepped onto the field shouting, "Okay everybody, hustle out to the handball courts and divide into your squads. First two squads get on the handball courts, everybody else take a seat here by the fence and rotate onto the courts to replace the people who get eliminated." Mr. Drego had been my physical education teacher since elementary school and I was now in the eighth grade. He was a good teacher, but I did not enjoy athletic endeavors. Still, I had to be there, dressed in my red shorts and red t-shirt with the Plainedge

Red Devils logo on it, so I accepted it and relaxed with my back against the fence.

I was thirteen years old. The sky was clear and bright blue, the air crisp and clean; the sound of robin redbreasts chirping signaled new life all around. I sat with my friends in the grass against the fence surrounding the courts. John Fitzpatrick was on my left and I don't remember who was on the right. Fitz and I talked about recent contacts he had made on his shortwave radio before I leaned my head back against the chain link fence and breathed in the smell of the grass wafting up through the air. Inhaling the warm aromatic air centered my attention in the moment and brought with it a calm sense of well-being. I looked out at the handball courts and momentarily observed the action of the players smacking the ball against the wall with their open palms. My eyes looked up, above the walls of the courts, to the clear blue sky. I felt relaxed, my mind clear.

Though I made no effort to do so, my attention was focused right there on the scene, with no thoughts in my mind, fully aware of the beautiful sensations coming into me from the outside world. In this very moment of observing the sky and feeling the simple beauty of the soft breeze blowing across my face, everything changed. Something shifted, forever transforming my view of God, myself, the world, and humanity's place in it. My mind went blank. Though no words can describe what happened and my young mind required time to grasp even the basic impact of the experience, in looking back on it I am able to express the nonverbal impressions that remained with me after I returned to normal waking consciousness. Something happened that, according to Mr. Drego and my classmates, took time to happen, perhaps twenty seconds or less. My friends and Mr. Drego later told me that I had apparently lost consciousness. That may have been the case from their perspective; however, I remained fully awake and intensely aware the entire time.

I say "something" happened because it is difficult to refer to what happened as an experience. An experience requires a subject – that is, a person or entity having the experience – and an object – the something that the person or entity experiences. During this event, what I had always thought of as "I" or "myself" disappeared along with the world I was accustomed to experiencing. There suddenly existed nothing – no things – not me, not my friends, not the grass or the sky. There was no noticeable transition between my experience of the world of subject (me) and objects (everything else), and what I call my non-experience of everything, including myself, as nothing. The shift occurred instantaneously and without warning. I was not thinking about having an experience or of doing or being anything other than sitting on the grass, looking up at the sky.

The last thing I noticed was the smell of the grass and the light breeze on my cheeks. I then became part of a different reality, a reality that I could not experience because I was the totality of that reality. The lines of distinction that separate us from the world no longer existed. My visual field was filled with nothing; I interpret and describe this no-thing as a blazing white light. I explained to myself that I had seen a white light, but I didn't. I saw and experienced and thought of nothing – zero – yet I was fully aware of everything. I was everything, and since everything is the same as nothing, I had no capacity or reason to think. I was in a state of timelessness and where there is no time, there is no memory. Memories are of things that happened earlier in time and without time, there is no past to remember. There is only right now and everything that occurs happens only right now.

The strongest thought that occurred to me later that day was that I had experienced a feeling of love beyond what the word "love" might ever have meant before. I was loved and at the same time I knew myself to be the creator of this love. This powerful sensation of unbounded love cannot be sufficiently described in words. Whenever I think about it, I am overwhelmed by it and made small in comparison to it. The ineffable feeling that enveloped me and penetrated my being that morning left me with an understanding that this love was unconditional, knew no boundaries, and would sacrifice anything, forever, for its beloved. Along with love, I experienced myself as infinite, unbounded power. This was not the kind of power that humans might use to control circumstances. It was the gentle power of all that is, the power that creates universes without effort and has no need to be used. This power simply is.

Though this non-experience in no way resembled anything I had ever heard or thought about God, I immediately knew that I had been touched by everything that ever has existed, is now, or ever could possibly exist. This was the immanent and transcendent God of all gods, the uncreated God of all creation. It is only in retrospect that I interpret and describe this non-experience with these words. The words are not the reality and cannot be used to touch or experience the reality; they are mere tools used in a tiny effort to describe something that defies description.

In that moment nothing was happening; I was everything, pure subject without object, so nothing could be happening. I was the singular nothing, the eternal mystery; I was all that is all at once, and that is what we all are. I use the word "God" only because it is probably the word most used worldwide to describe this indescribable something/nothing. Call it whatever you like: higher power, Allah, Self, Yahweh. It cannot be explained, understood, or experienced by the reasoning human mind. The conscious mind can only accept it. The bigger part of who we are transcends our reasoning minds and understands this truth innately and without doubt. In the normal, subject/object sense of "experience," I did not experience any of this that morning: I was it, I am it – and so are you.

Chapter 4

TRUSTING THE PROCESS

As suddenly as this non-experience came upon me, I abruptly found myself back in the temporal world with no time to reflect upon the power of what had just transpired. Something else was happening that I wanted to know about and it attracted my full attention. Although my thought processes once again felt normal, what I saw around me was not normal. I realized that I had no weight. I thought it unusual to be weightless, but I was unconcerned. I then realized I had no weight because I was floating around freely without a body, and it felt great.

I saw the sky all around me and the earth below me. When I looked down I saw the scene I had recently been part of. I was about two hundred feet above Mr. Drego and the students. Some were gathered around my body. Mr. Drego stood over me, bent at the waist, looking concerned. His apprehension was wasted on me, I thought, because my life couldn't be better; I wondered why he and my friends looked so anxious. I was in a beautiful place and my immediate desire was to remain there. I had a choice about it:

I could remain out of my body or I could go back into it. It was a free choice. Then I realized that choosing to remain out of my body would give people on earth the impression that I was dead. Indeed, if I did not return to it, my body would be dead, and that thought alarmed me.

I then perceived a voice that seemed to come from somewhere outside myself. It left me with the knowledge that the possibility of remaining alive without my body was available to me right then and there in that moment. I also realized that the choice to remain in the present state was what was known as death and the people around me on the ground would soon come to the conclusion that I had died.

My parents, brothers, sisters, and everyone else would bury my body and I would go off to who knows where. I assumed that the "who knows where" was the beautiful bliss of the love and the white light. But I wasn't ready for that. What had just occurred was something so good and natural that I wanted to tell everyone about it. I knew that if other people knew about this love and unity, they would like it, so I said to myself, "No, I will return to my body."

At that instant I was back in my body and it felt like cold, damp, heavy clay. It was so heavy that I could not move or get up. I looked out of my eyes and saw that I was on the ground, sitting in the same place from which I had looked up at the beautiful sky sometime earlier that day. Mr. Drego appeared relieved. I heard him tell someone to help me into the nurse's office. I tried to move but very little happened. I made an effort to talk, to tell them that everything was okay, but I couldn't get words to come out. My thoughts were clear but nobody heard them; the thoughts never made it out of my mouth.

Mr. Drego and some of the boys pulled me up and mostly dragged me to the nurse's office where they sat me in a chair opposite her desk. I felt coherent in my mind but my body felt heavy and difficult to move. The nurse asked me what my phone number was and I heard myself say it in my mind, but the sounds that came out of my mouth were unintelligible. She gave up on that idea and impatiently pushed the phone toward me. "Can you dial your number, Jimmy?" I looked directly into her eyes, focused my thoughts on making the telephone call, and willed my arm to move toward the telephone. I struggled to move my arm and it slowly responded. With all of my mind energy focused on the telephone, I finally removed the handset from the cradle; it felt as heavy as the desk. With a slow and deliberate effort I finally extended my right forefinger into the dial and with intense concentration was able to move the dialing ring around to the stop, slowly dialing each digit of our home telephone number: Pershing 5-2453. The nurse told my mother to get to the school as quickly as she could. Looking back on this, I wonder why no one called an ambulance. My collapse was not normal; it could have been something dangerous. I did not think about it at the time, but it now occurs to me that this was an oversight on the part of the school nurse.

My mother walked into the nurse's office wearing an expression of concern. The nurse explained what had happened while Mr. Drego and the boys helped me into the car. I had already regained the ability to walk, and during the drive home I rapidly gained more control over my appendages and was able to speak more clearly. My mom parked the car in the driveway and I sat in the seat while she came around and opened the door. She stood there next to me, calmly asking how I felt and what had happened. I shook my head and said nothing. I had so much I wanted to tell her about this amazing experience, but I was still more focused on thinking about it than explaining it.

Less than a minute later I put my feet on the driveway and mom helped me into the house; she immediately called our family doctor. Within a few minutes the experience of being in my body felt nearly normal. Most of my strength returned; I was able to move around and speak. I explained to my mother that there was nothing to worry about. I reminded her that I had been praying for God to visit me and told her that it had finally occurred. I told her a little bit about what I had perceived, emphasizing that God did not fit the description that she or my father or her mother or the priests or nuns at St. James Church had given me. She was doubtful but wanted to know more. I had not yet thought through the details, but I told her that God was everything, that God was me, that God was her, and God was definitely not an old man in a place called heaven. She was concerned and told me to relax until the doctor arrived. I think my new ideas about God disturbed her as much as my previous inability to move.

Our family doctor, Hank Fassino, was also my dad's best friend. After my mother explained to him what she knew and what she had seen at the nurse's office, he opened up his black bag and began to examine me. He asked me how I felt now. I told him I felt great the entire time and was now in control of my muscles. Dr. Fassino declared that I was fine and he could find nothing wrong with me. He proposed that I may have been bitten by a spider but showed no signs or symptoms of anything out of the ordinary. He told my mother that she should probably keep me home for the next two days and he would return both days to re-examine me. Before departing, Dr. Fassino assured my mother that everything was fine.

After the doctor left, my mother needed to turn her attention to my youngest brother and sister, Thomas and Eileen. Gary, Kathleen, and Gerard, ages eleven, nine, and eight, were still in school. This gave me time to go upstairs to my bedroom and think about what had just occurred. I was excited but tired; it was difficult to sort out my thoughts. Replaying the events in my mind reinforced the fact that the experience of oneness with everything had been an experience of God. I had no notion of the phrases *non-experiential experience* or *higher power* so, at the time, it was simply "God." Though I had heard no voice during the experience, I was left with the impression that God had spoken to me, saying: "Here I am, plain as I can be, the answer to your prayer." God had answered my prayers by revealing Himself to me. I used the male pronouns, though there was nothing masculine or feminine or anything resembling personality about the presence I had experienced. I was aware that there was much more to the experience than my mind could comprehend at that moment. When my father arrived home from work, my mom told him that she brought me home from school and Dr. Fassino came to examine me, but she left the God part out of the conversation.

Although aware that the experience was miraculous and huge, I lacked even the slightest glimmer of the depth and breadth of what had just occurred. I was humbled by the experience, feeling tiny and insignificant in the face of the mystery that had presented itself to me. I knew the experience would change my life and that it could change the lives of many others as well, so I thought about the best way to explain it. I thought everyone would want to hear about God from someone who had actually seen and communicated with God, but I soon discovered that most people did not want to hear my version of God.

The priests and nuns who taught Catechism at St. James Church were not at all sympathetic, my grandparents and parents were stuck in their Roman Catholic dogma, and my friends were not really interested. My ability to speak about the experience was limited. I said that God is everything and if God is everything, then we are God. I said that God is made of love and so are we. This love that we are has substance; it is not just a feeling like we get when someone says "I love you," and it is much stronger than and totally different from the love we have for our parents. I also said that God's love is not based on obedience to a bunch of rules. I spoke with very few people about this. Most of those with whom I did discuss it were either disinterested or disagreeable, so I stopped talking about it and kept the experience to myself.

Chapter 5

WHO AM I?

My dad had given me an illustrated physics book for young people, and it described something that reminded me of my non-experience: a quantum leap. A quantum leap occurs when an electron becomes too energized to remain in its orbit and jumps from one energy level to another within the atom. The atomic transition occurs in a very small amount of time, measured in billionths of a second. This is rather like what happened to me; the vibrational level of my entire being shifted in a very small amount of time. This shift affected the way I thought and the way I processed information, initiating an awakening process that continues today and, I suspect, will never end. My thirteen-year-old human mind made a quantum leap that changed forever the meaning of my past, present, and future.

If we had a vessel that could fly us around the universe, we would find unlimited stars, asteroids, planets, unknown things, and different life forms that we cannot begin to imagine today. The farther we travel into the expanding universe, the more there is to explore, revealing to us new possibilities that we were previously unable even to imagine. So it is with our selves. The exploration of who we are is an infinite adventure that never ends, with new discoveries to be made about ourselves each moment, forever.

I chose to continue the process of exploration. People that I respected, including adult relatives, teachers, priests and nuns, attempted to convince me that their explanations were more fitting and they would not consider looking at anything different, at least not from a thirteen-year-old child. However, I knew that, at a deeper level, their traditional descriptions of reality could be viewed from a different perspective. I pursued the question "Who am I?" in spite of their opinions or the fear those opinions fostered in me. Who am I? Who is God? How do we connect? Why did I have that experience? What practical difference does it, or will it, make in my life?

These questions led me to books. My Roman Catholic background brought me initially to the words of Christian mystics and saints. During the next several years I discovered Meister Eckhart, Saint John of the Cross, and Saint Teresa of Avila. Dad bought books about Einstein's theories of relativity and quantum physics for young people. I connected with these books because some of what they said reminded me of aspects of my experience.

Meister Eckhart, born in the thirteenth century, described God as both manifest and un-manifest. He said that Christ is born anew in each of us. These were, and are, radical notions that, along with his mystical writings and sermons, so upset the Catholic Church that Pope John XXII deemed him a heretic and would have put him on trial had Meister Eckhart not died before the trial date. His rejection far exceeded what I experienced in the 1960s. St. John's *Dark Night of the Soul* was difficult to understand so I read what other people said about it. St. John warned that I might face difficult spiritual and emotional days in my future, and those days certainly came. St. Teresa of Avila, a sixteenth-century contemporary of St. John, wrote about the four stages of the soul's ascent, the fourth stage being complete union with God where the individual soul is no longer conscious of being in a human body. This resonated with me, reminding me of what I had experienced. These books and others that I explored in my last year of high school helped mitigate my sense of rejection and built my confidence in what I had experienced. Although my confidence increased, I was not ready to leave the Roman Church so I continued the practice of Catholicism with commitment and vigor.

I continued to think about the non-experience and was interested in finding a way to replicate it intentionally, but I had no further direct experiences of God during this time in high school. I noticed that sometimes when I was alone, I perceived a unity with the world, and while I found this interesting, it was not the same as my experience in eighth grade. I suspected that I was still processing the non-experience of 1961, so it made sense that no others had occurred; an experience of similar intensity may have overwhelmed me at the time.

I was a high school senior in 1964 when I read about the 1954 defeat of the French Army at Dien Bien Phu, a city in a country called Vietnam, which I had never heard of before. Several months later I read an article in the *New York Times* stating that more than three hundred American military advisers had been killed in Vietnam. After that, I started hearing about Vietnam a lot. In March 1965, the evening news showed clips of United States Marines coming ashore on the beach at Da Nang, Vietnam, a city about halfway between Ho Chi Minh City and Hanoi. I knew nothing else about Da Nang at the time. Our nation soon became deeply involved in that tiny country so far away.

What this meant for me and the rest of my high school graduating class of 1965 was that we would either go to college or be drafted into the Army and go to Vietnam. Some of my friends actually wanted to go to Vietnam, believing that their involvement was necessary to stop communism, our national enemy of the day. I thought it ridiculous that anything we might do in Vietnam would stop the spread of communism or help protect the United States in any way. Even without Vietnam looming, there was never any doubt in my mind about going to college; the only question for me was which college it would be.

I wanted to go to a local school and was accepted to Hofstra University on Long Island. I was also accepted to St. Norbert College in West Depere, Wisconsin and St. Vincent's in Latrobe, Pennsylvania. The decision was made when my dad said, "I'm paying for your education and you will go where I tell you to go." He wanted me to go far away so I would grow up and not be distracted by friends or family. He decided that St. Norbert was the school for me.

St. Norbert is a coed Roman Catholic school in West Depere, a small town on the west bank of the Fox River, about five or six miles south of Green Bay. Dad flew with me to Green Bay in late August 1965 on my first trip away from home. We left JFK in a Boeing 707 and landed two and half hours later at O'Hare Airport in Chicago. From there we flew in a Piedmont Airlines DC-3 to Green Bay. We arrived at the campus, completed some documents, carried my suitcases up to the third floor, and put them in room 302 of Bern Hall, the freshman dormitory. I was quiet and reserved in the chaos; all around me other freshmen talked loudly and walked up and down the hall meeting each other. Dad and I sat in the room for a few minutes while he told me not to worry because everything would be all right. His return flight to New York was that afternoon, so after about thirty minutes we walked to the parking lot, shook hands, he drove away, and I waved to him as the car pulled out of the parking lot. I was alone for the first time in my life.

I stood there for several minutes, wanting to go back home and get in bed. I was seventeen; it had been good being a kid, but now I had to take the next step and find some degree of independence and responsibility. Within a few weeks I felt at home at St. Norbert. Most of the students were from Wisconsin and the Chicago area with a few from other places in Illinois and even Iowa. One other freshman, with whom I became good friends, was from Syracuse, New York. I never knew I had an accent until the Midwesterners began making fun of it, which made me start working on overcoming the distinctive New York accent. Though I had feared being away from home in a strange place, it soon became a highly valued experience. I went home for Thanksgiving, Christmas, and spring break, which I appreciated. After finals, I went home in May 1966 feeling like I had accomplished something quite large.

During that first year at St. Norbert I did not pursue alternative avenues to the mystical experience and did not speak about it with anyone. A friend of mine offered me an opportunity to take LSD, which Tim Leary and others had touted as a pathway to higher consciousness. I declined his offer. I was glad I did because about an hour later my friend came running down the hall, yelling, "The devil's chasing me, the devil's chasing me!" That did nothing but confirm some of the more frightening stories about LSD that I had read in magazines and seen on television.

While home for the summer, however, I came across a book by Alan Watts called *The Joyous Cosmology* and another by Aldous Huxley called *The Doors of Perception and Heaven and Hell*. I knew that Alan Watts, an erstwhile Episcopal priest, was a philosopher and a practitioner of Buddhism. I had read Huxley's *Brave New World* and wanted to learn what these intellectuals had to say about altering their consciousness with chemicals. Aldous Huxley spoke about an experience with mescaline while Alan Watts wrote about LSD. These books opened my eyes to the possibility that chemicals, especially LSD, could, in some people, prompt an experience that sounded similar to the one I had when I was thirteen. After reading those books I read Huxley's *The Perennial Philosophy*. I also became an avid reader and follower of Alan Watts. Still, I had no immediate desire to ingest a mind-altering chemical for any reason.

Chapter 6

LOVE

I began my sophomore year at St. Norbert in August 1966. In October or November, *Playboy* magazine interviewed Dr. Tim Leary. When I read the article I thought again about the possibility of using LSD to experience higher consciousness, but did not pursue that option. I continued reading Watts, whose books covered much more than the spiritual aspect of life, including the connections between the universe and human psychology, and much more that I found interesting and beneficial. I also read a book by Maharishi Mahesh Yogi called *Science of Being and Art of Living: Transcendental Meditation.* I saw this book on the desk of a fellow student named Dennis, found it interesting, and secured a copy for myself.

Maharishi's words described something similar to the spiritual experience I had in 1961. He framed my understanding of reality in language I had not seen in any of the Christian writings I had discovered. Maharishi described in words my direct experience of having been all at once the creator, subject, and object of all experience, which he referred to as the *field of pure being*. Soon after my experience by the handball court I had found myself wanting to share it with everyone because I believed that if everyone experienced this unity of being then the entire world would be at peace. Maharishi said something very similar in his book. He verbalized what I had come to understand as reality, and this inspired me to practice the technique that he called Transcendental Meditation (TM), which Maharishi said could be a practical pathway to eternal being.

Maharishi had recommended twenty minutes of TM twice a day, but when I first started I found it difficult to sit still for more than ten or fifteen minutes once a day. Within about two weeks, however, I was enjoying it so much that it became easy to practice twice a day and twenty minutes seemed to flash by in seconds. For me, the experience produced a profoundly peaceful state of mind that I would describe as a continuity of consciousness, a smooth and steady state free of the storm of thoughts that normally came and went through my mind. It was not the same as my experience of 1961 in that I did not completely leave my normal waking consciousness and enter a state of unified oneness.

In February of 1967 I walked to Main Hall for my ROTC class, *Small Unit Tactics*. I was enrolled in ROTC only because it was required of freshmen and sophomores; I had no intention of continuing with it or ever being part of the military. The class was taught by a squared-away Army major with short red hair and glasses. He was a great instructor and did an excellent job of keeping us awake during an otherwise boring class that taught us World War Two tactics in the Vietnam era.

At the conclusion of the class I walked a few blocks to the barber shop. The shop was located a short walk from Main Hall. It was a peaceful walk even in winter if the wind was not blowing. This was a still day, bare-limbed trees lined the streets, and the sidewalk was covered in shiny ice. I took a short run and slid on the ice for ten or fifteen feet. I was relaxed because my Thursday classes were wrapped up for the day.

The shop was small, with three chairs and two barbers. The owner, Paul, cut my hair each week. He was slightly large around the middle and was about five feet ten inches tall. Dark brown hair fringed Paul's mostly bald head. I sat in the chair and after minimal small talk enjoyed peaceful silence while he rhythmically clicked the scissors through my hair. After trimming and combing my hair, Paul paused to allow me an opportunity to inspect his work in the mirror. I said, "Looks great, Paul, as always." He then turned the chair one hundred and eighty degrees to face the door. The chair and my body stopped, but I continued spinning – right out of my body.

I saw Paul standing there along with everything else in his shop, but none of it appeared solid. Everything in the room was a field of vibrating energy that extended around and through everything in the shop and beyond. Paul and I, everything in his shop and the space between everything, arose from that energy field. The material world was flexible; nothing was solid. I saw multi-colored waves of energy flowing out of me and as I shifted my thinking the energy waves changed color and moved in different patterns in time with my thoughts. These waves blended together with everything in the room; all of it was the same vibrating energy. I was entranced by this particle and wave world when Paul tapped me on the shoulder. I was able to pay Paul for the haircut and then slowly rose up from the chair with my energetic feet standing firmly on the immaterial floor.

Outside the shop, the ordinarily dull winter scene struck me as the most aesthetically pleasing view I had experienced in years. There was nothing particularly beautiful about the buildings and bare trees of the town, but my view of their underlying reality astounded my senses and captured my attention. I perceived this entire world as a living, conscious being. Beyond just the scene in front of me or the world around me, the entire universe was aware of itself, constantly generating and regenerating itself out of nothing. All of this creation remained in existence only because it was alive. Each thing that exists was not created at some particular time; it is always engaged in the self-aware process of creation. I was part of this world that constantly recreates itself, while I also somehow participated in this creative process. The self-aware, living universe surrounded me and was me. It was the energy known as thought that constantly brought all this into form, and what I had previously thought of as solid and immovable was as flexible and dynamic as my thoughts. I was experiencing the living universe, that is, I was experiencing myself, at the same time that the universe was experiencing me, moment after moment, over and over, forever in a dynamic interplay buzzing with life. This was the non-dual duality in action, creating itself as it chose to be. *Chose to be?* I thought. *You mean this world can look different from what I experience every day? Where was the choice being made? Who was doing the choosing?*

29

I was fully aware of everything that was taking place. While experiencing complete unity with all that is, I also maintained an awareness of myself as separate: one yet two, non-dual yet dual. This was a contiguous extension of the non-experience that occurred in 1961. This experience was different, yet both were insights into reality as it exists all the time. It was only my state of mind that had, for most of my life, caused me to perceive the world as individual solid objects in space. There is nothing solid about the world except that we believe it to be so.

I had not previously realized that my world had always been directly informed by my thought energy. Reality occurred to me in a new way now because an important, intentionally created data filtration system had opened up in my mind, allowing me to directly experience the living universe just as it is. Though somewhat disoriented, I maintained my sense of identity and continued walking toward the dorm. If my life experiences were even partially the result of my thinking and I had never before realized that, then anything was possible now that I had. This direct experience of reality showed me that because everything is ultimately me and I was not afraid of myself, there could be nothing to fear, ever.

As I walked past the Catholic elementary school across the street, I heard the sounds of the schoolchildren blending with the sound of the gentle breeze, revealing once again the intimacy of the link that ties all of life together as one. We all are one within that One from which all of this arises. We individuate and walk around with these bodies so we can have objective experiences of ourselves on this beautiful planet. Before this universe existed, God was all alone, pure subject, with no way to learn about itself.

God's urge to know itself, to answer the question "Who am I?" resulted in the creation of everything that exists. This entire universe, the whole of creation, is the answer to that question. Wherever God looks, God sees itself in all its various forms. Wherever we look, we see ourselves; in the sky, in the ocean, the rivers, the trees and creatures of our world, we see ourselves. We are the eternal, unbounded being who created all of this for the purpose of knowing and understanding who we are.

The me of which I speak is not the limited ego self; I speak of that which contains and transcends the ego self: the ineffable mystery of life that we are. This experience was qualitatively different from the experience of 1961. The resulting understanding is basically identical but there are differences in the nature of what occurred. I did not leave my body this time; I maintained awareness of my ego self and did not experience a visual field of white light. Though the world looked much different on this cold Wisconsin afternoon, I always saw the objects around me and was able to navigate among them. I think the initial experience prepared my consciousness for future experiences that would allow me to learn the details of the workings of the universe.

I thought that I had been disconnected from God energy since 1961, but there is no way ever to be separated from the higher self. It is as impossible to be separated from your higher self – God – as it is to be separated from any other part of who you are. Everything is one; no separation is possible. I had perceived myself as separate because I had not directly experienced the unity I came to know in May 1961. It was, however, only my perception of disunity that resulted in my feeling of separation. There is no way to run from God. No choice we make, nothing we do, can disconnect us from our true and original nature. From the time before time and beyond what we call life today we are always connected and forever one with all that is. My perception of separation had caused me to think of myself as genuinely separated from God, so I committed to developing a practice that would help me stay consciously aware of my connection to my higher self.

What I experienced in 1961 and 1967 was not explained to me, taught to me, or passed on to me from someone else; the experiences did not come to me from books. The books I had read between these two experiences helped me put my thoughts into words but did not cause me to have these experiences. One moment my world looked like it always did and in another moment my reality was transformed. I saw that I had been alive forever and that this moment, now, was a part of that continuous forever. We are not separated from our eternal source simply because we are at this moment experiencing this objective, material reality. The time/space continuum is not something that exists on its own, separate and distinct from the timeless essence from which it arises. This experience right now is that timeless essence and so are we. This essence is love and we are love.

What stayed with me as a result of my experience of God consciousness was a deep sense of peace. In knowing this peace I realized that peace is what we all really want in our lives. Everything we do, all the money we make, all the relationships we form, is all aimed at securing that sense of peace, and none of those things accomplish it. There is nothing we must do to bring us peace. Peace is always with us, always there waiting for us. It is really another word for God, for higher self, for love. When we know who we are, we know lasting inner peace.

These experiences and their fruit of ideas were now in my awareness forever. I was nineteen years old and well aware that many individuals had dedicated their lives to experiencing the great mystery and died without ever having known it. I mistakenly believed at this time that God had chosen me, selected me, from among the billions of people on the planet to have these extraordinary experiences. I naively considered myself enlightened, thinking I had achieved the goal of life and had no further work to do in this department. I became spiritually arrogant and overconfident, completely brash and possessing a cocky attitude. I did not know that these experiences alone meant essentially nothing – I was literally blinded by the light and could not see this. I failed to realize that I did not know myself nor did I understand the meaning of what had just happened to even a small degree. Socrates said that the unexamined life is not worth living. Thinking these experiences had completed me, I had certainly never examined my inner being. Were these experiences the blessing of God or the curse of Satan? I entertained the possibility that perhaps the devil was trying to trick me by disguising himself as God. Was I walking the path of good or was my track leading me to evil? The question of good and evil would occupy my mind for many years. Do good and evil exist, and if so how do we identify them, how do we know the difference, and how do we reconcile them?

Even in the peaceful priest-populated setting of St. Norbert College, Roman Catholic doctrine and everything else in my life was overshadowed by the light of these experiences. In my sophomore year I made the difficult choice to cease my practice of Catholicism with no alternative religion in mind. I said nothing to my mom or dad; only my brother Gary knew that I had excommunicated myself. I no longer went to Mass, but just before flying to Puerto Rico on spring break, I went to confession for the final time, just in case of aircraft problems.

Chapter 7

CHANGE OF COURSE

The journey to Puerto Rico was my first visit to a country outside the United States. I enjoyed the tropical climate from the moment I arrived and knew that I would like to live in a place where it never snowed. While Wisconsin was freezing, the temperature in San Juan was in the mid 70s. For two weeks I toured points of interest across the entire island and traveled by boat from Luquillo to St. Thomas in the U.S. Virgin Islands.

Upon returning to St. Norbert I continued my normal studies while also reading books about philosophy, religion, witches, and anything having to do with different ways of looking at God. Eastern religions interested me so I read about Hinduism and Buddhism, especially Zen Buddhism. Finals week arrived in May and after the last test I caught a ride to the Green Bay airport and arrived home in New York for the summer of 1967 – the summer of love. The war in Vietnam raged while Lyndon Johnson and Robert McNamara increased troop levels to nearly 500,000 by spring of 1967. It was impossible to miss the news about Vietnam since it was on television each evening and in all the newspapers. The firefights, body counts, and shots of homeward-bound caskets depicted a nightmare that I chose not to participate in; the mere thought of going to Vietnam frightened me.

Though my grades were good and I had done well on my finals, I did not return to St. Norbert in the fall. I had been seen drinking beer in Lost Dauphin Park during finals week and an aggressive newspaper reporter wrote about it in the Depere paper. The newspaper published my name and described me as the only student from New York. Though it was legal in New York for a person under twenty-one to drink outside of a legal establishment, I'd broken Wisconsin law. I had thought nothing of it at the time – everybody did it. For this choice, however, I was expelled along with two of my friends who were seen at the same time.

I learned very quickly how powerful any choice can be. I was completely casual about the choice I made to drink beer that day. This apparently casual choice, for which only I was responsible, resulted in my failure to graduate from college on time, causing a complete change in my life plan. More critically, however, that choice put my life at risk because the draft board immediately reclassified me as 1A. Nineteen-year-old men with a 1A classification were first in line to be drafted, and within weeks of arriving at home for summer vacation I received a draft notice from the United States Army. Instead of accepting a commission in the Army I enlisted in the Air Force on October 31, 1967.

A pair of opposing forces was at work within me: one led to the path of peace and the other took me off my feet and rushed me along in a direction that I did not realize I had chosen. While at St. Norbert I was still connected to my parents financially and emotionally. Joining the Air Force severed both of those connections. My dad was extremely upset with me for getting kicked out of school and I did not blame him. He made an extraordinary effort to get me admitted to another Catholic school, but at this late date and with the pressure of the draft increasing college enrollments, we found no vacancies. My mom saw my plans change dramatically in a way that could, and did, ultimately lead me into combat; she was completely devastated the morning I said goodbye.

I was sworn in at Fort Hamilton, New York with all the other new recruits. We were bussed late that afternoon to JFK airport where we boarded an airplane bound for Amarillo, Texas. After six weeks of basic training at Amarillo I was assigned to Lowry Air Force Base in Denver, Colorado, where I became a conventional and nuclear weapons systems specialist. The rigors of basic training and the intensity of technical school kept me from thinking about the reality of my situation and allowed no time for meditation or spiritual practice. When my mind found enough time to go off on its own, I ruminated with deep regret about the painful results of the choice I had made. I knew I had to accept the fact that I could not change what had already occurred. If I could accept what I had done to myself and move forward in the present to make the best out of the future, I would be all right; if I stayed stuck in the past, thinking about my bad decision, I would not succeed.

Though the experiences of God, or *higher power*, had inspired me, I did not know how to implement the power revealed by these experiences in my life. Sometimes I felt like the creator of my life and sometimes I felt like a victim of it. I had mistakenly assumed that these mystical experiences alone would cause everything in my life to occur smoothly and happily. I learned this was not the case when some of my choices had unintended results that were 180 degrees out of phase with my definition of smooth and happy. I did not understand that on some level I had chosen all of it, all the time. My experiences of higher power were meaningless without an understanding of who I was and how I related to these experiences. My lack of self-understanding made it difficult for me to accept the challenging results I had created. When I finally accepted the reality of my situation I was able to begin resolving the challenges. Through the process of resolution I discovered that these apparently rocky circumstances contained gold within them in the form of previously unknown strengths and abilities.

I graduated from Lowry's fighter weapons training school at the top of my class in May 1968. After thirty days leave in New York, I went to my first duty assignment at Seymour Johnson Air Force Base in Goldsboro, North Carolina. I was part of a weapons loading crew in the 335th Tactical Fighter Squadron, one of three squadrons in the 4th Tactical Fighter Wing.

After living on base for a few months, I rented a fifty-year-old home with a co-worker and friend named Ray. The four-bedroom house was located about fifteen miles from the base, in a small clearing surrounded by what appeared to be endless woods. It was painted turquoise on the outside and was filthy on the inside. We spent our entire first weekend in the house cleaning grease from the tops of the kitchen cabinets. Every night after work for the rest of the week, we cleaned the wood floors and the bedrooms. The next weekend was devoted to painting the walls. We exercised our creativity by painting the living room walls purple and the ceiling black, with our footprints, handprints, spider webs, and other arcane designs on the ceiling in day-glow orange and yellow that shone brightly in the black lights we installed around the room.

The only heater was a kerosene stove in the living room. A narrow copper tube ran from a big fuel tank in the backyard along the surface of the ground, under the house, and up through the living room floor where it connected to the stove. The bedrooms remained very cold throughout the winter. The house was mounted on concrete blocks, which offered little support for the floors, causing them to slope at varying angles and making it difficult to walk a straight line from one point to another.

Ray stayed only on weekends, leaving me and my redbone hound, Zeke, alone in the dark, silent woods during the week. Hidden from the main road at the end of a quarter-mile driveway, our house was an ideal place to continue my practice of Transcendental Meditation. I had also read a book by an Englishman who claimed to have been possessed by the spirit of a Tibetan monk named Tuesday Lobsang Rampa. The book included instructions for what Rampa called astral traveling. He claimed it was possible for one's spirit self to leave the body and travel anywhere in the universe while remaining connected to the physical body by a golden cord. Breaking the golden cord, the author explained as a caveat, would set the soul free, leaving it unable to find its way back to the body. Having had the experience of actually being out of my body, I thought his explanation made perfect sense.

I practiced TM every day and each night after dinner. Alone in the silent darkness, I intentionally attempted to leave my body. Night after night I lay in my bed practicing the detailed instructions in the book. Sometimes I thought I was on the brink of leaving my body when fear overtook me and the process stopped. On several occasions I did leave my body. I experienced a strong sensation of moving around outside my body with apparently accurate visual experiences of my surroundings. I found these astral travels very interesting, though not as clear or as powerful as the out-of-body experience that had occurred when I was thirteen years old.

I met a local girl named Linda and lived with her for about a year. That relationship was interrupted in November of 1969 when I was suddenly ordered to rotate with the 335th to Kunsan Air Base, Korea. My last night with Linda was a sad one. I had to board a C-141 Starlifter for a flight out of Seymour Johnson at five o'clock in the morning. Linda and I stayed awake all night listening to the radio. The last song to play before I left was *Leaving on a Jet Plane*, written by John Denver and performed by Peter, Paul and Mary. How strange and how sad, I thought, that just as I have to say goodbye, that song comes on the radio. It was very painful for me when Peter, Paul and Mary sang that line, "Oh babe I hate to go."

The mission was a reaction to North Korea's capture of the U.S. Navy ship *Pueblo* and its crew in January 1968. Though the crew had been returned to the U.S. in November of '68, the North Koreans kept the ship. Our job consisted of maintaining F-4D Phantoms loaded with AIM-7 and AIM-9 guided missiles and M-61

20 millimeter cannons on five-minute launch alert. I thought our intention was to get the *Pueblo* back, but the North Koreans never returned it; the ship is now a museum in Pyongyang.

The work schedule at Kunsan left little time for anything else. I worked twelve hours each night without a night off through Thanksgiving, Christmas, and the New Year. Finally, in January 1970 I was granted one night off. I used that time to visit Kunsan City, which required riding in an old Korean bus along a nine-mile stretch of pot-holed dirt road. The Air Force had paved the entire nine miles with asphalt in 1968, but when subzero weather arrived late that year, the poverty-stricken Koreans began digging up the road to burn for cooking fuel and heat in their shacks. During the winter of 1968-1969 the entire nine miles of asphalt had been consumed. The fields on either side of the road were inhabited, the homes constructed of flattened soda cans, sheets of cardboard, and anything else their residents could find to keep out the wind and rain. The missing asphalt made the bus bounce wildly on the way to the city, but that was trivial. I wondered what the people in the field were doing for heat that winter now that the asphalt was gone.

The bumpy ride reached its terminus somewhere in downtown Kunsan. The bus door opened and twenty-five or thirty freezing kids crowded around to sell sticks of gum to the G.I.s. Already saddened by the sight of the hovels, I became overwhelmed with compassion for the little red-faced children waiting for the bus in the bitter-cold night so they could bring a few pennies home for dinner. I paid extra for the gum. Many of the same kids were there each time I went to town during the following four months.

I became acquainted with some of them, deeply connected with others. I met the parents of one of these kids and spent time with the family in their one-room apartment in town, eating their food and celebrating their happy occasions. They were just like Americans, I thought, except they looked a little different.

There was one window in that apartment and it was too close to the ceiling to see out of. Cylinders of charcoal, burning slowly in a small metal stove beneath the floor, supplied heat. The cylinders were about eight inches in diameter and ten inches high, with a number of holes bored through them lengthwise making them burn easier. The heat radiated up through the floor upon which the family lived and slept. To prevent carbon monoxide poisoning, vents under the floor led outside. The family had no furniture other than a small wooden stand with a metal bowl on top and some cushions and blankets for the bed. The place measured about twenty feet on each side and was home for the three kids and their mom and dad, with no space for privacy. Cold running water was located outside in a covered breezeway where there was no heat. A few steps away from the lonely water faucet stood a small, unpainted wooden shack housing the latrine – what the Koreans called the *binjo*. The family kept a pot in the apartment to preclude the need to visit that binjo in the middle of the freezing night.

This was my first personal contact with Buddhists. With the small amount of English words that he knew, the father of the family explained basic Buddhist practices to me as he understood them. He also showed me how he meditated by paying attention to his breath while sitting in the lotus position on a floor cushion. I did not totally grasp his instructions, which were almost entirely in Korean, so I decided to look for some books about this meditation style in the Base Exchange.

I was in Korea on top-secret orders with the departure point, dates, and destination left blank; this meant I could use the orders to travel anywhere in the world on military aircraft. Having been granted one week for rest and recuperation, I chose to travel to Japan to see if I could learn more about Zen. I visited several places in Japan where I observed practitioners of zazen in sitting and walking meditation. Some of them focused on their breathing, some focused on nothing, and others focused on koans, expressions of ancient Zen Masters or questions that cannot be understood or answered by using rational thought processes. I learned the basic ideas of Rinzai (koan) and Soto (simply sitting) practice, which were similar to the way the man in Korea meditated by focusing on his breath, but received no personal, practical instruction. When I returned to Kunsan I began reading books about Zen and the practice of zazen.

The realization that I was learning something very powerful prompted me to think about how, or if, I could apply what I was learning to help people around the world who had so much less than us Americans. Is it possible for all of humanity to at least have consistent supplies of clothing, shelter, water, and food? Yes, it is. I wanted to apply my learning to advance individuals' experiences of inner peace, since I believed that individual peace would lead to what the Buddha called "right action" and ultimately resolve the conflict, poverty, and deprivation I had witnessed along that dirt road to Kunsan City. I desired to make a difference in the world and didn't know where to begin. I wanted to help people be peaceful but I wasn't consistently peaceful inside myself. I was afraid even to speak about my spiritual experiences because I thought no one would believe what happened to me or, if they did believe it, they would reject my ideas as people did when I was younger.

Chapter 8

CHOOSE

The 335th TAC Fighter Squadron returned to Seymour Johnson in May 1970. Linda had been living in her apartment by herself. We got back together but did not live together full time; instead, I stayed at her place two or three nights each week. Life returned to normal with eight-hour workdays and most weekends free. I lived in the old house where Ray had stayed with Zeke, excited to be back and happy that Zeke was still there and healthy.

I began practicing the meditation technique I had learned in Korea and Japan, supplementing the little I had learned there with books by D.T. Suzuki, Dogen, Paul Reps, Alan Watts, Christmas Humphreys, and others I had read in Kunsan. From these books I learned some of the technical details of zazen, the meditation practice that I had chosen to replace TM. I began by focusing on my breath to calm my mind and assist in entering a state known as Samadhi, or single-pointed concentration.

When practicing zazen in the morning, I sat on an old cushion with my legs crossed in a half-lotus position and my back erect.

Breathing in and out slowly and deeply, I paid attention to the air moving past my nostrils. To learn to keep my attention on my breath I counted each in-breath until I reached ten. I then counted ten out-breaths, added that to the first group of ten breaths, and called the total "one." I did this until I had counted ten groups of twenty breaths each without losing count. If I forgot where I was at any point, which happened all the time, I started the whole thing all over again. I practiced for about fifteen minutes every day for the first few days and quickly increased to forty-five minutes each morning; even that seemed like only a moment.

After about six or eight weeks I was able to count my breaths more accurately and consistently and started to feel more peaceful. The meditation practice seemed to help me relate to the ever-changing circumstances of life more patiently and calmly. After about two months I stopped counting my breaths and simply sat there observing the content of my mind. As various thoughts arose I observed them, allowing them to pass out of my mind like clouds blowing through the sky, without spinning them off into stories. By noticing the flow of thoughts entering and leaving my mind, without attaching my thinking to any of them, I arrived at a peaceful place within myself. Dogen referred to this in his Shobogenzo: "Sitting fixedly, think of not thinking. How do you think of not thinking? Nonthinking. This is the art of zazen."

Around the end of July I received orders assigning me to the 405th Munitions Maintenance Squadron at Clark Air Base on Luzon Island in the Philippines. The orders instructed me to report to squadron headquarters in early September. Leaving the many solid relationships I had formed in Goldsboro was a difficult mission. Saying goodbye to Linda was the most difficult. We had told each other "I love you" many times and she had stuck with me during my six months in Korea. Her frequent letters had helped me keep a good attitude while freezing every night on the flight line. I did not want to leave her and did not know what to do to avoid it. Linda took my beloved dog, Zeke, who I brought to Linda's home on my last day. We held each other as long as possible and were weeping as we kissed our last kiss. I had been saying goodbye to people I cared about since I first left home for St. Norbert at age seventeen, but I was not used to it, and never would get used to it. Saying goodbye was not easy, and in the Air Force it became the normal way of life.

After arriving in the Philippines, I was put in charge of the weapons release shop. Instead of my desired position on the flight line loading weapons, I was responsible for ensuring that the aircraft weapons release systems functioned properly and the various weapons that we had on airplanes, including the guns, were properly maintained. Though I did not enjoy working in an office, I did enjoy managing the team.

I had been in the Philippines nearly four months when I awoke one Saturday morning in early January 1971 with an upset stomach. I lay in bed, my stomach burning. The sound of the dripping faucet in my intestines brought me close to vomiting. I began mentally complaining about the pain, which only added to the discomfort. Then I tried to block it out, but the sick feeling and the burning sensation increased. I could not run from it and I could not push it away, so I stopped thinking about it. My mind must have gone somewhere else; I was empty of thoughts and didn't realize it until I returned. When I came back to normal awareness, I had been completely pain-free for several moments and remembered nothing I might have done to make that happen. I remembered nothing because that was the content of my mind at the time the sensation of pain faded away. I was thinking of nothing, feeling relaxed and detached in the same way that I became detached from my thoughts when I meditated. Instead of running from the pain or attempting to get rid of it, I accepted it and it went away on its own.

As soon as I realized I was pain-free, however, the pain immediately returned. I chose to be pain-free again but did not know how to get there, so I did the first thing that occurred to me: I used the principles of my meditation practice. I started by noticing the sensation in my stomach that I called pain; I did not think about it or judge it, I simply allowed myself to feel it. I then focused my attention on the feeling created by the air moving past my nostrils as it entered my lungs. When extraneous thoughts came into my awareness I allowed them to pass by freely like dust particles moving with the breeze. Sometimes I realized I had grabbed onto a thought and was spinning a story around it. As soon as I realized what was happening, I gently observed that I was having a thought and allowed it to move on. I continued paying careful attention to each breath as I inhaled and exhaled.

Suddenly the pain and rumbling stopped; the nausea was gone. I lay there breathing and noticed that I felt complete relief from the sickening symptoms that just moments ago had prevented me from getting out of bed and beginning my day. I was very grateful for this relief and in my mind I said, "Thank you God for showing me a way to heal my discomfort." I mentally reviewed what had just happened:

Woke up with pain in my stomach, feeling like I might vomit at any moment

Thought about how great it would feel to be pain-free

Made a mental declaration to be pain-free

Stopped resisting the ill feeling and accepted it

Focused my attention on my breath and almost instantly became well

I do not believe in coincidence. Carl Jung wrote about a phenomenon that he called synchronicity, and this helped explain to me why meaning could be derived from certain life events, especially those that occurred close together in time. I paid attention to the healing I had just experienced, because there was meaning in these connected events. That same energetic connection that allowed me to know in advance the next card in the deck also allowed me to heal an uncomfortable digestive condition that would have otherwise persisted. The key to the healing was the relaxed acceptance of the original condition. Until I accepted the current status of my being and allowed myself to feel the pain, I could not transform it. When I accepted it, I relaxed, and that allowed me to focus on my healing intention, which ultimately relieved my pain and illness.

About a week later, near the middle of January 1971, my crew and I flew an ancient C-47 across the South China Sea from Clark Air Base to Tainan on the southwest coast of Taiwan. It was a little scary flying over all that open water in that old twin-engine bird watching the pilot casually flick his cigarette ashes out the small window on the flight deck. We landed at the main base and drove the Nuclear Alert Vehicle several miles to the Nuclear Alert Detachment, where we loaded MK 61 and MK 43 tactical nuclear weapons on F-4Ds.

Two weeks later we returned to the Philippines. A friend of mine had introduced me to a young Filipina lady near the end of 1970, and after I returned from Tainan in early February I asked her to have dinner with me. Her name was Maria. I became distracted and took a break from my spiritual studies and experiments when we began seeing each other regularly. After a few months I suspected I was falling in love. I had planned to leave the Air Force early, which had been officially approved, and continue my education at Arizona State University, where I had already been accepted. This was not to be. My previous plans and intentions fell by the wayside of love. I had never felt that way before. Nothing like what came over me with Maria had ever happened with any of the women I had known in the States. I could not conceive of leaving the Philippines without her. She became the dominant thought in my mind and I visited her nearly every day.

As my departure date drew closer, I grew more concerned about leaving without her. How would I ever return to the Philippines and what would life be like without her? I believed this was the one woman in the world with whom I was meant to spend the rest of my life. So I bought a small diamond engagement ring and asked her to marry me. She accepted and we were married in a Catholic church in the Philippines on June 7, 1971. I canceled my early-out and instead we returned to New York in September and

I was discharged from the Air Force. I worked at my grandfather's company until late December of 1971. Working for my dad and my grandfather was not good for me. I didn't like the work, the environment, or being dependent on family. I told them I was leaving and reenlisted in the Air Force at the beginning of 1972. About that time, Maria and I discovered that our first baby was due in August.

Near the end of January we moved into an apartment in Bordentown, New Jersey, near McGuire Air Force Base where I was temporarily assigned until further orders. Those orders arrived in early February and instructed me to depart immediately for Da Nang Air Base in Vietnam. Due to our pregnancy, I requested and received a reprieve from Vietnam until October. Beautiful little Elisa Agnes came into the world on August 8, 1972 at about 7:25 P.M.

Elisa was a wonderful baby and the center of my life. Now I really didn't want to go to Vietnam, or anywhere else. I stayed with her as much as possible and the sixty days passed much too quickly. The mystical experiences of 1961 and 1967 showed me that anything was possible, but looking down at my two-month-old Elisa lying in her crib looking up at me, I despaired at the necessity of leaving her and believed that nothing I wanted was possible. I was on my way to Vietnam and was unable to stop it. Although unaware of what was going on, Elisa began crying loudly as I opened the door to leave. I turned around for one last look. I expected to be back in one year, but it would be September of 1974 before we would live together again.

Chapter 9

SURRENDER

Gary drove me to JFK airport, where I boarded a plane for San Francisco. I then flew on to Hawaii, Okinawa, then finally Tan Son Nhut Air Base, near Saigon, about twenty-seven hours later. The arrival was as peaceful as landing at an airbase someplace in the United States. There were no obvious signs of war at Tan Son Nhut. The heat and humidity hit me in the face as I descended the aircraft stairs to the tarmac. I boarded the blue bus to the terminal, where I discovered that the next flight to Da Nang departed the following morning. I waited in the terminal until I caught a jeep to the barracks where I would spend the night.

It was about eight P.M. when I was finally assigned a bed in a decrepit barracks. The plywood walls extended about three feet from the ground; solid screen ran from there to the roofline. Inside was one large space filled with triple-tiered bunk beds lined up against both walls and down the middle. The scene inside the building was chaotic, with soldiers, Marines, and airmen all seemingly talking at the same time. This was where G.I.s slept for one or two nights while awaiting transportation to other locations throughout Vietnam. It struck me as shameful that plywood shacks packed with beds covered with inch-thick mattresses and saliva-stained pillows were all the government could afford to spare for us front-line troops.

Mine was the top bunk directly beneath a fluorescent light fixture that could not be turned off. I climbed the rails of the lower bunks and pulled myself onto the mattress. Stretching out on my back, I noticed a big spider living happily within that light fixture about six inches above my face. He sat in his web waiting for me to go to sleep so he could come down and eat me. I couldn't take my eyes off the Vietnamese spider. When he dropped down on a thin thread of webbing, heading straight for my mouth, I flipped out. "Jesus Christ, that's it," I yelled, jumping from the bed as fast as I could. I was tired from the twenty-hour flight but not so tired I could fall asleep under that beast. I walked outside behind the barracks and leaned against the wall. Bright white flashes and huge fireballs lit up the night sky; it was Bien Hoa, about 40 kilometers northeast, defending itself from the Viet Cong. I wondered what was happening to the people in the middle of all that.

Most anybody who wakes up at home one day and sees something like this the next day is going to be affected; I certainly was. About midnight I walked into the barracks, crawled back up into the bunk, told the spider to stay where he was, and appreciated how good I had it compared to those folks just a few clicks away. I fell asleep with the light in my face while the busy spider sucked the life out of an unfortunate bug. Early the next morning I caught a flight to Da Nang.

The aircraft flew almost directly over Da Nang at cruising altitude before making a steep dive to avoid enemy fire. We landed quickly and taxied to a stop on the ramp. As I walked down the aircraft ladder onto the tarmac in the heat of the late morning Da Nang sun, I marveled at the beauty of the countryside. It was sad to think that this visually beautiful place had endured the nightmare of this long war. At the bottom of the ladder a young airman handed me a helmet and a flak vest and told me to put them on right away. We could see signs of war, in the form of craters and blown-up buildings, as he drove the jeep toward my residence – a long, two-story plywood shack. I followed him up an exterior wooden stairway to the second floor; a thin plywood door opened into a dark narrow space lined with walls of unpainted plywood on either side. Makeshift plywood doors indicated the separate rooms that the resident airmen had created out of what was once an open bay barracks. My guide pushed open one such door, revealing the room I was expected to live in for the next twelve months.

I couldn't believe this place: one naked light bulb hung from the ceiling by a cord; a bare and lonely mattress rested on the floor. The two airmen who called this dump home, who were away at work when I arrived, had constructed a loft for their two bunks. Below the bunks on an unfinished plywood counter were an open loaf of bread, an open jar of jelly, and an open jar of peanut butter. Feasting on all this stuff was the largest swarm of two-inch-long cockroaches I had ever seen. They didn't even run away when I walked over to see what was creating the noise. It was early afternoon, but the windowless room was lightless save for the small amount of sunshine that found its way through a small hole where a broken exhaust fan hung uselessly. I turned on the light bulb and watched the roaches as they enjoyed their lunch. This was not going to cut it.

After a few hours my "roommates" came back from work. "You guys know anywhere else where I can find a room?" was the first thing I said to them. They didn't want me around wrecking their party and were happy to answer. They told me that the guys across the hall might be able to help me. That's when I got up and knocked on the red-painted door across the hall. A buck sergeant with a long mustache, long hair, and sunglasses opened the door about two inches. Smoke drifted from the room into the narrow hall. "Can I help you?"

I hesitated briefly before saying, "I just got here; I'm looking for a room." He looked me up and down before answering.

I must have passed the test, because he said, "Come on in" as he opened the door into a brightly lit, air-conditioned, beautifully appointed, smoke-filled room. It was like stepping into a different reality. I introduced myself to a group of happy airmen and NCOs who helped me find a new room that night in the barracks next door. I slept there in my fatigues, flak vest and helmet nearby, and moved in with the rest of my stuff promptly after work the next day. This place was like a castle. I now had fluorescent lighting, air conditioning, a refrigerator, a nice bed to sleep in with a heating blanket to keep humidity off the sheets, and a couple of cool weapons mechanics for roommates.

Working nonstop on the flight line twelve hours at a time was a good thing because it kept me focused in the moment instead of thinking about my family and the ever-present threat of attack. We configured the F-4Ds with a variety of weapons depending upon that day's particular mission. From Gatling guns and napalm to hard bombs and cluster units, there seemed to be no limit to the destructive power available to us. For the U.S. to be "losing" this war seemed, to the pilots and those of us on the flight line, impossible – a complete joke. Nixon and Kissinger had promised, "Peace is at hand" long before I had arrived in Vietnam, but so far no peace was forthcoming. While American diplomats negotiated an "honorable" peace with the North Vietnamese in Paris, the war raged on.

I gained an unexpected and undesirable reprieve from the raging, almost daily rocket attacks when my grandmother, Nanny, died in early December. I returned to New York on emergency leave, missed the funeral, but had the opportunity to be with my wife and daughter for a short time. That small amount of time was all we needed to conceive our second child. Though I did not know about this until I was back at Da Nang, I was thrilled to receive a letter from Maria informing me that our second baby was due in September 1973.

On January 23, 1973, President Nixon announced an agreement "to end the war and bring peace with honor in Vietnam and Southeast Asia." The official end of United States involvement would come at eight o'clock Da Nang time on the morning of January 28, 1973. The night of January 27th was like any other. We loaded our airplanes with bombs, guns, and rockets so they could kill more Vietnamese while the North Vietnamese were free to continue killing us. Why were we still trying to kill each other when the whole debacle would be over for the United States in just a few hours?

After loading the birds, I went with my crew to a specially fortified, rocket-proof wonder arch to get some sleep. The wonder arches were U-shaped structures made of concrete and steel. They were big enough to hold one aircraft up to the size of an F-4 and provided excellent protection, completely enveloping the aircraft except for the wide-open front of the arch. The arch where we went for the night was sandbagged in the front, offering protection from most anything the North could throw at us. Intelligence reports issued earlier that evening had predicted intense attacks by rockets, mortars, and possibly North Vietnamese troops intent on overrunning the base. The night had been completely silent up to this point but there was no solace in that. I knew that sometimes the rockets did not come until just before dawn. But mosquitoes were swarming around me and I could not sleep, so I left the protection of the arch and walked across the flight line to the office.

My office was in a prefab Butler building constructed of corrugated steel walls on a frame that was bolted to a concrete slab. Two sheetrock-walled offices occupied part of the interior space, with most of the building filled with load-crew toolboxes, a picnic table, chairs, and assorted weapons loading equipment. As expected, I was alone; all the other weapons troops were in the arch. The front of the Butler building faced a road while the rear backed up to the flight line. Directly behind the office building ran a concrete-lined drainage trench and behind that was a revetment wall about ten feet high. The wall was constructed of corrugated steel on two sides with earth in the middle. Since there were relatively few wonder arches, most of the planes were protected on three sides by revetment walls. I threw my flak vest on the floor in front of the desk, took off my helmet, and promptly fell asleep using the vest as a pillow.

Less than one hour later I was awakened by the attack siren, accompanied by the well-known words screaming out over the loudspeakers around the base: "Rockets, rockets, rockets. This is the 366th command post. Da Nang is under attack, Da Nang is under attack. All personnel please take cover; Da Nang is under attack. Rockets, rockets, rockets." These were the words we all feared. One's distance from the explosions could be determined by the sound they made, and within seconds I could hear the distant whump, whump of rockets exploding far enough away that they were not a problem. Seconds later I heard several of the six-foot-long weapons roar overhead like freight trains in the sky. They were not a problem for me. The next group hit without warning, cracking all around me. When the detonation sounded like a big stick breaking, the rocket was within killing distance. My head left my flak vest as I pressed the left side of my face into the concrete floor.

There were so many explosive cracks I couldn't determine ex-actly which one blew supersonic molten metal through the steel wall an inch above my head. I felt it whiz past as it ripped gashes through the metal above and in front of me. Tears streamed out of my eyes as the explosions continued. I thanked God I was still breathing. I asked myself about twenty times, *What are you doing here, you dumbass?* I prayed out loud, "Please God keep me alive and please let me live through this disaster." The rockets kept coming and coming, exploding all around the building and the flight line. The intensity of the explosions was deafening. Then a feeling of calm surrender came over me and I quit hugging the ground, realizing that these rockets could easily come right through the roof at any second; I was surprised, in fact, that none had. If that happened, it wouldn't matter how tightly I was hugging the floor. With that thought I rolled over on my back, my arms spread out perpendicular to my body and my eyes gazing at the ceiling. I thought, *What the fuck, it either is or it isn't.*

The unbroken darkness outside turned to gray and the frequency of explosions reduced. Finally the rockets stopped coming. My heart was pounding; I was frightened. I had lived through many rocket attacks but none of them ever came close to what we experienced that final morning of U.S. combat involvement in Vietnam. Walking to the window at the front of the building, I saw three unexploded rockets sticking out of the road. Explosive ordnance disposal personnel promptly wrapped chains around the rockets and dragged them away with their jeep. Large slabs of concrete from the drainage ditch behind the building had been thrown over the revetment wall and a tower of water shot high into the air from an exploded pipe.

I later learned that about 440 rockets had exploded on base that morning and one man was killed – one of the last combat deaths in Vietnam. He had remained in the barracks hiding in the latrine. Because the rocket had detonated right next to his head, the "V" pattern of the explosion caused the shrapnel to miss his body, but the concussion of the explosion had scrambled his brains. The impact point was marked by a missing piece of concrete that the tip of the warhead had removed from the latrine floor. Of that half of the barracks, only bits of wood remained.

I walked back to the wonder arch and rounded up my crew; we drove to the end of the runway to recover the birds as they landed. We disarmed the M-60 machine guns on the OV-10s and drove back to the line to watch the last planes hit the chocks for the final time at Da Nang. Our flight line mutt was asleep on the ramp as the last OV-10 taxied about two feet away from him, coming to a stop with the prop blades of the right engine spinning above his sleeping head. The very moment that our airplanes shut down at 8:00 A.M., the fully loaded Vietnamese Air Force A-37s came screaming down the runway, taking off for targets in the North. The war did not end for the Vietnamese. Nor did it truly end for American forces either. We carried this war forward from bases in Thailand and elsewhere, launching attacks into Cambodia and Laos for another eighteen months.

Nor did the end of the war mean I was leaving Vietnam any time soon. Troop withdrawals were controlled and nobody was in control. I was ordered to the flight line many times to catch a bird to Thailand and was either kicked off, sadly watching the plane take off without me, or the flight was cancelled at the last minute. Then, on March 3, 1973 a big security policeman roused me from my bed at six o'clock in the morning. "Get yourself down to the flight line immediately," he said. "There's a 130 waiting with your name on it." That's all I needed to hear. Within minutes I was downstairs in a pickup truck on my way to the line. I threw my stuff, including my Sanyo three-speed oscillating fan, in the back of the C-130 and took off for Ubon, Thailand.

Chapter 10

A NEW PATH

The flight to Ubon was, thankfully, uneventful and short. After the C-130 taxied to a stop and the rear ramp opened I felt an immediate rush of hot, wet air enter the aircraft. Ubon was even hotter and more humid than Da Nang, most likely because Da Nang was directly on the coast and Ubon was far inland surrounded by jungle. This heat was only a small sample of what I would experience each day on the flight line. A bus took me to the squadron headquarters where the First Sergeant awaited my arrival.

I was excited to get downtown, impatient and frustrated with the squadron First Sergeant who took several hours to get me checked in. Upon completion of the procedure I immediately took a shower and shaved in preparation for my first night in Ubon. About five o'clock that afternoon, on a Saturday or Sunday, I found my way to the base taxi stand and caught a cab into the city. The taxi dropped me off near a bar frequented by airmen from the base. The bar was not yet open so I stopped a samlar, which is a

Thai pedicab, and rode around looking at the sights. After a relaxing half-hour ride with no fear of rocket attacks, I asked the driver to take me to the Ubon Hotel, where I spent my first two nights in town for five dollars, one hundred baht, each night. It was a good hotel but until I could find a bungalow I would have to live in the barracks to save money.

The barracks was an especially unpleasant place to live. It consisted of a large open area lined with bunk beds and lockers. All of the radios, stereos, and conversations blended together, making privacy and rest nearly impossible. Given that the barracks was filled with shift workers, the noise continued nearly round-the-clock. The heat and humidity of Thailand made this space distinctly hot, sweaty, and unpleasantly odiferous. The bunk bed I shared was adjacent to a pair of lockers, one of which was mine, and since the lower bed was already occupied I was assigned the upper bunk. In this bed I benefited from the cooling effect of a large ceiling fan, but other than that, the location of the fan was an intolerable negative. The blades were nearly as large as the propeller of a C-130 and seemed to roar at the same volume and spin at the same speed. With the fan rotating rapidly about two feet over my head, I risked decapitation if I sat straight up. Climbing in and out of this bed required a refined roll in-roll out approach, adding to the inconvenience of living in the barracks.

My primary concern about the barracks was the constant noise and confusion, which made it very difficult to practice meditation. I wanted to move off-base as soon as possible so I could resume my meditation routine, but did not know where to begin looking for a bungalow. I was pleasantly surprised when I met two weapons mechanics, Chuck and Jim, from Udorn. They had volunteered for reassignment to Ubon and were looking for a third person to share a four-bedroom bungalow in a quiet neighborhood outside of town. I drove with them to check it out and it was exactly what I wanted: a middle-class bungalow with an American-style bathroom and a shower with hot running water – a rare find in Thailand. We made arrangements with the manager, whom we called Papa San, to move in the following day. To avoid paying a dollar a day for a round-trip taxi ride to and from work, I purchased a ten-speed Japanese made bicycle and settled into a regular meditation practice in my new home.

Other than the lack of rocket attacks and the difference in countries we were bombing, nothing had changed about fighting the war. The workload was even more intense than it was at Da Nang. We worked twelve hours a day loading 2000-pound laser guided bombs, 500-pound snake-eye hard bombs, guns, rockets, and cluster bomb dispensers nearly non-stop. I was grateful for the one or two days off we received each week. On my second or third day off, I found myself reflecting on the war we were secretly fighting in Cambodia and on the people in South Vietnam, who were now fighting the Viet Cong and the North Vietnamese Army and Air Force by themselves for the first time in thirteen years. I began thinking of things that had not occurred to me while in Vietnam. I was an Air Force NCO paid to assist in the destruction of people, places, and things. Looking back on myself in the combat environment, I saw a side of myself that was capable of cruelty to innocent people and unremorseful over my personal contribution to the deaths of hundreds, even thousands of human beings. I did not see them dying directly, but I knew they all died horrible deaths from weapons I had loaded and there was essentially no difference between them and me.

Sometimes our Vietnamese enemies were women and children and there was no sure way to tell them from the women and children who wanted to help us. The flashlight batteries used to launch the 122 mm rockets that bombarded Da Nang came mostly from the base, carried through the gate and given to the Viet Cong by women and children. I thought about the Vietnamese woman shot to death six feet in front of me as I left the shower one morning; she was carrying high explosives in a small canvas backpack. The Vietnamese people appeared to me as something other than human and it was this perception that helped justify my actions at the time and caused me to experience pain and guilt later. If I could rationalize my actions, I was certain the leaders of nations were easily capable of excusing theirs as well.

I believed I valued individual peace within and peace in the world. Yet, in the face of those values, I found myself killing people while avoiding being killed. None of this was an accident. It was all a result of choices I had made. I could not excuse my actions by saying I needed to make a living and somehow found myself killing people so I could feed myself and my family, but that was exactly what I was doing. The reality was that I had made choices that began as thoughts in my mind. I spoke those thoughts and then took action to make those thoughts real in the world. Mentally reviewing the impact of a few key choices, I became aware of connections between my thoughts and my everyday experiences.

However, I could only evaluate and consider those thoughts of which I was consciously aware, and those thoughts did not explain all of my experiences. I apparently also operated according to thoughts and choices occurring outside of my conscious awareness, so the part of me known as the unconscious must actually have a mind of its own. It made its own plans, and though I was consciously unaware of those plans, I then acted in ways that made them real in the world. The real power to create my life must lie in the unconscious. But what can I do about something of which I am totally unaware? I strongly believed it was possible to consciously connect with this inner power. Uniting my conscious and unconscious selves could enable me to choose and manifest my plans and intentions with awareness rather than acting out intentions created by my unconscious self. I chose to find a way to become aware of this powerful part of myself and started by forgiving myself and accepting my past actions. There was nothing I could do about them now anyway. I was only able to affect what was going on right now, so I focused my attention on the present moment.

After abstaining from women in Vietnam, I made a conscious choice before arriving in Thailand to find a compatible woman who wanted to move into my bungalow with me. A synchronistic series of events in early April led me to the home of a beautiful twenty-four-year-old Laotian woman named Noi. She told me that an American, who had departed Thailand about six months ago and was living in Florida, had promised to come back to Thailand, marry her and return with her to Florida. She had strong doubts that this would ever occur. I explained to Noi that I was married to a woman from the Philippines, had two little girls, and intended to return to them when I left Thailand. The fact that I was married did not preclude me from asking Noi to move in with me about three weeks after we met. I was aware that others, my own parents especially, might judge my actions as immoral because I was married to Maria while living with Noi. This did not cause me to think that I was bad or lacking in a strong spiritual character. I saw God as nonjudgmental and I did not judge myself for my relationship with Noi.

One afternoon on a day off, she and I were upstairs eating a mango when I stepped outside onto the balcony. Looking across the neighborhood and out toward the jungle, I was surprised to see an old friend standing on the balcony of a bungalow about two hundred feet away. It was Jim from Da Nang. I called his name and he heard me, clearly shocked when he looked in the direction of my voice and recognized me. He and his girlfriend walked to my bungalow immediately. This was certainly not a coincidence. His Thai girlfriend, Tao, visited with Noi while Jim and I discussed what had happened since we had last seen each other in Vietnam. Jim was an F-4 crew chief; he had departed Da Nang when the F-4s left and had lived in a small downtown bungalow before moving into this neighborhood just a few days earlier. We had formed a close friendship in Vietnam and maintained that relationship in Thailand, seeing each other nearly every day on the flight line and spending time together when we had the same day off.

It was about noon on the last day of April 1973 when Jim rang the big bell I had attached to the side of the bungalow; he came upstairs immediately, apparently very excited about something.

"Hey, what's happening, bro?" he asked with a big smile on his face.

"Not much," I said. "Just hanging out waiting to go to the job later on." He and I were on the night shift at the time.

"I want to show you something," he said, reaching into his pocket. He pulled out a folded piece of aluminum foil and opened it up. Wrapped in the foil was a small sheet of paper about two inches on each side. "Take a look at this."

"What?" I asked.

"It's LSD," he explained, smiling. "Very good LSD. I got it in the mail yesterday from a buddy back in the world." I do not know what inspired him to tell me this, but he did. "Want to try some?"

"Jeez, I don't know, man; I've never done it and don't know if I ever will."

In the past I had considered taking LSD to see if it would do for me what I heard it did for others who had taken it. It was offered to me while at St. Norbert in 1966 and when I was in Greenwich Village after returning from Korea in 1970; I turned it down both times. I had read about people's positive experiences with LSD under the supervision of a psychologist or psychiatrist and the accounts of certain well-known Hollywood actors and actresses of the 1950s who claimed their lives had been very positively affected by LSD therapy. I also had read what several Zen monks and mystics had to say about their LSD experiences. This is what most interested me – the possibility of a mystical experience – but fear had always held me back. I had read the accounts of Alan

Watts, Gordon Wasson, Aldous Huxley, and Carlos Castaneda, who had experienced psilocybin mushrooms, mescaline, or LSD and written about the power and beauty of their experiences. I had also studied the pharmacology of LSD, psilocybin mushrooms, and mescaline. However, I had never seen or ingested any of them.

"Why not?" asked Jim.

"Man, I want to take it; I've heard a lot of good things about it. But what happens if I go crazy? I can't stand the idea of being out of control or scared shitless even for a second, let alone twelve hours." There was no way I could know if my mind would spin out of control for a day or forever, but pieces I had read in popular magazines and seen on television – kids taken to Bellevue and shot up with Thorazine, Diane Linkletter jumping out a window – had indicated this was a definite possibility. When I mentioned this fear factor, Jim made an interesting proposal.

"Of course, it's up to you," he said, "but I have an idea in case you're interested."

"What might that be?" I trusted Jim and was willing to listen to his plan.

"You know Tom, the crew chief on the bird next to mine?" I had seen and spoken with Tom several times while at work.

"Yeah, sure," I responded.

"Well, he and I are going to take some on our next day off. If you want, you can hang out with us and see for yourself what happens."

"What good is that?" I wondered.

"Well," Jim began, "if you see what happens to us and hear what we've got to say about it, that might help you make up your mind. I mean, you said you're interested in it and you have some fears. If you see how it affects us it might help you make up your mind. And whatever you decide is fine, no pressure."

Though there could be no guarantees, I thought that was a good idea, and his willingness to share the experience with me was very gracious. "I've got to think about it," I said. "Let's do this: when you and Tom are ready, let me know. Then I'll tell you if it works for me or not."

"Good enough, we'll do that."

Two nights later I saw Jim driving his aircraft tug down the line. He saw me also and stopped; I climbed into the big vehicle. These powerful machines, with independent all-wheel steering, were used to move aircraft around on the flight line.

"Tomorrow morning after work Tom and I plan on taking some LSD. What do you think?"

"I've thought about it. If you want, you and Tom can come to my bungalow in the morning and I'll hang with you while you do your thing."

"Okay then, sounds good," Jim said. "We'll pedal our bikes to your place and go from there."

"Great, I'll see you about six."

Chapter 11

A DIFFERENT WAY TO BE

After the night shift wrapped up, Jim, Tom, and I met at the weapons shop and rode our ten-speeds back to the bungalow. It rained a little on the way back but we pedaled leisurely, enjoying the ride through town and then into the countryside. A large lake bordered both sides of the road. Fishermen in their makeshift boats, constructed of expended Styrofoam flare cases, floated around the lake catching the fish they would later take to market and feed to their families. We arrived at my bungalow about 6:30 in the morning and left our bikes in the empty carport.

We ran up the stairs into the guest room. Jim removed the aluminum foil packet from his pocket, opened it, and separated one square from the rest of the small sheet. He cut that in half and he and Tom each put the small piece of blotter paper in their mouths. It was only about fifteen or twenty minutes before they started talking a lot and laughing at silly jokes that I didn't think were funny. I never saw two people laugh so hard; they settled down after about an hour. They stayed at the bungalow most of the day, thoroughly enjoying themselves for the seven or eight hours that we were together. Sometimes they were quiet, not saying a word, while they stared at the most ordinary things as if they had never seen them before. The ceiling fan was an especially big hit for them. At one point Tom spread out on the floor, looking up at the rotating fan. He talked about it like it was the greatest thing he had ever seen. After watching it spin for a minute or two, Tom said loudly, "I think I'm losing it." I wondered what he thought he was losing when he suddenly began laughing and moved on to something else. Several times one or the other of them lit a match in front of the other's face, pulling it back rapidly and laughing at the other's facial expressions.

They had no intention of using the LSD as a therapeutic or spiritual tool and I don't think either one of them had ever heard of a mystical experience. They just wanted to have some fun, and it looked like they did. In their actions or conversation, I saw no sign that they were experiencing what one might call enlightenment or anything remotely spiritual. Neither did they display any anxious or fearful behavior. When they weren't caught up in something else, both of them answered my questions, explaining what they were experiencing and how they felt about it. After a few hours they started to look tired as the effects began to wear off. They sat around for a while and then decided to go home. The whole adventure looked completely safe to me, so I decided I wanted to experience it myself, as long as I could do it with someone else. I told this to Jim and we arranged to get together on our next day off.

Three days later, at the completion of the night shift, we would be free from work for the following thirty-six hours. This time we

rode our bikes to Tom's bungalow, which only took a few minutes because he lived just outside the perimeter fence at the end
of the runway. After the first F-4s of the day took off roaring
down the runway in full afterburner, I said, "Hey guys, this noise
is not working. We can't even hear ourselves speak." Tom and Jim
agreed. We jumped on our bikes, pedaled to my place, and parked
the bikes in the carport. The first floor of the bungalow consisted
of a Thai bathroom, a small kitchen, and a large living room. The
three of us took our seats in the living room where Noi joined
us with glasses of orange juice from the kitchen. Jim removed an
envelope from his shirt pocket; the aluminum packet was inside
the envelope. Jim's girlfriend Tao walked in from their bungalow
as another friend parked his bike in the carport. They joined us in
the living room.

Jim removed a rectangular piece of blotter paper from the envelope. Perforations divided the paper into sixty squares. This was
his main supply. I got up close this time to watch what he was doing. In the center of each square was a faint colorless circle about
three-eighths of an inch in diameter; this was the LSD. According to Jim, this acid was so powerful that one half of the circle was
a full dose that would provide a powerful LSD experience. He cut
the required number of squares in half with a pair of surgical scissors that he had obtained from a medic on base. Each of us except
Noi placed one half of a square in his or her mouth. As I placed
the piece of paper in my mouth, I felt a connection with the sacred
that reminded me of the first time I had received a Holy Com-
munion host in church when I was seven years old. I prepared
myself for the presence of God. I don't know what the others had

intended or thought about as they were taking their LSD, but I was pretty sure they were ready to party. I said nothing about my spiritual thoughts or expectations. "Keep it in your mouth for a while," Jim advised, "so the LSD can dissolve with your saliva. That will get you off quicker." The only flavor I was able to discern came from the paper itself. After a couple of minutes I swallowed the paper. I had no idea what to expect – from myself or anyone else. I felt excited but secure; this was my home and each of my guests was a friend.

I had waited many years, passed up several opportunities, and right now was the moment. This morning in Thailand was beautiful, with a cloudless sky and a light, intermittent breeze. From the front window I saw the green of the dense jungle contrasting with the blue sky above; colorful birds chattered in the trees. Being here was a gift.

Tao and Tom went upstairs to the big room with the balcony. I remained downstairs with Jim and our other friend, an F-4D fire control technician whose name I cannot remember. After about fifteen minutes I began to feel cold although the outside temperature was about ninety. I laughed loudly when I suggested we warm the place up by closing the screen door to keep the cold air outside. After that, anything anyone said occurred to me as uproariously funny in a totally nonsensical way. Our entire world, our lives, everything, appeared as a funny joke told by a cosmic jokester. Who cared if life was nothing more than a joke played on humans for an unknown reason or for no reason at all? There was nothing to be known and nobody to do the knowing. It was clear to me that we all are here running around on earth for a purpose completely different from the stories we are told and the reasons we make up. We are not what most of us think we are. No. We are much more capable and powerful than we realize. We could all be spending our time creating love, fun, good food, and joy. The rich aesthetic of this meaningless, effortless life could set us free to create beauty in all we see. Instead, we all go around with masks on acting like it is all so seriously important while most of what we do is senseless.

Everything we were doing looked so funny to me because it really was, and is, pointless. Even the awful killing we did every day was mostly just to give us something to do. The way we have structured our world causes us to think we have to be doing something all the time, and most of what we have created to do centers around making stuff for other people to buy and throw away. What a waste of time. But if we don't occupy our time with something, we might go crazy. The thought that some of us consider killing each other and destroying property to be critically important and meaningful made me think we had already gone collectively crazy. What difference will any of this make in twenty years or two hundred?

These thoughts were not funny. After laughing for about twenty minutes, I now felt serious. I walked upstairs and went out onto the balcony alone. I stood at the rail, surveying the neighborhood and the jungle from an elevated vantage point. A palpable sense of perfection and harmony poured over me, flowing into and through me. We sometimes use "perfection" to mean that everything looks the way we planned it, or that we got the result we wanted from one of our personal, insignificant plans. Perfection occurred to me in that moment as something different. I had no preconceived notions about what should be going on or how any of it should look. The perfection I perceived was the harmonious order of the entire universe exactly as it exists from moment to moment.

The perfection of our lives on earth is a reflection of the perfect music of the spheres, the motion of the planets revolving around the stars that make up the billions of galaxies in the universe. From exploding stars to the turn of a new blade of grass popping out of the soil into the light of day, everything flows together in harmonious order. Our hearts beat rhythmically, synapses of the brain fire in perfect sequence; each beat, each burst of electricity connects to the farthest reaches of the universe, giving and receiving the energy of life. From the birth of a child to the death of a hero, not one thing occurs anywhere that is not intimately connected, indeed at one with, everything else everywhere. We live, breathe, and move in a vibrating field of beauty and all of it is us. Nothing happens out of order or in isolation from anything else.

The sun captured my gaze as it crept above the roofs of the bungalows, casting its light directly on the jungle trees. The light reflected off the trees, focused through the lenses of my eyes, and sparked images inside my head. The universe, all that is, exists only here, in me. My senses constantly generate an objective reality that appears outside myself, designed by me to show me who I am. It's a beautiful story, all of this, woven by me and by you to describe the arc of a life that goes on without beginning or end.

Everything we experience reveals to us our unified oneness with each other and our true identity as the creator gods that we are. That revelation is the ultimate purpose of the universe and our lives here on earth. Everything we've been told and all the stories we have made up about our jobs, our investments, and our eventual retirements are proximate fantasies designed to lead us to an understanding of our ultimate identities. This is a cooperative effort, created by all of us together, as we harmonize with each other on a level that remains hidden from our sight. When we tune our vision to the one vibration that we all are, we see with clarity that we are all in this together. Until we collectively realize this unity, we will continue to function separately, missing the peace available to us right now. And the tuning is so simple it would be a disgrace to miss it any longer.

Chapter 12

THE UNBORN NOTHING

Our small enclave of bungalows stood alone outside of town, surrounded on three sides by dense green jungle that met the blue sky at the horizon. On the fourth side, a wide river formed a border with a grassy meadow beyond the bungalows. A few small clouds floated far away in the sky like intermittent thoughts floating through the emptiness of my mind. I looked out across the neighborhood to the jungle beyond. This beauty is the unborn nothing that we call God. It extends into forever, leaving self-aware universes in its wake as it plays hide and seek with itself everywhere all at once. The beauty of creation and the awareness that appreciates it are both God – immanent yet transcendent – fully present in each moment, forever. The surrounding multiplicity of trees, bungalows, birds, lizards, sky, and rocks is an illusion we create to give us different ways of looking at ourselves. We are this reality we perceive and we are the uncreated nothing we know as God, blended together in the complete and total unity of oneness. The underlying reality that is God and our everyday experience of life always have been and always will be the same, identical, one. Standing there on the balcony, suspended above the world, I was the subject having an experience and the object being experienced all at once. This experience of shifting perspectives was strange, but I rolled with it and let it happen, allowing truth to flow over me and carry me away like a rushing river headed for a waterfall.

I knew without doubt that what I perceived was the natural state of everything that exists around me all the time. My mind had peeled back its filtration system and the data that inform reality came through all at once. The flowing river really did come to the falls and I flew over, spinning into eternity. There was no danger in going over the waterfall and nothing to fear about everyday life. I am not a thing and it is no-thing that underlies all of reality. This no-thing is what allows this experience to happen; I am nothing and I am the experience and one day I will separate from my body again. When that happens I will not lose my identity, I will regain it. I will be right here where I am now, but it will all look different as my identity continues on as the singular, conscious, nothingness that always was and always shall be. From nowhere onto the blank white table of my mind, thousands of pieces of a jigsaw puzzle tumbled, each taking its place in the meaning of the whole. As the pieces came together they created an image of the universe, of God, as a formless nothing informed only by thought: my thought, your thought, our thought. It is nothing that creates the space for the creation of anything we can think of, and it is our thinking that creates anything we choose.

I gasped as my eyes opened wide and I said to myself, "This is exactly what happened when I was thirteen." What had just

78

occurred was in many ways identical to the non-experiences of May 1961 on Long Island and of 1967 in Green Bay. The primary difference between now and then was that I had intended this experience and was prepared for it. These mystical experiences were not a random sequence of coincidences. The similarities between the spontaneous experiences of 1961 and 1967, the intended experiences of astral travel and meditation that I had practiced since 1968, and this experience with LSD shifted my perspective from believing in an idea to knowing it as reality.

The direct, intense, experience subsided but I was still under the influence of LSD. I felt an increased situational awareness and sensitivity to my surroundings; other than that my mind was clear and I was ready to go inside and find my friends. They were mostly engaged in antics similar to those I had observed during the trip with Jim and Tom. In between periods of goofing around, listening to music, and laughing, they sat and said nothing. There was one negative highlight when Jim's girlfriend, Tao, began crying. She said she was afraid that nobody liked her or wanted her. She carried on for what seemed like a long time and, feeling that it was my responsibility to calm her, I went over to her and began speaking with her. Shortly thereafter she calmed down and seemed to be herself once again. In a few hours the effects of the LSD wore off and our guests decided to go home.

Later that evening, Noi and I sat on the balcony. A faint glow in the west was all that remained of the sun. A dog barked in the distance, momentarily breaking the utter silence of the moment. We sat there quietly, two tiny, insignificant dots in the midst of an infinite ocean of creation. This is what it comes down to, I thought. The gentle peace and beauty of full immersion in the moment is what we all live for, strive for, and what money cannot buy. This priceless instant never ends and is freely available to all of us all the time. I then felt a deep appreciation for the gift of the moment, so rare that it will never again be duplicated in the entire saga of the universe.

Something had shifted, leaving me with a different perspective on everything that had transpired and all that had not yet occurred. Although my previous transcendent experiences had occurred naturally and this one resulted from my having taken LSD, it was this experience that served to strengthen my confidence in the others. My observations of the people I had spent the day with made it clear that not everyone experiences this substance in the same way. As with life itself, it has different effects on different people.

I began speaking about my experiences to my friends and others who visited my bungalow. I also found myself discussing things of which I had no previous knowledge. When talking with the doctor during a physical examination, for example, I found myself able to speak about medicine almost as if I had been educated in the field. The mathematics I had struggled with in high school suddenly made sense. I understood the history of evolution and could explain details of quantum mechanics. I had dreams in which I was reading passages from the New Testament and Old Testament that I had never read before, and upon awakening I checked the Bible and confirmed that my readings were accurate. This happened with other books that I had never heard of or read before. I felt like I had access to what is known in Sanskrit as the

Akashic record, a nonphysical library that contains all the information about everything in creation. I simply opened my mouth and initiated conversations that so fascinated the listeners that they began returning to my bungalow with cassette recorders. I realized I was touching on knowledge that was always there but had previously been blocked from conscious view. Now the filter was removed and, like a huge reservoir when a dam is removed, knowledge rushed out with great velocity and volume.

I didn't have to say a word and people, even strangers, interacted with me like I was a wise holy man, though I did not see myself as particularly spiritual, wise, or holy. I meditated frequently, finding a place of great peace within me, but it was through the course of everyday life that I learned more about the meaning of spirituality and holiness. My actions in the world continued producing both intended and unintended results. While it was clear that my conscious thoughts and actions contributed to the results I created, I also saw something else behind the scenes informing my life events.

Bringing the vibrational field that is the totality of creation into what we call our everyday experience of reality involves a complex interplay of energies. We spend most of our lives completely unaware of what is going on, experiencing only a tiny fraction of what exists all around us and within us. Through meditation I looked into my unconscious self to see if I could become more aware of the cosmic dance that generates human experience. These brief glimpses inspired me to believe that I could align my conscious intentions with the energies within me and learn to create my everyday experiences in accordance with my conscious choices.

Most of us don't know how the volume control knob on a radio changes the volume coming out of the speaker. All we know is that when we turn the knob, the volume changes. I suspected that a "knob" might exist for the power inside me, and would give me access to that power even if I knew nothing about how it worked. I thought I could discover such an interface, though at the time I did not know if it was possible or how to go about it.

While on the flight line loading bombs, I often thought of discovering the interface between my ego self and my transpersonal self. It was a strange juxtaposition of thoughts. How could I load these death devices on these powerful killing machines while thinking about creating peace within myself and peace in the world? It wasn't the stress of the workload or the heat that weighed so heavily on my mind. Now more than ever, my conscience weighed on me. When I met the returning birds and the pilots climbed down the ladders to the ground, I always asked, "Where did you drop that stuff?" or "Who did you shoot at?" Sometimes the bombs went straight into the ocean; most of the time they destroyed a bridge or wiped out a bunch of people with hard bombs, cluster units, missiles, or 20 millimeter bullets, which were small bombs themselves. This guilt started in Vietnam and intensified at Ubon.

Chapter 13

UNIVERSAL ENTELECHY

Near the end of August, Noi's American boyfriend arrived in Thailand. About two weeks later they flew back to Florida. I knew the day would come when I would have to say goodbye to Noi but was unprepared for the emotional crash I suffered when she left. Shortly after Noi's departure, a young Thai boy came to my bungalow. I did not hear him arrive and I did not let him in. He simply walked into the upstairs room over the carport. He did not speak but handed me a small piece of lined paper that had been torn from a larger page. On the paper was written in clear English, "Your daughter was born yesterday morning."

I was happy that my daughter was born healthy and very sad that I was not present for the birth. Maria, pregnant with Frances, had returned to the Philippines with Elisa in February. I had attempted to fly to the Philippines earlier that month for the birth of our second child, but the Philippine president, Ferdinand Marcos, had declared martial law, preventing me from entering the country. So I found out that Frances Ann was born at Clark Air

Base hospital on September 11, 1973 from a little Thai boy bearing a small piece of paper. Here was another link in the chain of events that caused me to wonder how all this fit together and why the fitting together didn't appear to be in line with my conscious choices.

Yes, the U.S. was still fighting a war and war can cause all kinds of disruptions in the lives of the people involved in fighting it. I had not seen my oldest daughter since she was two months old, and now Frances was in the Philippines and I had never seen her. Looking back in time, it was clear to me how some apparently small choices that I had made had resulted in these difficult experiences. The choices we make on a conscious level are only part of what is going on. This is why positive thinking and using our thoughts to create our reality fall short of consistently producing our intended results. Our positive conscious thoughts can be headed in one direction, but our unconscious thoughts, in combination with universal entelechy, can create a current that overpowers our positive thinking and sweeps us away to an unknown island far from our planned destination.

I use the word *entelechy* to represent a directing force, inherent in the universe, that results in the actualization of one of many potential possibilities. The entelechy of the universe applies to each of us because we are microcosms of the greater whole. Something bigger than we are, which exists outside of our conscious awareness, drives each of us to actualize our potential in a particular way. The particular ways that our life experiences actualize may not always be identical to the conscious choices we make for ourselves and can therefore cause us to be surprised by the results of those choices. We have the power to enhance the actualization of our potential in accordance with our choices, but, because of this combination of unconscious thoughts and the entelechy of the universe, we can have no guarantee that all of our choices will manifest exactly as we envision them.

My experience showed me that my choices and their results are not always the same, and I therefore set for myself the goal of bringing my unconscious thoughts, along with the energies of the universe that contributed to my life experiences, into conscious awareness. Realizing that I am the universe, I understood the potential difficulty of attempting to completely understand, and work on, myself. It is like trying to view my eyeballs with my own eyeballs. Knowing, however, that anything is possible, I continued pursuing this level of self-examination.

Living without Noi was initially very difficult. Quickly realizing I had no choice, I accepted my reality and used the time alone to practice meditation. During the previous six years of practice I had learned to quickly settle into a centered state of peaceful emptiness. I followed a daily routine of one to two hours of deep meditation that left me feeling peacefully energized when I returned to a state of normal waking consciousness. Various thoughts typically wandered in and out of my awareness for the first ten to fifteen minutes of meditation before I drifted into a state of no mind that left me merged with the singular nothing. I sometimes did not notice that distracting thoughts had entered my mind. When I suddenly realized that I was thinking about something, I allowed the thought to drift away and once again became aware of my breath. These meditation sessions resulted in non-experiences that brought me to the same place I had spontaneously visited years ago. The differences, however, were profound, in that I now maintained my faculties after the meditation.

Letting go of and transcending ego mind takes us to the quiet place from which all of creation arises. In this state of no mind we know nothing other than peace. I learned to enter this place at almost any time that I chose. Not all meditation sessions had this result; each of them, however, left me feeling relaxed and energized. From this place of peace I made a choice to learn how to create anything I chose and experience it in my everyday life. As for my everyday work, I was reminded of the old Zen saying: "Before enlightenment, chop wood, carry water; after enlightenment, chop wood, carry water." Was I enlightened? Yes. Do I know what enlightenment is? No. According to Van Morrison, "It keeps changing into something different."

In my mind it was about what I called self-understanding. There is nothing we must do to know enlightenment and nothing that can prevent us from achieving it. We are talking about our true nature – the true and original nature of all human beings, of all life. You already are your true nature; you are your God self, right now. If you ask yourself the same question that God asked – "Who am I?" – you will be answered and the answer will reveal your true nature. The entire universe came forth from nothing for the sole purpose of answering that question and there is a reason that most of us have forgotten the answer. If you came into the world with a complete understanding of your God self, knowing that you created everything that exists and that your life was a self-created illusion intended specifically to reveal yourself to yourself, then your life on earth would have no purpose and you would not have needed to create the universe in the first place. That is why when we created the universe, we caused ourselves to forget that we did. I practiced daily meditation for the remainder of my time in Ubon, continuing to look for an accurate way to move the volume control knob within me to create consistent results.

In anticipation of my departure from Ubon on October 30, I had gathered most of my things together into somewhat organized piles. I happened to be at home on the morning of October 16 when a taxi carrying an Air Force clerk pulled up in my carport. I walked downstairs and met the airman outside, where he handed me a set of revised orders instructing me to get on a plane for San Francisco the following afternoon. Completely unprepared for this sudden departure, I told him to forget it. He referred me back to the printed orders in my hand. The young airman was surprised at my response because everyone else leaving early was happy about it. With sufficient notice, I might have been happy about it also. There was nothing to be done now except pack and say goodbye to my neighbors and friends. I sold my bicycle to the man next door for $20. I made a quick trip around town to say goodbye to my Thai friends and then took a taxicab to the base. After saying goodbye to some good friends, I ate dinner at the chow hall and took a taxi back to the bungalow for the final time.

After I packed the last of my things in the morning, Papa San gave me a ride to the flight line in his new Datsun five-speed. A C-141 took me to Clark Air Base in the Philippines where I visited with Maria, her mother, brother and sisters, and my two little babies, Elisa and Frances. This was the first time that I had seen

Elisa since I departed for Vietnam in 1972 and the first time I had seen Frances, who was now one month old. Elisa was fourteen months old. She was beautiful, her hair dark brown and trimmed short with light brown skin and dark eyes. I took a picture of her as she kissed her little sister Frances on the cheek. Frances weighed almost ten pounds, a beautiful baby with light skin, wispy blond hair, and green eyes.

After a relaxing two-week reunion in the Philippines I returned to New York for fifteen more days of vacation. While at my parents' home in New York I planned the return flight for Maria, Elisa, and Frances, made the reservations, and purchased the tickets. I was scheduled to be in Myrtle Beach, South Carolina in the middle of November 1973. After loading my possessions into my new car, I drove down to Myrtle Beach and moved into the barracks while looking for a place for my family to live.

Chapter 14

WAR REDUX

When I reported to the weapons shop in the morning I was referred to the squadron commander's office. Meeting the squadron commander on my first visit to the administrative office on a new assignment was unusual. "Good to meet you, Sergeant Wilhelm," he said with a smile. After about fifteen seconds of small talk he got to the point. "I know you just returned from Southeast Asia and you are probably not interested, but we need you in Khorat for six months."

"Excuse me sir, you need me personally?" I asked with surprise. "There must be other people with my skills that could fill that slot."

He narrowed his eyes and spoke slowly with a measured rhythm. "I apologize for the lack of details, but Nixon's extension of the war outside of Vietnam has put a squeeze on experienced weapons people. The 354th TAC Fighter Squadron has a commitment to Khorat, hundreds of our people are there now, and you will join them."

I arranged for a telephone call with Maria to explain why I was on my way to Khorat, Thailand for six months. She said she understood, though I know it must have been very difficult for her to accept. It was difficult for me to accept, and I tried rationalizing that six more months was not that long. Maria was happy in the Philippines with her mother but she wanted even more to be back with me in the United States. I was on a flight to San Francisco the next day.

Almost from the moment I deplaned in Khorat, I felt a negative vibe. I did not like being there and wanted to go home. The only redeeming quality of Khorat Royal Thai Air Force Base was the library. I found a lot of excellent books about higher consciousness and had time to read and to continue experimenting with my mind/body/universe interface. I lived in an old wooden barracks on a deserted section of the base at the end of the bus line. Every day I rode the bus to the main base and worked on the flight line all day, looking forward to the evenings when I rode back to my nearly empty barracks. I saved money by living on base rather than spending it on a bungalow downtown, and the peace and silence of the barracks afforded me the opportunity to meditate and practice other mind exercises. My practice was similar to those I had followed in Ubon and in the North Carolina woods in the late sixties.

Sometime in my second month at Khorat I came down with a bad stomach virus that lasted for a couple of weeks. I went to sick call two or three times and took the medicines that the doctor prescribed for me with no relief. As a last resort the doctor told me to stop eating solid food for a week; I was already feeling weak but he would not excuse me from duty. After the third day without food I went to work at six o'clock in the morning and was confronted with a frag change affecting about 25 birds – a major operation. The temperature was one hundred and five degrees and the humidity was very high. My crew worked alone download-ing bombs from each aircraft while several other crews replaced the hard bombs with cluster units. I was on the flight line for six hours and was exhausted when I finally headed to the chow hall for some much-needed food. I had to eat in spite of the doctor's instructions.

After standing in line for my meal, on my way to the table, I suddenly and instantly lost consciousness with no warning. Al-though completely unaware of it at the time, I fell straight for-ward, hitting the concrete floor with my chin. Returning to con-sciousness was a slow and very strange process. I started waking up in complete blackness and silence when a thought entered my mind. I somehow realized I was lying down, which made no sense to me because I had already gotten up from bed that morn-ing and couldn't figure out why I was again in a prone position. I reached another level of awareness and, feeling my mouth hang-ing open, attempted to close it. I was unable to do so and realized that something bad was happening, whereupon I told myself to remain perfectly still.

At that point I became more aware and heard the Thai wait-resses screaming. I felt people touching my body and then heard a medic say, "Roll him over on his side before he drowns in his blood." Now I was fully awake, lying on the floor completely dis-oriented with no understanding of what was taking place other than knowing that it was not good. I felt no pain and still had no idea why I was on the floor or how I had gotten there. The medical team put me on a stretcher and rolled me into an ambulance. Within minutes I was in the emergency room while one doctor stitched me up and another removed the remnants of my front teeth.

I discovered later that day that I had dislocated and broken my jaw and knocked out several of my teeth, which had gone in one side of my bottom lip and out the other. Khorat lacked the facilities to treat the broken jaw so I stayed at the base hospital overnight. After a painful night and morning in Khorat, in the early afternoon I was placed on a plane to U-Tapao Royal Thai Navy Airfield south of Bangkok. The next day I went into surgery and my jaw was wired shut. I remained in the hospital for three weeks, undergoing every available test to determine the cause of the blackout; the doctors finally advised me that I had passed out due to hypoglycemia. My blood sugar got very low that morning and the next thing I knew, I was waking up on the ground, broken and bleeding.

What a nightmare. This was the biggest disaster that had occurred in my life up to that point. Days passed before I gained the courage to look in a mirror. My appearance was changed forever and I would undergo years of ongoing dental work because of this accident. I looked into my thinking to find the reason for the accident. What had I been thinking about that would lead to such a tragedy? I did not want to know the answer to that and successfully blocked it from my mind. I did know that everything that occurs in the universe, and therefore in our individual lives, occurs in order to guide us toward self-knowledge. That provided little solace, as I was unable to see the benefit of the situation at that time.

Upon my return to Khorat I was placed on restricted duty and no longer loaded bombs on the flight line. Instead, I was given an office job supervising the organization of equipment in preparation for the fighter wing's return to Myrtle Beach. I never enjoyed pushing paper, feeling much more comfortable where the action was out on the flight line. Day after day I sat in a hot Quonset hut office managing the mobilization team.

I departed Khorat in early June 1974, returning to Myrtle Beach in time for the beginning of the city's summer celebrations. My old friend Jim had been in Myrtle Beach since he left Ubon in '73. I was surprised to see another close friend in the weapons shop, Bob Helmig, an AC-119 Stinger gunner I knew from Da Nang. Jim had a small apartment with a spare bedroom, which he invited me to occupy while looking for my own place. I soon discovered an affordable apartment that would be available on September 1st and scheduled my family's arrival for a few days after that.

Chapter 15

FOCUS

Maria, Elisa, and Frances were scheduled to arrive in the first week of September. I planned to use five consecutive Sundays during the summer to continue the exploration of my inner self. To this end I intended to employ the meditation techniques I had learned in Thailand in conjunction with the astral travel practice I used in North Carolina. I selected Sundays because I generally did not work on weekends and was alone every Sunday while Jim worked his second job at the Holiday Inn. I chose specific goals for each meditation session and planned to keep a notebook and pen nearby in case I wanted to record my thoughts.

I spent the first two Sundays reviewing various decisions and events of my life, making no attempt to select them in any sequence or according to any standard. I closed my eyes and began mindfully breathing until I reached an altered state of awareness. I observed and waited for an event to arise in my mind. My memory amazed me as choices and experiences from my youth right up to the present moment began showing up in my awareness; whatever showed up, I examined. I then fragmented those events into the details that occurred before, during, and after the experience. I was able to see motivations and results that had previously remained outside of my consciousness. When I became satisfied that I had thoroughly analyzed that particular decision or event, I moved on until another popped into my mind.

In this manner, over the course of those two full Sundays I reviewed many of the landmark events, thoughts, and decisions that had occurred since I was a child. This retrospective overview left me with the impression that my entire life, literally from the moment my parents met each other, fit together like a novel written by an unknown master author. Events that had seemed to occur randomly now appeared linked together like pieces of a jigsaw puzzle. Various decisions that I had initially interpreted as big mistakes now made sense when viewed as a whole; every experience could be a growth experience if I chose to see it that way.

On the third Sunday of the sequence, as I was sitting on the couch with my legs crossed, my mind quiet, I suddenly felt like I was being attacked by some outside force, some unrelenting and powerful monster. I was frightened and immediately began defending my mind against what I now saw was not one monster but many, possibly thousands. I thought that if I did not defend myself and these unseen monsters got through to my brain, I would be destroyed, perhaps actually killed or maybe turned into a mental vegetable or automaton.

Then, counter-intuitively, I decided that the best thing I could do was to stop defending myself and allow them in. I was afraid to try that but I did it anyway. At the moment I relaxed, giving up all of my defenses and basically saying, "come and get me," the experience of being attacked disappeared like a dark thundercloud after a storm. That's when it occurred to me that, like darkness, fear has no substance of its own. Shining a light under the bed blows the darkness away, and shining the light of awareness on my fear blew my fear away. There was never anything to fear because fear has no reality of its own. I had contributed to the creation of this fearful experience and its solution in the same way that we all play a major role in the creation of everything we live through. Moreover, I came to realize that all of our life experiences are created by the confluence of four elements:

1. Our conscious thoughts and choices: these are thoughts and choices of which we are consciously aware and which we are able to articulate clearly in our thought and speech.

2. Our unconscious thoughts and choices: these thoughts and choices occur outside our conscious awareness, and we are not able to articulate them. For example, if we are walking and suddenly begin running, our hearts will begin beating more rapidly to satisfy our brain's need for more oxygen. We do not consciously choose our heart rate because our unconscious minds choose the exact heart rate that we need at all times.

3. The collective unconscious: according to Carl Jung, the collective unconscious is shared by all members of humanity and inherited by each of us. Individuals have access to and are influenced by the contents of the collective unconscious without having personally had the experiences or memories that are contained within it.

4. Universal entelechy: this is the underlying momentum or vital principle that drives the universe to fulfill its potential in a particular way. Not only does the universe have a par-

ticular entelechy operating within it, but so does everything in the universe. An example would be a caterpillar's entelechy to be a butterfly, or the entelechy of a human fetus to fulfill its purpose as an adult human being. Because each human is part of and one with the universe, this purposeful thrust of the universe impacts the experiences of our individual lives.

We are free to choose our individual conscious thoughts and appear to have a degree of control over them. We can use conscious intention to reprogram much of what happens in our unconscious, thereby causing the activities of the unconscious to conform to our conscious preferences, which strengthens our manifestation abilities. Because all of creation is one we can impact the collective unconscious by choosing to understand our original, true identity.

We can be aware of universal entelechy and flow with it just as we can float downstream with a river's current. By moving with the energy of universal entelechy, we can use it to manifest our preferences. We can learn to flow in the direction of the universal energy by accepting, appreciating, and integrating every experience that comes into our lives. If we are not aware of universal entelechy, we are controlled by it, and we wonder, "What just happened?"

This is the case with everything we experience. Every wonderful thing that happens, every disaster, every great relationship, and the relationships that don't work are all influenced by the individual having the experience within the context of these four forces. When we understand and accept this level of responsibility for the way our lives go, we gain the freedom and the power to transform ourselves and our experience of everyday life. These four elements of manifestation help explain the way the universe works as one unified whole. Each of us is that whole, and as such we are the ultimate creators of our lives. We write and direct the script, and everyone else is simply playing the part we give them.

The threatening monsters in my mind caused me to experience genuine fear, including an increased heart rate and everything else that goes along with a life-threatening experience. The instant I confronted that fear, the imagined threat disappeared and the fear went away. When we see how these four energies work as one, we know without a doubt that the material world is flexible. Since it is flexible, we can change it by changing the way we perceive and think about it: the way we perceive any scene or event is our own choice, and when we change that choice, we can change our world.

When I realized that the event and the fear it inspired were self-created, I opened my eyes and witnessed visible waves of energy rushing out from my heart chakra into the unified field from which all experiences arise. This was the process of the four elements of thought energy coming together to become physical reality. All aspects of my thought energy were transforming into physical matter right before my eyes. There was no distinction between mind and body, the spiritual world and the physical world, other than the difference that we create. Everything that exists everywhere is all the same thing and it all comes forth from nothing. The thoughts occurring in my mind in that moment manifested as the experiences of my life later that day, the next day, or the next year. This holds true for all of us. What we think powerfully influences what we live. If our world of experience fails to correspond with our conscious thoughts, it is because the thoughts we are conscious of are not all of the thoughts that we are having. Our hearts beat and breath goes in and out of our lungs whether we think about it or not. Clearly, some part of us makes that happen. There is more happening outside of our conscious awareness than within it, and therein lies the challenge of accurately manifesting our intentions.

The ground of all being is an ever-present vibrating field extending infinitely and forever, never born and never dying. It is just as it is. We are that vibrating field and when we choose to inform the field with our choices, we transform ourselves along with everything else. The energy we put into the field is the field, and as our energy alters the appearance of the field, it loops recursively back into ourselves, thus altering us along with everything else in creation. As we think, consciously or unconsciously, we impart form to the field, causing us to experience the infinite field as individual and distinct shapes and experiences. I watched as the energy waves emanating from within me became matter one particle at a time. I saw these vibrations leave me and enter a tiny machine. Millions of these miniscule devices continually processed energy waves into tiny vibrating particles we know as the building blocks of matter. My choices determined which machines the waves entered and different machines produced different kinds of particles. The individual whirling particles emerged nameless; it was human thought that named these essential elementary particles, which form from the energy of God to create everything that exists.

Particular kinds of particles bumped into other particles, creating atoms, molecules, and ultimately the things called walls, chairs, record albums, my body, and everything I saw in every direction that I turned. There was nothing solid about the particles that came together to create the physical world; they all began as energy waves that I perceived as multicolored, translucent, squiggly lines emanating directly from my heart and flowing around, through and between everything. The material objects that I saw around me did not exist in space but only in my mind. This was an active experience, not a passive observation. I distinctly felt the connection between my mind, the objects around me, and the space between those objects. I perceived myself as the creator, the object, and the subject of a continuous, unbroken whole. I experienced reality as one because oneness is its nature. The moment I began thinking analytically about this experience, it stopped. My perception of the world returned to the way I was accustomed to seeing it: a bunch of solid objects spread out before me in space.

Questions arose immediately. I knew that this experience of reality did not apply only to me. I wondered how everybody could be creating the world all at the same time while mostly agreeing about the way it looked. We might have different perceptions of red or blue but we are able to drive cars on the road because we all see each other, and if we're not paying attention, we will feel it if we bump into each other. Was I responsible only for experiences that directly impacted me or was I somehow creating everything, whether I knew about it or not? I remembered naming the cards before lifting them from the deck and thought that this principle, if I understood it at all, might apply to the experience I just had. My mind felt connected to all of those energy waves, tiny particles, and massive objects. Did that mean that I could change their structure; did that mean I could walk through them or make them disappear entirely? If my thought energy gave form to the infinite unified field, could I then alter the appearance of that field by altering the way I thought? One thing that struck me was that I was the creator of whatever came into my experiential field. Could I heal my body; could I create wealth and health? This was a rare and powerful idea to comprehend. It did not occur by magic, accident, coincidence, or luck. I witnessed this creative process because I had intended to witness it.

Before the first Sunday of the series I had outlined my goals for each week. During each week, that particular goal was on my mind, off and on, for the entire week. During the week, I was not aware that thinking about the goal for the coming Sunday was energizing or priming the unified field to deliver the intended result. I had a plan and I consciously chose each element of the plan, but I did not choose each detail of the plan. My goals were stated in more general terms with my focus on the final outcome. While I was doing this, I did not know that this was the way to do it; I did not know how or if it would turn out. I chose to see how creation worked, how my experience of the world showed up. I did not choose to see energy waves emanating from my heart chakra. I could not comprehend how such goals would be fulfilled; I knew only that I wanted to experience their fulfillment. The beautiful waves of multi-colored light that moved out into space and transformed into the tiniest elements comprising the physical world were the fulfillment of the goal, the answer to the question. I picked up on this because I thought deeply about the experience immediately after it occurred while it was still fresh in my mind. At the time, I knew this experience was satisfying but I did not know and could not predict how important this would become in that malleable dream world we call the future.

After I settled down from that intense observation, I closed my eyes and reflected on the state of existence prior to the Big Bang, when there was only the nothing we sometimes call God. Because nothing else existed in that time before time, God was pure subject, and as such, had no way to reflect upon itself. God therefore had no way to know anything about itself. That caused God to wake up to the question, "Who am I?" In questioning its identity, God launched the creation of the universe, thus becoming creator, object, and subject of all experience.

Similarly, I had just woken up to the idea that my everyday reality was a movie that I wrote, produced, acted in, and directed. In waking up to my own power I also woke up to the fact that we all create our own movies. The movie we produce in the world tells us everything there is to know about ourselves, and that is why we create it – that is why God created the universe. Our interpretation of reality that we call our personal life guides us to self-knowing by showing us all the various aspects of ourselves. Everywhere we look all we see is a reflection of our thought, and everything we do reveals another aspect of who we are. Now I wanted to know how flexible reality really is. To what degree and how quickly are we able to alter reality with the power of thought? I suspected that perhaps one day I might gather the energy and the nerve to find out.

I once considered the mystical experience an isolated, discrete experience that revealed to an individual his or her true nature – God. It occurred to me that day in the hot South Carolina summer of 1974 that every moment of life qualifies as a mystical experience revealing the nature of God to God, God to man, and man to God all the time.

The following Sunday, the fourth Sunday in the sequence, I started out by putting a Moody Blues album, *Every Good Boy Deserves Favor*, on the turntable. I tuned in to the music, became aware of my breathing, and listened to the words, "All my life I never really knew me 'til today, now I know I'm just another step along the way" (Moody Blues, 1971). Questions streamed rapidly through my awareness. When God creates, how much control does he have over the creative process? Does God bog himself down with decisions about every star he creates and the details of mitosis in the cells of earthbound animals? Does God at some point call his creation complete, never to be changed? Does God calculate the amount of adrenaline per milliliter of blood required in the human bloodstream to ensure survival in specific emergency conditions? Or does God take a more macro approach to the creative process? Does God have anything at stake in his creation, like time or effort, something that might keep him in the game? Or does God blow off universes and start fresh if they are not working out as he had planned? Does God have a plan? Do the building blocks of reality, from quarks to quasars, protons and electrons, remain the same for all places in all universes and all types of creations? And the question that loomed largest in my mind on that Sunday and for many years thereafter was this: whatever it is that God does, HOW does God do it? What specifically does God do, if anything, to bring this incredibly miraculous experience of life into existence? What are the details of the process that turn the primordial thought energy of God into a living, material being?

While searching for the "how" of creation I closed my eyes and waited for the answer. On the movie screen of my mind I saw myself walking along a city street, peering into the shop windows, anxiously seeking knowledge of the creative process. Suddenly, up ahead at the next intersection, I caught a glimpse of God standing there, waiting. He had white hair and a thickly flowing white beard. He glowed brightly in his long white robe, eyes twinkling, smiling a warm, loving smile. God raised his right arm, his hand beckoning me to come to him so he could show me the how of creation. With eyes wide open, I ran to him to learn the answer. Then, just before I reached him, he whipped around the corner. I called to him, "Wait, please wait," but when I got there and looked, he was gone. The only sign of his presence was a pile of dry leaves stirred from the ground into a whirlwind as he whisked past. I watched the spinning circle of leaves fall slowly to the ground and hung my head in sadness; the answer to the how of creation had eluded me once again. I considered the possibility that the details of God's process may be forever unknowable. That was unacceptable, so I continued pushing, trying, following clues in my mind in pursuit of this elusive knowledge.

Many times we may ask ourselves the question: How can I accomplish it? A young person may dream of being a fighter pilot or a university professor and ask, "How do I get from college student to fighter pilot? What are the steps that will take me there and what else is involved?" This is actually the same as asking, "How does God make an atom, or a universe? How did God get from nothing to here – to me and you?" I continued asking and later that day God gave me the answer: He said, "I chose it." In the beginning God chose to know who and what he was, and everything that ever has been, is now, or ever will be is the answer. Beyond asking, "Who am I?" God does not know how he does anything. God makes a choice and the universe happens. God does not know, control, or attempt to track the details of "how." It is only our desire to anthropomorphize God that has us think that God's mind works like our own. Understanding God's non-doing made it clear to me that I or anyone can consciously choose to create our lives in the same way that God created the universe: choose something and let go of any attempt to control how it manifests.

I had also learned that the choices made by my conscious mind did not always produce desirable results, often dragging along unintended consequences with them. Though these results and consequences were necessary growth experiences, I preferred to grow and change with less pain. My goal was to understand and know my essential self so I could align my conscious thinking with the infinite wisdom within me, thus allowing my actions to be guided by the unlimited wisdom of my God self. This was what I had started thinking about in Thailand. It involved finding a way to connect my conscious thinking with my unconscious self, just like the volume control knob changes the radio's volume because it is connected to the internal electronics in a way that I do not understand. Though this unconscious part of me seemed as remote and unavailable to my normal waking consciousness as the distant galaxies of the universe, I now knew it was possible. Believing in the possibility was a step beyond where I had been that day in Thailand, though I still did not know how to accomplish it.

Chapter 16

THE EASY WAY

I devoted the next two Sundays to exploring the connection between my conscious and unconscious mind while preparing myself mentally for my family's arrival. A blend of excited expectation and nervous trepidation called me to do what I could to ensure a smooth transition to family life. I had created a lot of responsibilities to many people in Myrtle Beach, living a lifestyle that would be unsustainable after Maria, Elisa, and Frances arrived. I had become accustomed to living as a single person, managing my time as I chose, meeting people, and driving from place to place with complete freedom. Among others, I had commitments to the people who had been attending my talks at various venues around Myrtle Beach. To segue into family life, I planned to fulfill existing commitments, make fewer in the future, and announce a reduction to one or two talks each week.

With the end of summer the tourist population decreased, shops closed, and car traffic thinned. I picked up my three girls at the airport around September 4th. Elisa was two years old and

Frances was about a week short of her first birthday. A wave of love washed over me as soon as I saw them. I had not planned for the fact that they did not know me and were afraid to be alone with me for the first week or two after their arrival. That became apparent shortly after we arrived home from the airport and their mother went into the bathroom. Standing right next to me, Elisa saw her mother disappear; she looked up at me and immediately began crying. The pain and fear on Elisa's face caused me to feel pain and woke me up. My priority was clear. I wanted to spend most of my time with my little daughters.

Each day before work, I dropped Elisa and Frances at the day care facility on base. After work I picked them up on my way home. Maria was already at her job when I arrived home with the girls. I prepared our dinner, bathed them, played with them, and read stories to them. Two nights each week, after Elisa and Frances went to bed, five to ten people came to the apartment. This plan got out of control and the number of people soon increased to an untenable level. Now I was in a difficult position; I wanted to focus on my family but it seemed impossible to stop the swelling interest I had generated before my family had arrived. This was no longer just a few friends; I started receiving phone calls from relative strangers at various times of the day and night. Maria was home on the weekends with Elisa and Frances, so I visited several different homes where small crowds waited to hear about what I began calling self-understanding. By the end of each weekend, I had possibly touched one hundred to two hundred people.

These activities, however, consumed a lot of time, and since I also had a full-time job, I was not sufficiently available to my children and I definitely was not being the good husband I wanted to be. Where was this peace I was talking about? Maria asked me to dedicate more time to our family. She was right; I also wanted that. Increasing time with my family meant decreasing it somewhere else. I was so interwoven into the community that I thought our best opportunity for living like a family necessitated leaving Myrtle Beach. Maria agreed, so in February 1975 I filed papers for a three-year tour with my family in Spain. Within six weeks I received orders for Torrejon Air Base in Torrejon de Ardoz, Spain. We were scheduled to depart on November 5, 1975. In order to fulfill my responsibilities to the people and ensure that I left no one hanging, I began informing my community of listeners about my departure as soon as I got the orders.

Maria and I began arguing in early March. I could not blame her given that I had been separated from my family since 1972. Maria was unhappy about my weekly speaking engagements and wanted my full attention on the family. I agreed with her and was willing to reduce my time away from the house even more than I already had. Then the real trouble started. I was on base working when Maria discovered my journals from Vietnam and Thailand. There were five or six spiral notebooks and photographs, including many images of Noi. Maria later informed me that after looking through the photos and notebooks, she promptly dispatched them into the garbage, never to be seen again. Though the journals did not go into detail about the depth of my relationship with Noi, there was enough there to make the situation obvious. I understood my responsibility and did not blame Maria when she verbally lashed me that evening and for several days following. No amount of apologies, pleas for understanding, or restated commitments on my part made any difference.

Though she reduced her overt expressions of anger, I knew that animosity stirred within her. We had been married for three years but had only lived together for about half that time, never establishing a solid bond. As part of my reconciliation efforts I greatly reduced my time away from home. I chose not to completely cease my activities, so I invited a few guests to the house one evening a week after Elisa and Frances were in bed and Maria was at work. I had once loved Maria and wanted to have a lasting and solid relationship with her. When we were home together I devoted my time to her and our daughters and did what I could to re-create the relationship we once had. After about two months we began to relate to each other on a more peaceable level. It was, however, obvious to me that Maria did not completely forget or forgive what I had done.

During this time at Myrtle Beach I continued my normal meditation practice, read constantly, and began experimenting with psychic energies. When I had read *Concentration and Meditation: A Manual of Mind Development* about four years earlier, I had learned about what Christmas Humphreys referred to as *Siddhis*, a Sanskrit term for various powers that some students of the spiritual path acquire. These are psychic or energetic powers, such as the ability to know the past, present and future, knowing the thoughts of others, and achieving whatever one desires in the material world. Christmas clearly stated that these powers are not the goal of the spiritual path; as incredible as they are, they may actually serve as traps, preventing one from achieving enlightenment. Knowing this, I pursued them as a way to demonstrate to myself that what I had perceived as real was real and what I knew as the path was the path.

I began using what I had learned from meditation and from previous interaction with the unified energy field to create new experiments to teach myself how to align my conscious awareness with the power of my unconscious mind. My most profound mystical experiences and everyday meditation practice had shown me that we cannot force enlightenment to happen. It is impossible to achieve any results by using power in a forceful way. This understanding is reflected in the Japanese word *judo*, which means "the easy way." Judo teaches us to defeat an attacker with ease by using his own power against him. We do not force anything to happen; we allow things to happen by creating a space within which something can manifest. We can create an environment that allows power to act in accordance with our conscious choices, but we cannot force the energy of consciousness to make something occur.

This became apparent to me when I was eleven years old. I did not concentrate on seeing the card or knowing the numbers. My ignorance helped me because I simply looked at the deck of cards and named the next one in line when I "heard" it in my head. I simply stated the suit and number of the card and then flipped it over. Later in life, every time I had merged with the unity of being, it happened when I was relaxed and not thinking of it or trying to make it happen. When meditating, I did not try to experience enlightenment or unity with all that is; I simply noticed my breath and followed it as it moved in and out of my body. When practicing astral traveling in North Carolina, I only left my body when I was relaxed and not waiting for it to happen. When my spirit separated from my physical being it surprised me.

One evening in the summer of 1975, while listening to music with three friends, I decided to see if I could know in advance what album my friend would choose to play next. I made no effort to read or inject anything into anyone's mind. Before the current record ended, and before anyone stood up to choose the next album, I simply made a mental note of the music I thought would be chosen. Either the name of the album and the band popped into my mind or I heard music in my mind and named the album and the band. A couple of minutes later, my friend pulled an album from a shelf containing about two hundred albums. When the record began to play, it was the one I had named. This happened with seven out of seven albums that night.

Was I transmitting to their minds or was I hearing their thoughts? I had asked these same questions as a child: did I control the numbers that turned up on the dice or did I foretell that the dice were going to end up on those particular numbers? I had wondered about how this happened; I had wondered how the information could be transmitted without wires and why some people were aware of this ability and some were not.

In 1975, I discovered that information is not transmitted or received anywhere by anyone. All of reality is a unified whole that in some ways resembles a hologram. The hologram is based on the fact that every discrete unit of data that composes the hologram contains all of the information necessary to produce the entire hologram. How that relates to the nature of our universe is that all of the information available in the universe is available everywhere, to every part of the universe, all the time. There really is no person doing the thinking and another person doing the receiving. We are all one and none of us is actually doing any of those things. All the information that exists is available to all of us instantly all the time. There is no time in the created universe, only change. We use the concept of time to track the change. What we call time and space are flexible bits of information; the way we perceive these bits is informed by our beliefs and choices.

Nothing resembling control or manipulation was involved in the experiment that night, or in any other experiment with which I had been involved. The results of this experiment were not due to my controlling other people's thoughts or actions. That was not the case at all. The name of an album or the sound of a song came to my mind and I paid attention to it. This was the universe simply functioning the way it functions, and it doesn't matter whether we know how it functions or not.

The exercise with the record albums could be said to demonstrate the potential of human minds to communicate with each other directly, without the need for external devices and systems. Our minds can certainly do this. However, this is a limited explanation that fails to encompass all available data and falls short of realizing the unity of all that is. Our minds are one mind. Everything we perceive is information; the universe is information, we are information, and we create the information that we are. The information we create appears to us as the lives we live every day. From our human perspective, communication occurs when two or more separate entities exchange information. What we call communication really isn't necessary because there are no separate entities to exchange anything. We are all one and we already know everything there is to know.

The sum of it is, I relaxed in a chair, thought of a piece of music, did nothing, and then almost immediately heard the music playing through speakers. A person with closed eyes, who did not know what was occurring behind the scenes, might consider this a miracle. It was no miracle, however; it was a natural result of the structure of the universe. The universe is not a miracle. The creation of the universe was driven by the act of making a clear choice. I knew in advance the albums that would play because I chose to know them. It was not necessary for me, or my friends, to know the details of how it was possible for one person to think of a piece of music and another person to somehow know it, select it, and play it. Those things occurred as the result of a clear choice and that is all we can, or need to, know about how it works.

The following morning at seven o'clock I was back in my office in the weapons training hangar. I briefed my team on the work schedule for the day and they drove out to the flight line to inspect the weapons crews in action. I trained a crew in the hangar all day with the number four man on my training team while two other teams inspected the other squadron's weapons mechanics. After work I picked up Elisa and Frances, drove home, and prepared dinner. After their bath we read stories together until they went to bed at eight o'clock. I went to bed myself, put on my headphones and listened to Richard Harris reading *The Prophet* by Khalil Gibran. This is how most of my evenings passed since I had committed to being alone with my children every night. Listening to *The Prophet* gave me some ideas for the upcoming Saturday's discussion meeting.

It worked better for Maria if I held the meetings on Saturday mornings for a couple of hours instead of at night during the week. Several people were happy to have the meetings at their homes, which worked very well for me because the number of attendees exceeded the capacity of our apartment. I always felt nervous excitement before a meeting and this hot Saturday in August 1975 was no exception. The format of the meetings was casual; I generally opened by asking if there were any questions remaining from the previous meeting. After answering two or three questions I quoted a portion of Gibran's poem, *The Prophet*.

> No man can reveal to you
> aught but that which
> already lies half asleep
> in the dawning of your knowledge.

That provided an excellent lead-in to the main topic, which arose from the experiment with the record albums. It was the first time I had explained the relationship between the singular nature of creation and our ability to communicate nonverbally. Beginning with a description of the experiment, I concluded with the details of what made the profound results possible. This topic stimulated more questions than usual. I enjoyed seeing the excitement in the eyes of the listeners as I simply opened my mouth and allowed words to flow out. In addition to the people I knew from the Air Force who came to every meeting, I noticed an airman from the training department who was attending for the first time; his name was John.

After answering the final question I touched on some of the points that I planned to discuss the following Saturday and concluded the meeting. After that, all the guests departed except John. It was not unusual for people to stay behind to ask their questions privately. I approached him. He seemed distant, as if we did not know each other. Before I could say hello, he asked, "Are you God?" His question surprised me; it was the first time anyone had asked me that. It was not, however, the first time I had thought about it.

I responded, "Yes, and so are you and so are all of us." John continued looking at me and said nothing. I continued. "No matter what we call it, we all have God, or higher power, within us and we can all experience it and know it. When we do, everything changes. The only difference between me and you, the reason you asked me the question and I did not ask you, is that I have some degree of awareness of God within me. It's a matter of self-awareness and self-knowing," I said. "It's not about personal ego; it's your essential self."

John stood there, perfectly still. I wondered about his demeanor. He approached me like he didn't know me. He had what I thought was a desperate look on his face, and standing there speaking with him, I felt compassion for him. Then he asked, "How I can know the God part of myself and what will change in my life when I do?"

"Those are good questions. Why don't you come to the meeting next Saturday," I said, "and I'll answer them. By the way, you look a little uptight. I mean, we work together every day but you walked up to me like you'd never seen me before."

"I think I'm just nervous, that's all. You're not an ordinary Air Force person. Since you took over the training department I've been thinking you're in the CIA or something, and that makes me nervous."

"Well, I'm not in the CIA, so relax. I've got to get home now, so I'll see you Monday morning."

"Okay, I'll see you then. And thanks."

"You're welcome." John returned the following Saturday and every Saturday after that until I departed for Spain.

I went home after the meeting, Maria went to work, and I took Elisa and Frances out to the park. After dinner I cleaned the kitchen and spread newspapers on the table so Elisa, Frances and I could play with modeling clay. I called them in and put the big piece of clay between them. They had a plan to make a little town of houses and people with the clay. They had no material available other than the clay. When they finished creating their model village out of the piece of clay, all of the tiny houses, cars, trees, and people were necessarily made from, and could only be made from, that original piece of clay. I thought about God, the original nothing from which all of creation arose. Before God created the universe, only God existed. There was nothing available for God to use in the creative process other than God. Everything that exists is, therefore, made entirely from the nothingness that we call God. Elisa and Frances started only with clay and God started only with God.

God was the singular nothing that existed before the creation of the universe and God does not stand separate from this creation. Nothing separate from God existed before the initiation of the creative process and nothing separate from God exists now. God is everything that exists and God is both immanent and transcendent. God is immanently manifest in all the apparently separate parts of the creation while simultaneously subsuming all of creation within God's being. The paradox of simultaneous immanence and transcendence is a verbal attempt to describe something that lies beyond description; it is a humble effort to clarify something that cannot be understood by the reasoning mind.

To help see this more clearly, I broke the thought process down into a short list:

- Nothing existed before the universe.

- Everything that exists today, everything that ever has existed, and everything that ever will exist, arises from this nothing.

- Everything now in existence can be nothing other than the original nothing.

- Many people refer to this nothing as God, Allah, Yahweh, and by other names.

- Knowledge of this nothing is available to anyone who chooses it.

This does not mean that a human being's individual ego self is God. For example, the part of me that is known as Jim does not command the world or the universe with a wave of his hand; indeed, neither does God. This means that our essence, our highest self, what Carl Jung calls our "transpersonal self," is God. Each of us has both the infinite God self and the limited human self within us. We each have the ability to consciously know our God self and to live our lives as conscious expressions of that God self right now. This does not mean that it is good to express our God selves and bad if we do not. It means we each have the power to live lives that we choose. The process of self-discovery transforms our humanity into Godliness if we choose it. Transforming our human aspect does not mean changing it or doing away with it. We need our ego and will always be fully human. Transformation, or enlightenment, means understanding our true nature and expressing it in all aspects of our being. We are now and always will be fully God.

Much of my time in the following weeks was dedicated to preparing our household goods for shipment to Spain. I also visited with many of the people who had been attending my meetings during the past eighteen months. It is never easy saying goodbye; it was especially difficult with some of the people that I had come to know very well.

Chapter 17

SHIFTING PERSPECTIVE

The first of November arrived with anticipation; the long awaited journey to Spain was only four days away. Maria had not said anything about it up until that point, so I was shocked speechless when, the day before departure, she informed me that she, Elisa, and Frances would remain in Myrtle Beach. She said she wasn't ready to go and would make the trip sometime in the future. How long had she been planning this? I felt like I was coming apart from the inside out. Based on Maria's behavior during the past several months, I thought our relationship was working; she had given no signals and said nothing about her intention to stay in Myrtle Beach. She had expressed nothing but enthusiasm about living in Spain for the next three years.

When I once again found my voice I asked her to reconsider. Nothing I said moved her. She stood there stoically, apparently hearing nothing I had to say. My pleas did not change her mind and I certainly could not force her to go. I could not change my assignment orders; I was committed to going and there was nothing

I could do to prevent it. Angry and depressed, I departed alone the next day. This was devastating. I could see no good in this event at all. I could not calm my mind or raise my spirits during the entire eight-hour airplane journey. Images of my daughters were painted on the forefront of my mind. Upon landing, the reality of the event hit me in the face again. I had orders for my entire family and was questioned about their status every step of the way, making me repeat the same sad story over and over. I felt like I had walked halfway across the Grand Canyon on a tightrope that had suddenly snapped, leaving me momentarily suspended in midair with no support. Before I knew it, I was freefalling toward the ground and no amount of flailing or waving my arms could stop my descent.

I arrived in Torrejon de Ardoz, Spain on November 5, 1975, fourteen days short of my twenty-eighth birthday and twenty days before the death of Generalissimo Francisco Franco. I was sad, disappointed, and temporarily powerless over the fate of my own children, who were now more than three thousand miles away.

Torrejon is about twenty kilometers east of Madrid. The city of about 100,000 had no industry of its own, serving mainly as a suburb of the capital and a convenient town for Air Force people living off base. I was assigned to the 401st Tactical Fighter Wing; our main mission was to counter the Communist nuclear threat in Europe. In addition to our mission in Spain we supported nuclear detachments in Aviano, Italy and Incirlik, Turkey. Because I arrived without my family, I was assigned a room in the barracks. I began a new journal that first night by reflecting on my spiritual situation, noting in the first sentence that I still had a strong desire to cling to the material world. I was in a state of shock without my family. How did I create this situation, and why? I continued my daily meditation practice, which helped me maintain focus and composure.

I was in Torrejon a little more than a week when I received my first letter from Maria. In anticipation of news about Frances and Elisa, I opened the letter before exiting the post office and began reading it as I walked slowly out the door and toward my barracks. Maria told me about our children, saying they were doing well and missed me. She also included beautiful photographs of them that brought smiles to my face and inspired me. I was thankful for this communication. When I returned to my room I sat on the floor with my legs crossed and began following my breath in and out. After about an hour of this meditation practice I wrote a long letter to Maria, Elisa, and Frances.

A couple of weeks later I bought a blue 1968 Volkswagen Beetle and began looking for an apartment. In December of 1975 I moved into a villa in a community known as Eurovillas, about thirty minutes through the hills from the Air Force base. The villa was nice but it was not worth the long drive on that rough road. Within a few months I moved, with one of my Eurovillas roommates, Carl, and one of my weapons team members, Dave, into an apartment in the city of Torrejon, about five minutes from the Air Force base. This furnished third-floor apartment had three bedrooms, one bathroom, a small kitchen, and a living room with a balcony; it was a beautiful apartment and much more convenient to my work. Thoughts of Elisa and Frances continued to dominate my mind: I wondered what they were doing each day, but most of all, I was concerned about their future. I knew I would have them back in my life; I did not know how to make that happen. One thing I knew I had to do was save my leave days for trips back to the States. I would see them as much as possible, at least once each year and possibly more.

In addition to the mission at Torrejon, the 401st Fighter Wing was responsible for keeping two nuclear weapons crews in Turkey and two in Italy on a constant basis. Because most of the weapons crew chiefs were married with their families in Spain, I volunteered to take most of the rotations in Turkey, the least popular of the two detachment locations. I went to Aviano, Italy only once on an unusual special assignment. About every six weeks my crew and I boarded a C-130 for the long flight to Incirlik, Turkey, where we remained for two weeks.

Whether in Turkey or at home in Spain, I practiced at least forty-five minutes of meditation each day and also maintained my spiritual journal. I resumed leading public meetings and conversations about human potential and God. I also experienced, through meditation and concentration, many more mystical experiences. Usually, after about fifteen minutes of meditation I would enter a state of unity lasting for about thirty or forty minutes. These experiences were not accidents, coincidences, or spontaneous events. They were intentional and came easily with practice. "Easily" is an important word. Any effort to achieve such a state prevented it. Only when I forgot about it and simply let go of thought did it occur. Each experience was like a visit to a heavenly place of peace; upon returning to normal waking consciousness I experienced a heightened yet highly relaxed state of being.

After returning from a trip to Turkey in September of 1976, I went directly to the Torrejon post office on my way home. My mailbox was stuffed full of envelopes. I grabbed the stack and walked to my car. In the big stack of mail was a letter from an attorney. I recognized the name, John Wilson Jenrette, Jr., in the upper left hand corner of the envelope. It gave me pause as I opened it; this was not an ordinary attorney. Sure enough, Maria had filed for divorce. I was protected by the Soldiers and Sailors Act, so Maria could not divorce me as long as I was stationed outside of the United States. If she and I could work out a reasonable custody arrangement, however, I would be willing to get it over with and sign divorce papers right that moment. With that decision made, it was a matter of returning to South Carolina, negotiating with Maria, and potentially signing the divorce documents. I intended to reach agreeable custody terms and complete the divorce on the same trip. I wrote a letter to Maria informing her I would be in South Carolina before the end of October. She called me after receiving the letter to tell me she was open to discussing everything when I arrived.

My leave was approved; to eliminate the hassles of a military space-available flight I flew commercial to New York with a connection down to Myrtle Beach. During the flight I closed my eyes and visualized my chosen outcome. I was willing to give Maria the car, everything in the house, and an equitable share of our cash, which meant whatever amount she wanted. All I really wanted was joint custody of my children with the right to visit them whenever I chose and have them with me for specified holiday periods. Under the circumstances, I was not looking forward to seeing Maria. After renting a car and checking into a hotel I called her and asked her to bring the girls to my room for a visit. She brought the necessary documents with her, which we signed while Frances and Elisa jumped up and down on one of the hotel beds. I asked Maria if she was divorcing me to marry another man and she said no.

I paused my thinking for a moment to observe this sad scene: so totally not what I had expected or wanted out of marriage or life. I didn't know Maria would be married within a month, but was certain she would eventually remarry. I dreaded the thought of another man raising my girls and was determined to see them regularly, maintaining my influence in their lives. In that moment of extreme sadness I watched my little daughters playing in complete innocence and happiness, oblivious to the implications of this poignant moment on the rest of their lives.

I stayed with Elisa and Frances the rest of the week, doing the fun tourist activities in Myrtle Beach. I imagined those moments lasting forever and cherished every second that I held them closely to me. In this once in forever, blink of an eye moment, there was no past, no me, no future – just now, and only now existed.

Chapter 18

JOURNEY OF THE HEART

I returned to Spain in the middle of October. The night following my return, while I sat in my living room chair reading *Time* magazine, a thought occurred to me – a thought about traveling to Amsterdam. The idea had been in the back of my mind for about a month, since a friend who had recently returned from the Netherlands told me about his trip. Two weeks remained of my approved leave. Instead of going back to work early, or driving to Barcelona, Benidorm, or Cadiz, I decided to take a train across Europe and stay in Amsterdam for a week. The very instant I made the choice to travel to Amsterdam, something different, strange, and somewhat fearful occurred. I felt my heart jump inside my chest then momentarily stop beating. My eyes opened wide as I waited for what seemed like an eternity for something to happen. The next instant my heart took one explosive beat, so powerful I thought it could pop out of my chest. Immediately after that extreme sensation it returned to its normal beating.

That really got my attention. I didn't know if it was a health issue or some type of response to my thought about traveling to Amsterdam – I had never experienced anything like it before. I considered the possibility that this was a communication from the collective unconscious confirming my choice to travel to Amsterdam. From that moment forward, without exception, every time I thought about the trip to Amsterdam I experienced an identical sensation like a missed heartbeat in my chest. Any time the thought of Amsterdam entered my mind, my heart instantly skipped a beat and resumed with a huge, explosive surge. Though the feeling was uncomfortable, there was no fear attached to it. I didn't bother going to the doctor because it only happened and always happened whenever I thought about the journey to Amsterdam. This thoroughly convinced me there was something about this trip that was important and the universe affirmed it every time I thought of it.

I departed in the third week of October. My roommate Dave drove me to Atocha Station in Madrid to ensure my car would remain safe at the apartment. I entered the huge station and found my way to a line where I purchased a ticket for a sleeper car to Paris. Supplied with reading material, bread, cheese, and wine, I felt secure about the overnight trip. I gave thanks to God for the opportunity to be on that train and did that by saying, "Thank you God," while feeling the appreciation within me.

As the train rolled eastward I drank wine and snacked on the bread and cheese. A few hours into the trip I visited the dining car for more substantial fare. By the time I returned to the cabin, a porter had converted the seats into sleeping compartments. I climbed up into my little bed, closed the curtain, and lay there listening to the wheels clacking along the rails as I pictured the train speeding through the darkened Spanish countryside. The book I brought was about quantum mechanics. Lying there in the bed I thought about the correlation between the quantum mechanical explanation of nature, as I understood it, and my personal observations of nature's inner workings. I was specifically interested in the role of the observer in everyday life, especially as it pertained to the mind experiments I had performed. Experimenting with particles and waves like electrons, light waves, and photons, quantum physicists had obtained different results from the same experiments depending upon the presence or absence of an observer during the experiment. The presence of the observer altered the results of the experiments, even causing particles to appear as waves of energy and energy waves as particles. From my perspective, this occurred because the energy of the observers' thoughts affected the actions of the electrons and photons. The observers made no effort to alter the results of the experiments; the changes simply occurred as a result of the observer's presence. If the mere presence or thought energy of an observer alters the behavior of electrons and photons, then my thoughts and observations of myself could affect my experience of life in every moment. If this were the case, then perhaps my mind energy could intentionally impact the movement of the unified energy field, thereby altering the outcome of life events.

Rather than sleeping, I intentionally focused on the sound of the wheels clacking over the rails. Those steel rails and wheels sounded solid, but our world and everything in it is a subtle body constructed mostly of empty space. With my eyes closed and mind focused, I perceived everything as energy. At the smallest levels of physical reality, we refer to that energy as neutrons, photons, quarks, protons, electrons, waves, atoms, molecules, and many other names. I pictured the power of thought energy that is driven by intention.

When our thought energy shifts, then in accordance with our intention we alter the energy that manifests as these miniscule entities; we shift their arrangement and behavior, thus shifting the appearance of our world. Each thought has an effect on every detail created in our life experience. Each thought disperses into and becomes the entire unified field. That means that our individual thoughts impact everything, including, most notably, our own life experience. Each thought we think is thought energy. Our thought energy is part of the unified field, as are our physical bodies. The unified field is a manifestation of God that can be described as an aspect of God. God is the original nothing; the unified field is a manifest something. God consciousness subsumes and imbues the unified field and everything that manifests from it. The unified field is the infinite reality underlying all that we perceive with our normal waking consciousness. Everything in the material world arises from the unified field of energy, including any universe that exists and everything contained within any universe.

Because our minds are always active, we produce thought energy all the time, even when we are asleep. Words of ancient wisdom tell us that we receive what we give, we reap what we sow. We constantly give all of our thought energy to the unified field thus affecting everything that exists. The experience of life that we receive back from the unified field is that same energy that we continually give out. This means that what we receive is not always and is not necessarily what we are consciously thinking about. If the thinking taking place beneath the surface of our conscious awareness differs from the thinking going on in our conscious minds, then our life experience may not resemble what we are actively and consciously thinking about. Instead, we may experience the thoughts that are moving through the depths of our unconscious, and when this energy manifests itself as our living experience we may wonder what happened.

With my eyes still closed I imagined my mind as an ocean. I divided the ocean into parts. Normal waking consciousness was the air above the surface. The earth below the seafloor was the deep unconscious, where my heartbeat was managed and where thought energy turned into individual thoughts. Thoughts originate far below the ocean floor long before we become aware of them. They percolate up through the sand, into the deep ocean water, rising through the depths to the surface where they burst forth into conscious awareness, manifesting themselves as our life experience. The earth below the bottom of the ocean is where we can create the biggest impact on our thinking and in our lives. If we wait for thoughts to bubble up into consciousness, some of them may be contrary to our conscious preference. Instead of waiting, we can transform our thoughts at their source by impacting thought energy before it becomes an individual thought. When we transform the energy below the ocean floor where our thoughts are created, we will experience results that are spontaneously in line with our conscious choices.

Later that night, the changing rhythm of the wheels on the rails woke me up. The train rolled slowly to a stop in Irun, a town on the French border in the northeast corner of Spain. Spanish trains ran on a narrower gauge track than all the rest of Europe, so they stopped at the border to change the wheels to the wider French gauge one car at a time. This very time-consuming process required several hours. When the train pulled away I remained awake, thinking of the ocean of my mind. How could I transform my thoughts before they were created in my unconscious mind, that is, before they even existed? After all, the reason it is called the unconscious is because we normally have no awareness of it or access to it. Maybe I needed to phrase the question differently: how could I make a difference in the universe that would change the quality of what I received from it? For a moment I felt like I knew the answer to the question of the radio control knob that I had thought about in the past. But it was only a feeling; the answer itself eluded me.

I considered the disconnects that had happened when my conscious intentions and plans suddenly changed direction and resulted in unanticipated pain, like the incident at St. Norbert that prompted me to enlist in the Air Force. Most people I knew who were under twenty-one drank beer outside of a legal establishment at some point and nothing happened to them. I did not drink a beer in the park that day hoping to get caught and thrown out of school so I could end up in the military. I drank beer that day just like I had on other days – to relax and have fun with friends. I did not know that a Little League coach a quarter of a mile away would notice us and report us for it. In retrospect,

I would have done things differently, of course, but that is what happened, and that is what I had to deal with. I did not accept, appreciate, or integrate that event immediately; it took a long time, and my life did not move forward until I finally reached a point of complete acceptance and appreciation for that event and what I learned from it.

I am responsible for that outcome and for all events that I experience. That does not mean, however, that I preferred those unintended results or caused them in a vacuum, devoid of input other than what appeared to arise in my individual consciousness when I chose to go to the park and drink the beer. As a hypothetical comparison, we might consider a person who contracts a disease. Most people, for example, who smoke cigarettes, do not smoke them with the intention of acquiring cancer and most people who smoke cigarettes do not acquire it. Some people who have never smoked a cigarette do contract lung cancer. There appears to be, therefore, something beyond simply our thoughts or conscious choices that affects the results we produce in our lives. Our results are more likely the product of a process involving a combination of universal and personal entelechy in conjunction with our individual minds and the collective unconscious.

I am, and we all are, part of and one with the entire universe. The universe itself is conscious (it does not think the way we do but it is, nonetheless, conscious); therefore, all thoughts entering my individual mind originate in the universe – in the whole. My sense of separation from the universe and my belief that I originate my own thoughts are due to the filtration system that removes most information generated by the universe from my individual conscious awareness. Because we see only a small part of what is going on, we believe that we are separate from everything else in the world and that our thoughts originate in our individual minds. However, what appears to be our individual mind is, in reality, the mind of God.

It was my perception of myself as separate that left me with the sense that my ego alone caused all the actions that resulted in the so-called undesirable outcomes, whereas really, the universe must have participated with me in the creation of these results. I am an individual instance of the one original self and as such, the experiences I manifest, whether I think I'm choosing and creating them entirely by myself or not, must arise from the universe, my higher self. Given that my ego self is not the sole actor, my experiences in the world must be the experiences that are ultimately most beneficial to me and, by definition, to the universe itself. Though these outcomes may seem tragic in the moment, they are part of the universal movement toward self-understanding, which individualizes as an urge to know myself. When viewed on a macro scale, all experiences ultimately produce results that lead me to increased self-awareness. The results that I interpreted as tragedy were not consequences or punishments based in my own thinking, but learning experiences that, if I could find the key inside of them, could potentially help me learn more about myself.

The process of learning who I am is called self-understanding, and that is the purpose of the created universe and the reason we exist. The existence of the entire universe, of everything that ever has been, is now, or ever will be, is driven by the urge of higher power, of God, to know itself. If this vast wonder that we call the universe exists for the purpose of self-understanding, then certainly the individual quest for self-understanding is a worthy one. Early that morning in France, the idea that resulted in these thoughts was articulated in my mind in an instant while I heard in the background the clicking and clacking of steel wheels on railroad tracks. Holding that thought in my awareness, it was then necessary for me to unwind the microdot of the idea into the long length of thread required to weave this tapestry of self-understanding.

This thought empowered me. It caused me to recall the expression that I heard my mother use many times, "Every cloud has a silver lining." In order to begin looking for that silver lining, or even to think about looking for it, I must have already accepted the undesirable results that I had created. My question was, "Is there something I did not know that, if known, would grant access to the inner power of my unconscious mind, my God self?" The answer is yes. We can gain that access by accepting, appreciating, and maintaining integration with everything that comes into our experiential field.

Before we can move forward to create a new life out of the ashes of what we perceive to be our mistakes, tragedies, and failures, we must first accept that these are not mistakes or tragedies. In order to create new experiences in conjunction with the universe, we first need to accept the present condition of our life exactly as it is, whether we think we have created it or, as was the case with Job, it was seemingly thrown at us from out of nowhere. When we fully accept and integrate our life experiences, when we become one with them, we send a clear message to both our individual and universal selves acknowledging that this creation is ultimately our doing and intended for our greatest good. We appreciate it because we know that we, together with the universe, have created it to enhance our understanding of who we ultimately are. Sending this message of appreciation plants the universal seed that helps our subsequent experiences align more accurately with the conscious preferences and intentions that we call our own.

Most people do not cause or choose to contract serious illness or to have apparently random automobiles smash into the rear of their vehicle while they are innocently stopped at a red light. If we take the perspective that an illness, for example a cancer, is a foreign body growing within us that we must "do battle with," we actually contribute to the growth of that very cancer. When we understand that if it is within us, then it is us, and if we come to accept and love the part of us that is growing there, we enhance our opportunity to heal, contract no further disease, and attract no further disasters.

These thoughts resolved the questions that had kept me awake, and I slept. When I woke up in France my mind was clear and my body energized.

Chapter 19

PHYSICS AND MYSTICISM

The light of the new day illuminated the beautiful French countryside as the light of my early morning thoughts had illuminated my mind. This trip was my first long-distance journey on a train and I liked it, I appreciated it. Paris was the next stop. I do not remember the visual experience of approaching the city; I do remember my strong inner feelings in that moment. Though I would not be staying in Paris this time, my presence there brought to mind some of the historical high points of the city. Two hundred years earlier, the landscape I was now looking at might have contained French peasants storming a landlord's manor, or maybe Benjamin Franklin and Thomas Jefferson. Might I have been near the location where the French people executed Maximilien Robespierre? Fast-forward 130 years and perhaps Ernest Hemingway and John Dos Passos strolled along that sidewalk before their relationship was ruined by the Spanish Civil War. Were these strong feelings stirred by the energy left behind by the men and women of Paris? That question shall remain forever unanswered; however, the mix of history, mystery, and excited anticipation left me feeling like a child waking before the Christmas morning sun rises.

After the train finally rolled to a stop at Gare du Sud, I disembarked and walked rapidly to the subway, not knowing which train to take and unable to communicate with the Parisians. After a period of frustrated confusion I worked out the color codes and caught the train to Gare du Nord. It was then a relatively simple matter to purchase a ticket and board the next train bound for the Netherlands.

Though anxious to get to my destination, I enjoyed the many stops along the way at small and beautiful villages in France and Belgium before arriving at Central Station in Amsterdam. I've lost track of how many hours I sat on the train anticipating the sights and sounds of the Netherlands. An express train might have made it in half a day, but as I look back on the journey it seems that it was much longer. Feelings of nervous excitement rose within me and my heartbeat increased as the train slowly approached the station. I recalled the moment I had first conceived of this plan and the outrageous faltering heartbeat I experienced, and the memory now left me with a sense of destiny fulfilled.

I disembarked from the train with my single bag and quickly walked through the brisk air, turning first to the right out of the station, then left a few blocks down, then right. There, across the street on the opposite corner, was the Arrive´ Hotel, a four-story nineteenth-century brick building with shops on the first floor and the hotel on the top three. Since there was no elevator in the building, I carefully carried my suitcase up the narrow staircase to the lobby, which was also the check-in desk, bar, and coffee shop. Two friendly Dutchmen greeted me and quickly signed me in.

All the usual alcoholic drinks were available at the bar, including Heineken, Amstel and other beers, and various types of hashish and smoking instruments. Several groups of people smoked small pipes made of clay or metal while others puffed on cone-shaped cigarettes from which the smoke of hashish mixed with tobacco spiraled toward the ceiling, dispersing slowly in the large room. Light entered through a row of beautiful arched windows opposite the entrance, as high as the ceiling and extending the length of the wall. As I leaned with my back against the counter, looking out into the room, I noticed a man seated next to one of the arched windows to my left. He looked to be about forty-five years old. His hair was long on his shoulders, thick and wavy, an uncombed mixture of deep red and gray. He sat there looking out the window to his left while his right hand dutifully dialed and redialed combinations, attempting to open a bicycle chain lock. Contrary to my normally reserved behavior around strangers, I walked slowly toward the man until he turned from the window and looked at me like he recognized me. I greeted him with, "Hi, my name is Jim." He stood up, reaching out his right hand. At about six feet tall, he was just slightly shorter than I.

"Hello Jim, I'm Richard," he replied in English with an American accent.

I smiled while shaking Richard's hand. "Good to meet you, Richard." Richard wore several layers of clothing to protect himself against the cold of the Amsterdam winter. Gray pants peeking through small holes in his blue outer pants, and a hole in the right knee of the gray pants revealing a third layer of white long underwear, told me that Richard had likely not purchased these clothes. Each layer had holes but no two layers had holes in the same place. The condition of his clothing and hair made him look like a person with no money, a person to stay away from. This felt different from most encounters, though, like I had been magnetically pulled to him, and now that I had introduced myself, I had no intention of retreating.

Richard had a full beard, thick and mixed in color like his hair; his green eyes revealed a bright inner light. He invited me to sit with him so we sat at the table together and began to converse. My conditioning would normally have caused me to fear an ill-dressed, unkempt person like Richard. In this case not only did I feel no fear but I was excited to be with him; there welled within me a sense of great import surrounding Richard. As he began speaking, my thoughts were confirmed.

Richard knew nothing about me other than what I told him during a brief introductory exchange. He knew I had come from Spain, I had a room at the Arrive´, and I wanted to wash the long journey from my body with a shower. Richard's table was in the corner of the room, near the bar and adjacent to a window. Sitting opposite Richard, I could look straight out the large row of windows down to the opposite side of the street where I saw pedestrians going about their business. The rest of the coffee shop space extended toward the back of the room opposite the bar. An assortment of about twenty round and square tables filled the low-ceilinged room; nearly all the tables were occupied, mostly with young people ranging in age from about twenty to thirty-five. A long rectangular table at the back of the room supported large coffee and hot chocolate urns with various associated supplies standing around them. I think the time was about ten-thirty in the morning, maybe a little later. The room was crowded, with some folks eating breakfast while others quietly drank beer and others smoked hashish and tobacco. A compact stereo cassette system played *Riders on the Storm* by The Doors. Hundreds of cassette tapes were stacked on shelves behind the bar.

I asked Richard if he was a guest at the Arrivé. He told me he was an American expatriate living on a boat on the Amstel River and had moved from London about three years ago. I told him I thought he must have a lot of time on his hands since he was sitting there this morning dialing a combination lock. "I enjoy observing people," he replied. "Have you ever noticed when you pay attention to a particular person you can gain insights into their history, their occupation and a lot of their life story?" I suddenly felt as if Richard and I were the only people in the room. This was not simply due to the words he had just spoken but more to the vibrations I sensed from him and the quality of his overall energy field. I silently nodded, looking directly at him. "And," Richard continued, "thinking of it from a different perspective, say like quantum physics or a mystical angle, you might say it's possible to know things not normally available to our five senses." I straightened my back and moved closer to the edge of my seat. In all the years I had been speaking about the nature of reality, whether about God, mysticism, or quantum mechanics, no one had ever before initiated a conversation like this with me. I was always the one to start the conversations and after that most people simply listened and asked questions.

I had that very morning on the train been reading about quantum mechanics, looking for similarities between mysticism and scientific explanations of the universe. Richard's mention of the words "quantum physics" and "mystical" immediately increased my interest in what he was saying. I sensed a connection between us, but before saying anything about my thinking, I wanted to hear more of what he was thinking. Because I was still suspicious of him, I wanted some assurance that Richard wasn't attempting to find common ground in order to satisfy some undisclosed agenda. I failed to consider the possibility that Richard might already have known everything I was thinking that morning, although he had clearly disclosed this possibility when, shortly after our introduction, he spoke about knowing a person's life story simply by paying attention to them.

"It's really quite amazing to me that you're speaking about this right now, Richard. This stuff about knowing things that we have no physical access to and the quantum mechanical explanations for it is exactly what I've been looking into lately. This has happened to me before. I was just reading about this stuff on the way here. I mean, how is it," I asked, "that when I discover information about a particular subject, more information on that same subject starts showing up all over the place?"

"What exactly do you mean?" asked Richard. "How does more information start showing up?"

"Well, I've been reading about quantum mechanics recently and was reading about it on the train here. Then as soon as we met, you began talking about the same thing." Richard short-circuited the conversation by going directly to its practical essence.

"Perhaps, instead of answering that question with words, I can show you the answer. Would you be willing to try an experiment?" he asked.

"What kind of experiment are you talking about?" I inquired.

"Let's try this," Richard continued. "When you go upstairs to take your shower, you can expect your mind will be filled with thoughts, as always. I'm suggesting that one of those thoughts will stick in your mind more prominently than the others. I'll do the same thing with one of my thoughts. Remember your thought and when you come back down, we'll compare them."

I repeated Richard's plan to make sure I understood and when he confirmed I said, "Okay then, let's do it." I then nervously proceeded to my room on the third floor. I was nervous because, suppose it didn't work? Or, suppose it did?

Chapter 20

NEW HORIZONS

The Arrive´ was a hostel; the accommodations were inexpensive and stark. When I opened the door to the room, the door hit the head of the narrow bed, which had a skinny mattress and a thin blanket. One straight-backed wooden chair was at the foot of the bed, by the window. When I sat on the bed there was just enough room for my feet between the bed and the wall. The community bathroom was down the hall. No one else was around so I was the only one in the shower at the time. Fascinated by my brief conversation with Richard, many thoughts ran through my head. One of them seemed to come from completely out of nowhere with a spotlight on it.

A clear image from fifteen years ago came into my mind. I was standing behind the Bible in the Old North Church in Boston, looking out over the empty seats. It was from the steeple of this church that in 1775, two lanterns were hung as a signal that British troops were headed for Lexington and Concord by sea as opposed to land. My mom and dad had taken the family on a vacation to explore various historical sites in Lexington, Concord, Sturbridge, Salem, and Boston. The church was one of the sites we visited and I actually did stand behind the podium with the huge Bible opened in front of me. The picture that formed in my mind while I was in the shower was a mental snapshot of what I saw as I stood in the church that day. It was this memory that I would relate to Richard. I would not reveal it to him, however, until he told me what his memorable thought was. After the shower I dressed and walked down the stairs to the second floor.

When we were seated together once again I told Richard that I did have an obvious thought that remained in the forefront of my mind. The experiment that Richard had proposed might help support the idea that information could intentionally flow from one mind to another or from universal mind to individual minds, with no physical connection.

If we both saw a connection between our individual thoughts then, anecdotally at least, we could state that our minds communicated with each other or had access to a common source of information, like the Akashic Record. I asked Richard to tell me about the thought that landed in his mind.

"My thought," Richard began, "was not a personal experience. It was about an actual sermon delivered in the Old North Church in Boston in 1775. I've been to the church several times," he continued, "and learned about the sermon from a book I read in college. This is the thought that stands out for me as the one to use in our experiment."

"What makes this particular thought stand out for you?" I asked.

"This sermon was delivered the Sunday before the British opposed the colonists at Lexington and Concord. While sitting here looking out the window a few minutes ago, I thought about the Old North Church; this particular sermon came clearly into my consciousness and I couldn't ignore it."

"That's interesting. I'm kind of blown away right now," I responded. "Check this out. The thought that occurred for me was a personal memory of a visit to that same church. I remembered standing in the Old North Church behind the Bible looking out from the lectern toward where the congregation would have been seated. My dad took our family there because those two lanterns were hung in the church steeple in 1775, setting the Colonies up for the shot heard around the world at the Old North Bridge in Lexington – the beginning of the American Revolution."

Richard shook his head from side to side as he laughed loudly, as did I. When we stopped laughing he began to speak. "Wow, that's fabulous. All of us are part of the same energy; we are the same energy and it connects everything, one to the other, so anything that you know, I can know – anyone can know."

"That's the way I see it, and our experiment certainly seems to verify it," I said.

I wanted to eat something and see some of the tourist places in Amsterdam. I didn't want to leave Richard without arranging to see him again while I was in town, so before leaving the hotel I asked Richard if he would be interested in eating dinner together that evening. He answered in the affirmative and I asked him if he knew a good spot. That was tricky for me because I didn't know my way around the city. We moved to a table where a map of the city was pinned to the back wall of the coffee shop. Richard used his finger to point out directions on the map and explained which trams I needed to take to get there. We agreed to meet at the restaurant at seven P.M. and I said, "See you later."

Richard stopped me before I departed and suggested we conduct another experiment. "This time," he said, "as you walk around the city, be on the lookout for any particular small object that might catch your eye in an interesting way. If something gives you the feeling, bring it with you to the restaurant." I then departed the hotel to look around Amsterdam. I visited a small restaurant first, one with a large yellow banana painted on its front window below a sign that read "Mellow Yellow." I went in and looked at the menu on the wall before taking a seat. While eating and warming up, I noticed a matchbox on the table. I picked it up and shook it; it was empty. My first thought was, this is garbage; if it still contained matches, it could be used for something, but as it is, it's useless. I looked for a trash can and then thought it would be a good object to bring to the restaurant for the experiment. I put it in the pocket of my navy pea coat, paid my bill, and went outside to catch a tram. After a couple of hours in the city I went back to the Arrive´ and napped in my tiny bed until it was time to meet Richard.

Rain was falling rhythmically against the window when I woke up. After washing my face, I left the hotel, walking through the cold evening from the hotel to the tram station without an umbrella. It was a short walk but I was damp when I got there. I took that tram to the change stop where I got off and caught a different colored tram. Disembarking at the stop Richard had specified, I then walked along the sidewalk past a long row of Dutch homes with large windows in front. In each home the main window curtain was wide open, allowing a full view into the living room so all who strolled past could see the family members going about their business. This sense of openness surprised and impressed me. Family after family conducted their evening activities just several feet from the eyes of all passers-by.

I arrived, wet and cold, at the restaurant at seven P.M.; Richard was not there. The interior was small and elegant with a short bar to the right of the entrance. Most of the tables were occupied by well-dressed older couples; no one was as seated at the bar. I took a seat at the end of the bar and drank soda while waiting for Richard. It was warm, cozy, and quiet inside so I removed my damp coat. Fifteen minutes passed and I became concerned that Richard might not make it. Just then, I looked up from my glass to see Richard closing his umbrella as he entered the restaurant.

Richard had changed his clothes and was wearing a pair of wool slacks with a nice-looking shirt and a herringbone sport jacket. I greeted him at the door and a waiter showed us to a table. No sooner were we seated than he suggested we compare our items from the experiment. "In my travels this afternoon," Richard said exuberantly, "I stopped at a friend's house for a chat. I spotted this new Zippo lighter sitting on the coffee table and picked it up. My friend had not yet filled it with lighter fluid so I asked him if he intended to use it. He had no lighter fluid and since the lighter would not light without fluid I asked if I could take it with me. I told him about our experiment and that his unused lighter was the object I needed to bring to the restaurant. It's obviously useless as it is but if I had some fluid for this thing I could smoke a cigarette."

I was initially nervous about agreeing to these experiments because of the possibility that neither would work. Instead I was completely blown away by both of them. I reached into the pocket of my jacket, which hung on the back of the chair, and proclaimed, "Here's my empty matchbox; if we had some matches to go with it you could smoke a cigarette." We both laughed too loudly for the quiet dining room. After talking to our waiter about the menu, we placed our orders. I started a new conversation about my experience in Vietnam, which led me to express my views on the absurdity of the war and of war in general. Richard told me about the real reasons the United States got involved in Vietnam. He said our government was aware that most of the Vietnamese people wanted the country to remain unified under Ho Chi Minh. Richard also explained the government fabrication of the Tonkin Gulf incident, which was used to convince the American people that we were attacked by North Vietnam and needed to respond. As with most, if not all, wars throughout history, our engagement in that little Southeast Asian nation was really about profit for what President Eisenhower had called the military-industrial complex.

We discussed Israeli nuclear weapons, specifically the fact that Israel was in possession of many deliverable nuclear devices, something that they have never admitted. The conversation extended to the Bay of Pigs fiasco, Rhodesia, South Africa and the injustice of apartheid, Idi Amin and his slaughter of fellow Ugandans, and other world issues present and past. The thought occurred to me that I could ask him literally any question that popped into my mind and he would have the answer. Later, when I returned to Spain, I went to the library and researched some of the books he had referred to. The books and subjects he had discussed, for which I was able to find references, proved Richard's facts to be correct.

Chapter 21

IT'S WHAT YOU THINK

I did not want our conversation to end after dinner; on the other hand, I did not want to impose upon Richard by asking him to remain any longer. "My boat is nearby," Richard suggested, "if you would like to walk there we can continue to talk."

The warmth of the restaurant was broken by the sudden chill of the night air. The rain had stopped, leaving behind a shining coat of water on the sidewalks and streets. We walked for about ten minutes before crossing a narrow canal on a small footbridge that connected the sidewalk to a long paved dock extending into the distance along the left bank of the Amstel River. While walking across that narrow footbridge I smelled something sweet floating on the still night air. Richard explained that the scent originated from a nearby factory that produced fragrances for laundry soaps and other consumer items. One houseboat after another was tied up alongside the dock, which dropped straight down to the river, with gangplanks or ladders bridging the gap. Some of these boats had glass sides, exposing the well-decorated interiors to our view.

They were beautifully furnished like any elegant home. Several of them were inhabited at the time, the people inside going about their business while completely in view of those passing by. Impressed by these houseboats, I thought Richard might live in quite a nice place, but his boat bore no resemblance to these.

We passed the last houseboat and traversed an empty section of the Amstel where no boats were tied up to the dock. After a gap of about thirty or forty yards, Richard stopped alongside an aged wooden board leading to an ancient river barge about one hundred feet long. It floated high in the water, unlike the fully loaded and nearly submerged barges I had seen plying the canals earlier that day. This was Richard's home. I was afraid to walk that rickety gangplank hovering about ten feet above the Amstel. The board was about ten feet long and sixteen inches wide, inclined slightly downward toward the boat with the near freezing blackness of the Amstel waiting patiently beneath. Richard crossed the plank as casually as he walked along the dock. After he made it across to the boat, I carefully stepped onto the plank, placing one foot in front of the other, one cautious step at a time, until I landed with both feet on the deck of the barge directly in front of the wheelhouse. The wheelhouse, located at the far rear end of the barge, was a small structure with wooden walls. Most of the paint had peeled off the walls, revealing the old weathered wood beneath. The walls extended about halfway up, with windows continuing to the slightly peaked wooden roof.

I grew colder as Richard fumbled with a huge ring of keys, trying one after another in the lock, until he finally found the one that unlocked the door. I wondered if he performed this ritual every time he came home. He swung the door open, held it for me as I walked through, followed closely behind, then closed the door and locked it. We were now in the little wheelhouse, complete with a wooden steering wheel, from which the boat was once navigated through the canals and rivers of the city. "What's that big blob on the back window?" I asked.

"That's a dead spider," Richard replied. "I squashed him there a few months ago. I told the spiders it was okay for them to stay anywhere they wanted outside the wheelhouse but if they came in I would kill them. This one serves as a warning to the rest. But don't worry, they only show themselves in the summertime." We descended a stepladder straight down to the small cabin where the crew of two had once lived and slept in years long gone. At the bottom of the ladder was a narrow sliding pocket door with another lock. Richard's unlocking ritual began again as he fumbled with the group of about twenty identical looking keys hanging from his key ring. These were old keys with two or three big teeth on the end of a shaft. After four or five attempts he successfully unlocked the inner door and slid it back into the bulkhead, revealing the living quarters below the wheelhouse. Little labels taped to the keys may have helped, but I soon discovered that saving time with the keys was not one of Richard's priorities.

The cabin was a very small space, perhaps twelve feet wide and fifteen feet long, with walls crafted of fine dark wood. Narrow cabinets with vertical doors, brass knobs, and several drawers beneath were built into both sides of the hull. The cabinet on the starboard side had glass panes in the doors with a small built-in desk below them and a small drawer on each side. A narrow shelf on the port side supported a couple of dirty glasses, several candles, and other small items. Two straight-backed wooden chairs and a small three-legged stool occupied most of the carpeted floor space. A small kerosene stove in the center of the floor left very little room to move around. The temperature inside the boat was about the same as the temperature outside. Despite the carpet on the deck I felt the cold of the river coming through to my feet.

The cabin was completely devoid of amenities and resources. There was no refrigerator, no food, no running water, and no electricity. On the desk were a portable typewriter, a kerosene lamp, which Richard had lit, and two large glass ashtrays, the kind with the glass inserted into a metal base with an attached metal handle arcing over the top of the glass. The small sleeping area was in the narrow stern of the boat with nothing separating the main cabin from the sleeping quarters. Two bunks, consisting of wooden platforms about waist high, were built into the port and starboard bulkheads; they were separated from each other by the tiny enclosed head. The head was open in the front with a wooden wall on each side. Each bunk had a sleeping bag with no mattress and one small porthole above it.

I was not there for the decor and within minutes our conversation became animated. There was no better place in the world for me at that moment than sitting right there with Richard in this ancient barge on the Amstel River. Our initial seating arrangement made me turn my head to the right to make eye contact, which strained my neck, so we moved our seats to face each other. I moved to the port side facing Richard, who now sat directly opposite on the starboard side, each of us against the wall with the kerosene stove between us. Richard began by explaining the history of Amsterdam from the Middle Ages through the Second World War. His stories about the Dutch people protecting Jews from the Holocaust emphasized his concern about historic and ongoing atrocities perpetrated by humans against other humans. Richard told me he intended to introduce me to a particular friend, the daughter of a Dutch couple who had hidden and protected many Jewish people during WWII. The facts were interesting and Richard's presentation was captivating. He stood up during parts of the stories as he related his brief history of the Western world. While still standing, he asked me why I came to Amsterdam.

"I'm aware, of course, of *The Diary of Anne Frank* and the role played by the Dutch during World War II. I wanted to come here to find out for myself what the Dutch people are like. Why were they willing to risk their lives to save people they didn't know while at the same time ordinary German citizens allowed themselves to be enrolled in mass death? I've also wanted to see the canals, windmills, and art museums, and when a friend of mine told me about his trip I got interested in coming," I said. "I chose this particular time for a couple of different reasons." I started explaining my emotionally difficult trip to the States to see Maria and my daughters when Richard interrupted me.

"Hold on just a moment, please, while I take a leak." Richard climbed up on his knees in front of the head a few feet away and quickly returned to his place standing across from me close to the starboard wall.

"I was alone in my apartment in Torrejon," I continued, "thinking about my children and what I would do with the rest of my time off."

"I'm sorry, one second," he requested. "I must move this ash-tray closer." Richard smoked continuously. Sometimes he lit one cigarette from another and other times he had two burning at the same time. Although there were two ashtrays in the room, one re-mained empty while he filled the other with ashes and the crushed ends of extinguished cigarettes. I grew impatient with the delays.

"Okay good, are you all set now?" I asked.

"Oh yes, yes indeed," responded Richard.

"Okay then. Well, I returned from South Carolina a little more than a week ago and thought about driving somewhere in Spain when I remembered that a good friend had recently suggested that I might like Amsterdam. I thought, 'That's what I'll do, I'll go to Amsterdam.' Just then, a very strange thing happened that never happened before." I paused for a second before continuing. "The very instant the word 'Amsterdam' flashed through my mind, my heart stopped; it skipped a beat. And when it started again a split second later, it made a huge beat, like it exploded out of my chest."

Standing near the opposite wall, maintaining eye contact, Richard spoke softly and without hesitation. "You mean like this?" As the words left Richard's lips, my heart skipped a beat then exploded back into action exactly as it had in Spain when I first chose Amsterdam as my vacation destination. It is difficult to ver-balize what I felt at that moment. Not only was I speechless, I was thoughtless – nothing happened inside my head for several seconds while I absorbed the impact of what had just taken place. Richard looked into my eyes with calm understanding. He did

154

not move. My mind was blank as my gaze met his. Those few moments before Richard broke the silence seemed like an hour. The skipped heartbeat following his question removed all doubt about the importance of my trip and explained why, while I was in Spain, I had experienced the heartbeat anomalies every time I thought of Amsterdam.

"I've been expecting you," he said. I suddenly felt like I was made out of thin air; like I had just been blown away with the wind. I couldn't move, didn't want to move, as I contemplated what I had heard. I felt surrounded by love.

"What do you mean you've been expecting me?" I asked in a soft voice.

"I didn't know what your name would be," Richard began, "but I knew that someone would come here, someone with the same intention that brought you here. You would not be here if you did not have the commitment, the vision, and the power to generate the transformation you've spoken about within yourself. I've talked with my friends about you also. That's why I said you would meet the young lady whose parents helped save Jews from Nazis. There are others you will meet here also, all of them sharing the common interests of individual enlightenment and uplifting humanity."

"I'm completely . . . I don't know; I am humbled," I said softly. "I don't know what to say right now."

Richard said, "You chose your path a long time ago; now your chosen path has let you know that your choice is recognized, that you are recognized."

"I want to contribute something that will make a difference for people. That's what I would like to be doing right now but I'm committed to the Air Force for several more years."

"That's fine," Richard said. "You are contributing to people this very moment; you are always doing God's work. I do think you may want to consider accepting an honorable discharge the next time you have the opportunity."

"That seems so far away, and yes, that's what I have intended to do and that is what I will do. In the meantime I think the best thing to do is continue to speak to people about the message that's in my head."

Richard told me to continue doing that, stating that although the whole history of humanity is full of violence there was a real possibility of human beings living together peacefully. By meditating and doing what I was doing, I helped increase the number of people who believed in the possibility of achieving those goals. He said there were many people in the world working towards that end and referred to them as members of what he called the "International Short-Circuit Club." He said that people interested in peace, liberty, and justice short-circuited the fabrications and injustices of international politics, which were largely the result of human nature, by focusing their mind energy directly on achieving those goals instead of running around joining groups that promoted various causes.

All transformation, all change, begins as a thought in the mind. When we focus our thought energy with intention, we geometrically increase our ability to achieve results. We may then take action based on our intentions. The most powerful aspect of the focusing process is its impact on the thoughts and actions of others in the world. Our thoughts are part of the collective unconscious and thereby become available to everyone, everywhere. We affect the entire world with our thoughts, allowing others to take actions to help manifest peace within themselves and in the whole of humanity. Everything Richard said made sense to me and fit in completely with my own thinking.

I was cold. Even with my coat on, my arms across my chest, and my hands under my arms, I was shivering. That unlit kerosene stove in the middle of the floor was looking pretty good. "What's the chance of turning on that kerosene stove?" I asked.

He said, "You're sitting there dressed in those warm clothes with that warm coat and I'm standing here with pants and a shirt. You're freezing and I'm completely comfortable. How do you explain that?"

"Simple: it's frigid outside, there's no heat in here, and we're sitting on top of a river that's probably just a few degrees above zero Celsius."

"James, wait a minute. We've been talking about this all day and we've done a couple of experiments that we agreed demonstrated it. This room is the same temperature throughout the room, true?"

"Yes."

"You have more clothes on than I do, you're hugging yourself tightly, yet you're shivering and I'm warm. How you experience the temperature of your body is like everything else – if you think you're warm, you're warm, if you think you're cold, you are. And the kerosene stove doesn't work."

"I'm not surprised the stove doesn't work," I said with a hint of sarcasm. "But there is another part to this that maybe you can help me with. I think there may be more to it than the thoughts I have in my conscious mind. I've experienced times when my conscious and unconscious mind, or my individual self and universal self, were unified and I think that's not happening now. It's a missing part of the equation that I am unable to exercise at will." I told Richard about my analogy of the volume control knob on the radio. I told him I had been experimenting with ways to synchronize my conscious and unconscious thoughts and intentions.

"That's a good analogy, James," Richard responded. "And I do have something to offer you in that regard. Listen carefully; I am going to tell you the secret of the universe." At that point Richard's mouth continued to move but I heard no sound until he asked me if I understood. I told him I heard nothing about the secret, but that was all he said about it for the rest of that night. In fact, he said very little about it for the next three years. Instead of using words to tell me, he used actions to show me.

Chapter 22

GO FOR THE SNUFFBOX

Richard was born in Pennsylvania in 1932 and attended Riverside Military Academy, a boarding school in Gainesville, Georgia. After graduating from the military academy he attended college in Los Angeles, I don't remember where, eventually becoming a TV scriptwriter and film screenwriter in Hollywood. He moved to London in 1973 and then to Amsterdam where he had lived for the past three years. He displayed many bound screenplays in the cabinet as well as a scrapbook full of photographs and newspaper and magazine articles about his work, which we reviewed together. Richard selected one of his screenplays from the cabinet, handed it to me, and suggested I read it. I did not want to sit there in silence reading, but sensed that this was important to Richard or he would not have mentioned it.

The story was about a medieval kingdom ruled for many years by a benevolent king. The king died when his son, the crown prince, was sixteen years old and naïve in the ways of politics. Members of the court, interested in nothing but themselves, attempted to trick the prince out of his throne. The symbol representing control of the kingdom was a small crystalline stone, hidden by the king in a silver snuffbox. The king hid the snuffbox to prevent the kingdom from falling into the wrong hands, but died before telling his son the location of the silver box. The prince's only friend was a white horse, which was actually an angel sent by God to guide the prince. The angel horse communicated God's messages directly to the prince to help save the kingdom from the evil high priest.

In their efforts to wrest control from the prince, the evil courtiers engaged in many different plots and subterfuges. All their dirty tricks, bribes, and midnight arrests of their enemies gained them nothing. In the end the equine angel helped the prince maintain control of the kingdom. Everything worked out prosperously for the prince and his subjects.

While I read the screenplay from my seat on the port side of the boat, Richard sat at the small built-in table on the starboard side, close to the ashtrays. He remained there the entire time and was too far away to see what I was reading or if I was reading. When I completed reading the story I said, "Great story, Richard. I like the good and evil theme with God advising the prince through his pet horse."

Still in his seat, Richard puffed on a cigarette before saying, "You missed a line."

With a disbelieving attitude, I thought, *Yeah, sure, how would you know?* "I didn't miss a line," I objected. "I read the entire thing." I knew I had carefully read the entire screenplay.

At that, Richard stood up and came over to where I was sitting. "Let me show you." Richard opened the binder in front of me and leafed through the pages, each one contained in a plastic insert, until he was near the end of the screenplay. He looked at the left-hand page and then placed his fingertip under the last sentence in the second paragraph. That sentence read, "The prince went for the snuffbox." When Richard's finger came to rest underneath that line and I read it, the universe instantly dissolved before me and I found myself at one with all that is. The same God experience that first swept me away as a child had guided me here fifteen years later to this tiny cabin in a boat moored at the edge of the Amstel River in Holland. I was no longer cold. When I came back to objective reality, I heard the voice of wisdom in my mind tell me, "Jim, you have nothing to worry about for the rest of your life." At the same time, I felt a powerful rush of confident, ecstatic energy. I was humbled by the feeling of infinite love that enveloped me. I lowered my head and said in a low voice, "Thank you God." It turned out to be true that I had nothing to worry about for the rest of my life; it was also true that I would create many things to worry about as time moved on.

I was surprised I had missed a line and amazed that Richard knew it. Had I missed almost any other line I may not have been affected as profoundly as I was by the line I had skipped. It summed up the concept of the International Short-Circuit Club. The idea that the prince cut through all the crap and "went for the snuffbox" impacted me as no other sentence I had ever read. It reminded me to always go straight to the heart of the matter.

In Richard's story the snuffbox was the source and the prince went directly to it. For us, the source lies within and the universe provides a way for us to go directly to it. The way to the source begins with our appreciation of life as it is right now. With appreciation comes acceptance and integration, the keys to transformation – the keys to the kingdom.

At about six o'clock that morning I told Richard I was ready to leave. He and I agreed to meet the following day at his boat. He fumbled with the keys, opened the cabin door, and I climbed the ladder to the wheelhouse where he repeated the key ritual until the door opened and I ran fearlessly across the gangplank to the dock. Two long, cold walks separated by two tram trips took me to the welcome warmth of my little room at the Arrive´.

From the moment I made the decision to travel to Amsterdam, I had been profoundly affected spiritually, intellectually, and physically. My spirit experienced new channels of communication, my intellect had been stretched, and I had been physically affected by strange heartbeats triggered by something I did not understand. The last twenty hours with Richard were unlike any other time. I had not yet begun to process even a tiny portion of what had transpired, yet I knew that meeting Richard was a major transformational milestone.

People come into our lives for many reasons; they always help us see ourselves more completely and in many cases, they help us fulfill our aspirations. When I told Richard about my heart skipping a beat and he asked, "You mean like this?" the resulting change in my heartbeat confirmed that I was in the right place with the right person at the right time in my life; I appreciated that. Traveling to Amsterdam, especially in the wintertime, was far more difficult than driving my Volkswagen to warmer climates on the Mediterranean coast of Spain. Higher power guided me to Amsterdam. Meeting Richard was both the result of my intention and the next step toward the fulfillment of the intention. I knew that Richard came into my life to contribute to my self-understanding and I was in his life to help him achieve his goals, whatever they may be.

There was no way to explain the details of how my heart had skipped a beat the instant I chose Amsterdam as a vacation destination. I have always wanted to know all of the details about how everything happens, how everything works. From my skipping heartbeat, I learned that as long as everything is working I do not need to know how. Knowing the "how" of things was not my job. Even God does not know the details of how things happen. God pays no attention to them and has no interest in them. Indeed, it is possible that the "how factor," the power that translates thought energy into material experience, may be completely and forever unknowable.

The universe arose from nothing when higher power chose to understand itself and even higher power, God, does not know the details of how creation happens. God has no need to know. God did not design the universe to provide self-understanding. God did not determine the detailed workings of the universe like a human engineer determines the details of bridge construction. God asked the question, "Who am I?" and entelechy drove the universe to take the form necessary to answer that question. I set forth a goal and, in ways I cannot explain, in ways far too complex to rationally comprehend, the universe fulfilled that goal and I followed my heartbeat to Amsterdam.

In order to accomplish anything, all we need to know is the first step toward the goal. The first step may be talking with a friend, writing a letter, or taking a trip; whatever first step we think of is all we need to know at that moment. From there, knowledge of the second step and all subsequent steps will be revealed to us at the ideal time. Our job is simply to choose what we prefer to have in our lives, for example, self-understanding, the ability to feed hungry people, a new home, or a new profession. When actions come to mind, take them.

I took a short nap that morning, toured the Heineken brewery, cruised some canals, ate a herring sandwich while standing outside in the cold, and returned to my room shortly before dark. I went to bed early and slept through the night. Cold rain greeted me in the morning so I borrowed an umbrella from Christiaan at the check-in counter before leaving the Arrive´. I arrived at Richard's boat and from there he and I traveled by tram to the apartment of the young lady whose parents had protected Jewish people during World War Two. Richard told me we were going to take a bus ride to visit another friend. We arrived at her apartment building and walked up the covered outside stairway and through the hallway to a door marked 207. Richard introduced me to a beautiful lady about twenty-five years old. Her name was Karen. She was tall and slim with blonde hair and soft cheekbones.

We three sat in her cozy, expensively appointed apartment talking and waiting until the last minute for the rain to stop before venturing out to catch the bus. The time soon came to depart for the bus station and the rain was still coming down hard. I suggested we carry a second umbrella and Richard responded without hesitation. "We don't need an umbrella. When we reach the sidewalk the rain will stop." Anything was possible given my previous experiences with Richard, but this prediction was a stretch so I thought, *I've got to see this.* Rain had been falling steadily since the night before; chances of the rain ending in the next few minutes or even hours were remote. Rain splashed on the apartment windows as we stood up, pulled on our jackets, and walked out into the hall.

The outdoor stairway we had previously ascended was covered with an arched canvas canopy on a metal frame. The rain beat loudly on the canopy as we descended the flight of about fourteen steps. The downpour showed no sign of abating as I led our trio down the steps. I continued walking down and prepared to open my umbrella at the bottom of the steps. When my foot reached downward from the final step onto the ground and my leg crossed the threshold beyond which the canopy would no longer protect me from the rain, the rain ceased falling. One drop fell from the edge of the canopy and landed on my head. That was the only rain that touched me the rest of that day. The clouds soon dissipated, revealing a blue sky and the shining sun.

Richard's friend lived out in the country, a good distance from the city. We passed many windmills and flat green fields on the way there. After visiting with Richard's friend for about an hour, we walked out into the sunshine to wait for the bus back to town. There was one main road outside the home. It curved out of sight into a wooded area about two miles away. That was the direction from which the bus would be coming to pick us up. The bus was about ten minutes late when I started complaining. About a minute after I verbalized my unhappiness, Richard told me to quit complaining because the bus would be coming around the bend right now. I moved closer to the edge of the road for a better view and just then the bus rolled past the trees and around the curve straight toward us.

During the ride back Karen, Richard, and I spoke about the work her parents did during the Second World War. She told me they risked their lives so Jewish families could be safe because that is what they believed in. She said her involvement in the International Short-Circuit Club was motivated by the same sense of peace, justice, and morality for all human beings. In line with this theme, I discussed my adherence to the Buddhist notion of the bodhisattva, one who seeks enlightenment in order to assist all sentient beings in achieving enlightenment.

Karen, Richard, and I agreed that peace will come when we all have peace. Each of us is born with this innate desire; each of us seeks security and a safe place to lay our heads when we go to sleep at night. It seems that fear causes many humans to desire control and dominance over others, thinking perhaps that this is the only way they can have peace. In reality, the only way any of us can have peace is if we give it away to each other. One way to do that is to seek our own enlightenment and then pass it on to as many others as possible. As more of us experience the abundance that peace brings, we will heal ourselves and our living planet. As the bus pulled into the station, Karen and I said goodbye. Richard and I made arrangements to meet at the Arrive´ in the morning, my final full day in Amsterdam. I wanted to spend that time with Richard visiting art museums while he explained the history and details of the paintings and sculptures. I ate dinner alone and returned to the Arrive´ for the night.

Richard and I met in the lobby the following morning. We drank coffee and ate croissants at the Arrive´ before departing on our journey around the city. We discussed, among many other things, the potential of meeting again in the future. Near the end of the day I told Richard I intended to return to Myrtle Beach soon to see my daughters and would make another trip to Amsterdam. I would inform him by telegram of my final arrangements. That evening Richard and I said goodbye for an indefinite number of months. I had a strong desire to remain in Amsterdam, but my commitment in Spain would not wait.

Chapter 23

CLARITY

A fter a short walk from the Arrive´ to Central Station the following morning, I purchased my ticket and boarded the sleeping car. Due to many stops along the way, the trip to Madrid was slow, providing abundant time for reflection on my experiences in Holland. Many nearly incredulous experiences occurred while I was there; some stood out more than others. Though I had in the past experienced the unity of everything that is, I learned more about what this means and how it applies to everyday life. The application to everyday life was meaningful to me because my main concern was the pragmatic potential of mystical experience.

I gained a new depth of insight into the reality that all human minds are unified within a singular consciousness that encompasses all others, whether we are aware of this consciousness or not. Most of us never seem to notice it, but our connectedness with each other and with God consciousness affects everything we think and do. Most of us are convinced that the events we experience in our everyday lives represent the totality of our reality. We believe that we generate every thought that enters our awareness. As I have stated since the first chapter, most of us are conditioned from before we are born to view the world in a certain way, a way that was structured and programmed into us for our survival many millions of years ago. This habitual perspective tells us that what we see and hear every day is everything there is to be seen or heard. However, as the mystical experiences that began in my childhood revealed to me, there is more going on than light striking our retinas and sounds vibrating in our ears. There is another reality, an infinite reality, that functions all the time and it is this reality which informs – that is, gives form to – the everyday experience we call life. The volume control knob that I have spoken about represents the connection point that allows us to communicate consciously with our ultimate reality, thereby transforming our lives.

As the train approached Madrid, I focused on my next phase of exploration and experimentation. I intended to discover a method or system that would grant consistent access to our ultimate reality, which is our original identity, thus giving us the ability to consciously change our experience of life in any way we choose. The train arrived in Madrid on schedule. I walked through the station to the street where Dave picked me up. He asked a lot of questions on the drive to the apartment, and asked them so quickly that he never received a complete answer to any of them. I wanted to take a shower as soon as we arrived home, but I sat with Dave answering his questions and describing some of the high points of the journey. After that I took a shower and went to my room.

About fifteen days later I received a letter from Maria informing me that she had married a man named George who had two daughters from a previous marriage. When I received the divorce papers from her attorney, I had suspected that she had intended to marry someone else, but when I asked her this question in Myrtle Beach she denied it. I was distraught but not surprised. My distress arose from the idea that another man would raise my daughters in accordance with his values. That troubled me more than anything.

It also caused me to focus on accelerating my next visit to Myrtle Beach. My mind was scattered for a few moments, but after I refocused I chose to regain custody of my daughters and raise them in my own home. I thought about them every day and some days affected me worse than others. Living with Elisa and Frances again seemed out of the question at the moment, but in the past, plenty of things that had initially seemed out of the question had occurred as a result of my focused intention. My absence from my daughters during my time in Vietnam, Thailand, and now Spain was so painful that I committed to returning to them permanently before serving out my entire two years in Spain. I did not know how this would happen, but trusted that anything is possible.

I continued developing experiments, some pre-planned and some impromptu. The experiments were intended to change reality in ways that could be experienced by me and by witnesses. After each experiment I looked back from the ultimate result to what I had been doing and thinking beforehand that may have contributed to the outcome. I searched for patterns in my mind that were likely to have created the event. I wanted to simplify the process of communicating with my original self, my higher power, so that I and others could see how it worked in our lives. The ultimate goal was to produce results in my life that I chose with purpose and intention. Following my role model, the bodhisattva, my primary intention was enlightenment and a pathway to enlightenment that others could follow without the need to devote most of a lifetime to it. Beyond enlightenment, I wanted to learn to guide my life in accordance with my conscious intentions.

On several occasions small lizards somehow found their way up four floors and into my apartment. They were excellent experiment subjects. I sat still and focused on the lizard until I felt my mind energy merge with the lizard energy. Once I was locked in with the lizard, I focused my attention on a new location in the apartment to see if the lizard would follow my thought energy to the new spot. Invariably, as soon as I relaxed my focus, the lizard immediately moved to precisely that new location. This happened probably three or four different times over the course of about a month. I created experiments that could produce results right away because the small amount of time between the changes in my thought patterns and the changes in the world allowed me to discern a pattern. It was the discovery of this pattern that gave me the confidence to slowly shift my focus from short-term experiments to long-term choices employing exactly the same pattern.

It was apparent that self-understanding had a major impact on the transformation of my thinking and my transformed thinking impacted my actions. Siddhartha Gautama, the Buddha, told his followers that he knew the pathway to liberation and could show them the way; they would, however, have to make the journey on their own. Without comparing myself to the Buddha, I believed it was possible to discover a new pathway that would help me and others find their way to enlightenment. I saw the possibility of replacing fear with love, so we could all live peacefully with ourselves and each other.

Chapter 24

LISTEN TO THE SILENCE

Some Tibetan Buddhist monks become proficient at using the wisdom and power of enlightenment to alter physical reality. Most of my experiments were designed to accomplish exactly that. I reasoned that if I could cause relatively small shifts in my world, then I could expand the principles of the experiments into my life on a larger and more profound scale. I wanted to learn to have faith in myself and in the higher power that we all essentially are. I had seen my thoughts alter this world many times, as did those who were near me when I altered it. Observing the outcome of the experiments and relating it to the thoughts and actions that produced that outcome, I learned that making a choice, focusing on the choice, and surrendering the choice without attempting to influence it could produce the chosen result.

The element of surrender, of letting go, represented a critical step in the manifestation process and was an important part of the roadmap. In every experiment, my choice became my living reality only after I released the energy around it to the universe. When

I released the energy I temporarily stopped thinking about how I would receive the result; I gave up any attempt to control the outcome and was willing to accept the results of my choice no matter what they were. When all thoughts of the result left my mind, the path was cleared for the universe, God, to deliver my choice in accordance with my highest good and the highest good of all.

I continued meditating nearly every day as I had since I was nineteen. I devised and performed many other experiments that taught me how to produce short-term results that provided instant feedback. The consistency of the short-term results began to open my mind to the possibility of producing long-term, life-altering results. I also experimented with the I Ching. It proved to be an excellent vehicle for disciplining my mind, strengthening my psychic abilities, and increasing my wisdom. The I Ching is an ancient Chinese system thought to date back to the first or second millennium B.C. Known as the Book of Changes, the I Ching was believed to serve two functions: one as a system of divination and the other to describe the operating principles of the cosmos. The book contains sixty-four hexagrams, each composed of six lines. The meaning of each hexagram is reflected in the various combinations of Yin (dashed) and Yang (solid) lines within each hexagram. The book also contains interpretive text, though, as I understood it, experienced Chinese oracles did not use the text but created their own interpretations directly from the combination of hexagrams.

To use the I Ching, I tossed three coins. The combinations of heads and tails guided me in the selection of particular hexagrams. By referencing the general meanings of those hexagrams in the text, I would then interpret the meaning as I perceived it to apply to an individual's question. People came to me with questions about their money, pregnancies, sex of expected children, personal health conditions, the health of their relatives, and other similar questions. Many people came to me to work with the I Ching because my answers were consistently correct.

In February 1977, I wired to Richard my plans for returning to the Netherlands in March. I included my date of arrival at Central Station and informed Richard I would go directly to his boat from the train station. I also suggested that he return with me to Spain after my trip to Holland. Richard's confirmation of my travel plans came across the wire two days later. He intended to stay a few days in Spain before traveling to New York for a business meeting he had arranged.

Dave, my roommate, and Craig, another member of my weapons team, drove with me to Atocha Station on the appointed day of departure in early March of 1977. While I was standing in the ticket line, a thought entered my mind with the clarity of the spoken word. The thought said, *You don't have time to take the train. Go to the airport now and fly to Schiphol.* The meaning was very clear but my internal resistance was strong. Was that my inner wisdom speaking or was it the compulsive, impatient side of my personality? We were already in line at the train station and the drive through Madrid to the airport would be complicated. I would also arrive in Amsterdam a couple of days before Richard expected me. The inertia of the original plan was difficult to overcome.

I attempted to ignore the mental command to fly, but my anxiety level increased rapidly. My inner voice spoke loudly. I suddenly felt very impatient standing there in line. I visualized myself sitting on an airplane for two hours and then saw myself hustling across Paris to catch the train to the Netherlands. I looked at Dave. "Listen guys, let's drive to the airport. I'm going to fly to Amsterdam." David and Craig did not hesitate; they grabbed my bags and we walked rapidly back to the car. I was soon in Madrid Barajas airport with a ticket to Amsterdam. I thanked Craig and Dave, shook their hands, and they drove my car back to the apartment.

Chapter 25

SYNCHRONICITY

Upon landing at Schiphol at about one o'clock that Monday afternoon, I proceeded immediately to Richard's boat. He was not expecting me until Wednesday so I knew there was a possibility that he would not be at home. I walked down the gangplank and found the wheelhouse door locked. I knocked and no one answered; that confirmed he was not at home. At that moment Richard's neighbors, Peter and Anna, came walking down the gangplank, both speaking German at the same time, "Herr Jim, Richard ist im Krankenhaus; er ist im Krankenhaus!" I remembered enough German to understand that simple sentence. My heart rate increased with this news.

"Was? Was Krankenhaus?" I asked. "Wissen Sie?" Richard's neighbors were Germans and their English was not fluent but it was better than my German. They were nervous, both trying to speak at the same time, until Anna finally made it clear that Richard was in a hospital and they did not know which one.

Peter's face expressed empathy. "We were told he was beaten and robbed, nearly killed." This kind of violence was very rare in Amsterdam. Peter went on to explain that Richard was found in the street about three o'clock Sunday morning and taken to a hospital. That was all they knew. I knew nothing about the hospitals in Amsterdam but I knew I would find Richard. I left my bags with Anna and Peter and began the search for Richard Craig.

I studied a map, focused on Richard's image, and began a whirlwind of tram rides, several kilometers of walking, and a cab ride. I spoke with admissions people at four hospitals. One hospital directed me to another and still no Richard Craig. In the fifth hospital a woman in a starched white nurse's uniform with a white cap led me to a large room with three beds lined up against each of two opposing walls. She pointed to the bed in the right corner farthest from the door. The nurse told me the patient's name was Richard Craig, but I did not recognize him so I approached the bed for a closer look. It was Richard. His face was red except where it was black and blue; it was swollen probably 140 percent of its normal size due to an upper palate fracture and broken cheekbones. Richard's upper front teeth were still in his mouth, but each of them was rotated ninety degrees so their edges faced forward like blades in a food processor. I thought, *Man, Richard could die.*

This was not a good situation. The doctor with Richard stepped away from his bed to allow me a few moments to speak with him. Richard said in a near whisper, "Every time you think of me send me your healing energy. I will use it to heal myself and I will be out of here on Friday." That was the day Richard and I had planned to return to Spain, which was no longer a priority for me. He gave me the keys to his boat so I would have a place to sleep. I visited every day and whenever I thought of him I sent focused beams of healing energy his way.

About five times each day, whenever the thought occurred to me, I paused to send energy to Richard. I began by taking two or three conscious breaths. I then formed an image in my mind of Richard completely healed and focused my mind on directing energy into that image. The entire process required about fifteen to twenty seconds. Richard grew stronger and looked more like himself every day. I traveled around Amsterdam, drank Dutch beer in bars, and met a sweet young German girl who came back to the boat to spend a few nights with me.

Five doctors surrounded Richard's bed when I walked into his ward on Friday morning. Each doctor wore a white coat and beamed, proud of having healed Richard so quickly. Upon moving in closer I could see that Richard was indeed dramatically healed. The doctors opened their ranks to allow me to approach the bed. Richard was sitting up; his face had only light blue discoloration around his eyes and most of the swelling had disappeared. The man in the bed looked like Richard again. His front teeth, however, were still turned perpendicular to their normal position. Richard remedied this by opening his mouth, grabbing the teeth and straightening them out one at a time as I watched in amazement. The doctors took credit for Richard's rapid recovery and discharged him later that day.

Richard's transformative healing profoundly demonstrated that whatever we imagine for ourselves, we can experience. Richard said he would be healed and out of the hospital on Friday and he was. He did not predict the future; he created it. He and I directly impacted the quality and velocity of his healing by declaring our intention and focusing our thought energy on that chosen intention. My energy, focused together with Richard's, impacted the unified field of the particles and waves composing the structure of Richard's face. Our thought energy and the energy that creates our bodies are interrelated parts of the infinite unified field from which all of creation arises, so when I directed the energy of my healing intention toward Richard, a ripple occurred in the energy field. That energetic ripple manifested in the physical world as an accelerated healing process within individual cells in Richard's body.

By declaring that Richard would be healed by Friday, Richard and I set in motion energy that promoted the knitting together of bones and the healing of flesh. Our intention resulted in Richard's accelerated healing that allowed his doctors to release him several days sooner than anticipated. What we accomplished looked like a miracle. This is the word the doctors used to describe the amazing healing they performed on Richard. We thanked them all sincerely for everything they did to help him.

Although Richard was largely healed, he was unable to chew food. On Saturday, we shopped in several grocery stores for soft foods like tuna salad, yogurt, and soup. Sunday morning, we carried these items with us to Central Station and boarded our train for Madrid. Traveling with Richard was more fun than my solo adventures. He did not speak about the trauma he had suffered except to say he was beaten with blackjacks and robbed for the few guilders that he had with him.

He told stories about historical events, works of art, and his own life. We strolled through the train discussing all of our mystical and political subjects and brainstorming new projects intended to make a difference in the world. We talked constantly and the time flashed by quickly. When the train stopped in Madrid we collected our bags and walked to the street to catch a taxi. A few minutes later we were on our way to the apartment.

My roommates Carl and Dave were very familiar with my thoughts about higher power. They trusted my judgment about bringing Richard into our home and I did not want to compromise that. Neither did Richard, and out of respect to Carl and Dave we reserved conversations about our wildest ideas to times when others could not hear us. Richard turned everyday moments into extraordinary learning experiences. He brought all the details together under the overall umbrella of making a difference for people. This is where Richard most impacted me. The pragmatic aspect of the mystical experience had been on my mind since I had first experienced an alternate way of looking at the world and immediately asked, "What difference does this experience make in my everyday life?" Richard not only answered the question, but he gave me the tools to shape my everyday life in accordance with my preferences.

Even while he was sleeping, Richard taught me to focus my mind like a laser beam. He taught by showing, not telling, using daily routines and ordinary life functions to teach the workings of the universe. He demonstrated that the mind was the source of all power and could accomplish things that most of us would never consider possible. I learned to focus my mental energy by nonverbally engaging with his mind. This allowed me to directly model his focusing techniques in real time. When my focus achieved laser quality, Richard let me know by subtly shifting his mental frequency, suddenly changing the rhythm of his snoring, or making a sudden movement with his head. Each new experience, each new bit of learning, contributed to the development of the simple roadmap to self-understanding that I was in the process of creating – a roadmap that anyone could follow.

About six-thirty one Sunday morning I walked from my bedroom into the living room to find Richard relaxing in a chair. I sat down in the chair opposite his. Suddenly I heard Richard speaking to me with words inside my head. I heard him as clearly and naturally as if he were speaking out loud into my ears.

"What are you doing here?" I asked without saying a word.

"What am I doing here? I'm here all the time. What are you doing here?" Richard asked.

"Nothing; I didn't even know I was here until I ran into you," I said, surprised. "I still don't know where I am if not in my own head like I usually am."

"This is everywhere. I'm everywhere all the time. This just happens to be the first time you noticed me." The idea that I had been unaware of Richard's presence for so long took me by surprise. "You are everywhere all the time also; it's your awareness of it that makes the difference." By a combination of demonstration and brief, wordless mind-to-mind explanation, Richard then showed me the step-by-step pathway to this state of openness and awareness. Once I learned the pathway, I was able to use it whenever I chose. Through further experimentation I discovered that this state of openness was a doorway to the power of unlimited creative manifestation.

Richard helped me catch a glimpse into the mystery of power. I had initially felt guilty about wanting power. But why do we live our lives if not to realize our preferences and to assist others in achieving theirs? This requires the discovery, acquisition, and implementation of energy in a focused way that consistently produces results that we, or anyone, can experience and duplicate. That is power – the power to realize our preferences with ease and grace.

Chapter 26

ONE STEP AT A TIME

Normal human power sources such as electricity, cooking gas, and gasoline did not function properly when Richard was around. Our apartment was equipped with two very efficient, butane fueled, flash water heaters. A flash heater heats water only when the hot water faucet is opened, causing a diaphragm to open a gas valve, a pilot light to ignite the gas, and the flame to heat the water as it flows through a circular tube above the flame. Carl and I never had any problem with hot water in our apartment – until Richard arrived.

After Richard arrived, both flash heaters – in the kitchen and the bathroom – failed to work. I suppose that could happen – both units failing at the same time. Our landlord came and repaired them and I watched the water heaters ignite when the hot water faucet was opened. When he finished he picked up his toolbox and walked toward the door. Before he reached it, I tested the flash heater in the bathroom and it failed to ignite again. He got completely fed up with me as I continued to call him back to repair the flash heaters.

Richard was in the living room when Carl and I came down the hall after walking the landlord to the door. Carl was angry about the lack of hot water and he blamed Richard. He said, "Richard must be doing this on purpose and if he does it again I'll kick his ass."

"Richard is not doing it on purpose," I explained. "He doesn't like it either; the gas just quits working around him, it won't light." I wasn't making excuses for Richard, but this was simply the case. I spoke with Richard a few minutes later and asked him why the water heaters stopped working when his presence was the only new variable in the apartment. He told me that he had a situation with electricity and other energy sources that caused some power systems to fail intermittently in his presence. Richard was not happy about this but said that he accepted it as part of who he was.

"I live on a boat without electricity," Richard said quietly, "because there's no sense in me having electricity anyway." I stood up to change the tape on the reel-to-reel machine while Richard continued. "It wasn't always this way and I don't think it always will be, but for this past year and a half or so I've been short-circuiting electricity without even thinking about it."

My eyes opened wide with understanding. "So that's why," I said with an apologetic tone in my voice, "you didn't want to light the kerosene heater that night in your boat."

"That's right," he explained, "and now I see that you did get that understanding."

The next day we walked around the city of Torrejon for hours looking for a particular ingredient that Richard needed for the chili con carne he was making for that night's dinner. Unable to find it, we decided to drive to Madrid. I told Richard I did not enjoy driving in Madrid because I usually got lost and could not find my way to where I wanted to go or back to Torrejon. Richard said not to worry about it; he would direct us to the place where we would find the necessary ingredient. He had only been in Madrid once about fifteen years ago but he would give me directions.

I knew how to find the freeway to Madrid and as we approached the city Richard directed me to a particular freeway exit. Madrid traffic was intense as always. My normal response at this point was to get nervous, and even with Richard in the car I was on edge. Richard was perfectly relaxed. He told me when to turn left and when to go right and in about twenty minutes he told me to stop. We were parked in front of a large market, which we entered. Richard led the way through the maze of aisles. We stopped in front of a counter displaying a variety of vegetables and spices. Richard found what he wanted and purchased the necessary items. After that, we walked around in amazement at the quantity of food and variety of goods for sale in this vast market. Everything was under one huge roof without walls. We bought some cheese, olives, and other good things before walking back to the car.

About twenty minutes later we parked on the street in front of the apartment building. While riding in the elevator to the third floor I asked Richard how he navigated so accurately in and out of Madrid. "Let your inner wisdom guide you, James," he began. "First you must know what it is you want or where you want to go. Establish that clearly in your mind then don't think about it anymore."

"Don't think about it anymore, that makes sense," I said.

"That's right; don't think anything about it, just drive. As you are driving along you will hear instructions in your mind that will take you to your chosen destination one step at a time. The instructions may not come until the very last minute; follow them without hesitation."

"Okay."

"It's simple. Don't expect to receive more than one step at a time. Keep your mind clear, as we discussed that first day in the Arrive´. Have confidence that you will receive the instructions and that they will get you where you want to go. If you do that you will get there. As you see, we got there and back directly without one mistake."

Richard worked all afternoon to create a huge pot of chili. The tallest pot we had in the house was filled to the brim and overflowed onto the stove as it bubbled. Carl, Dave, Richard and I ate the chili for dinner with bread Richard found at the market. The chili was not good. Most of it sat in the pot until mold grew on top, whereupon I threw it out.

Richard packed his bags after dinner, I went to bed early, and Richard and Carl sat in the living room talking. I woke Richard the next morning to prepare for the drive to the airport. Looking professional in his sport jacket and slacks, Richard said goodbye to Carl and Dave. I think they were glad to see him go. Both of them thought his behavior was over the top and embarrassing and neither of them saw his mystical side.

It was a sad parting for me at the airport. Richard planned to return directly to Amsterdam from New York, leaving me unsure about when I would see him again. Like our first meeting, our next meeting was in the hands of the universe. We hugged just before Richard boarded the 747.

Chapter 27

MAKING THE CONNECTION

fter Richard's departure I had more time available for reading, meditation, and visiting with friends. I was at home one
night with two married couples who were friends from the security police squadron. All four of them, the husbands and the
wives, were security police. They brought along a cop friend who I
had not previously met. Music was playing in the background on
my Akai GX 365D tape deck. Because this machine automatically played two complete albums, it was more convenient than
the turntable, which required flipping or changing the album after
each side. As the two couples discussed their recent trip to Cadiz,
my thoughts wandered to the music. I began to focus my attention
on the music, hardly noticing the volume of their conversation
fading from my awareness.

My breathing fell into a rhythmic, meditative pattern. I slowly
inhaled and exhaled while focusing my attention on the musical

sounds streaming forth from the Bose 901 speakers. With five witnesses present, one of whom I did not know, this was an ideal opportunity to attempt an experiment. The idea of altering the flow of electrical power in the apartment occurred to me. As I inhaled, I focused my thought energy on the electrical energy powering the apartment. I imagined the energy of my mind becoming one with the energy of electricity. On each exhalation I amplified my mind energy like I was increasing the pressure in an air compressor's storage tank. As I inhaled I merged my thoughts with the flow of electrical energy through the apartment. On the exhale I focused my thought energy, increasing its pressure and power. Using this process I increased the energy to an intense level that I perceived as pressure inside my skull. As the pressure increased, I felt as if my brain might at any moment explode inside my head and I would be dead. I considered the real possibility of suddenly dying right there.

I quickly put that thought aside and continued focusing on my breath, inhaling energy and pumping it into the reservoir on the exhale. When I sensed the energy in the reservoir had reached critical pressure, I relaxed my mind. This opened the reservoir and released the pressurized thought energy into the unified field. The thought energy generated ripples in the unified field that manifested in the world in accordance with my intention. In this case, I had chosen to engage with and consciously alter the flow of the electrical current through the apartment; I would know that this was happening if all electrically-powered objects in the apartment began oscillating in harmony with variations in my thought.

When I set the focused energy free, I felt myself become one with the electrical current flowing through the apartment. I lowered the frequency of my thought energy and in that instant the current in the apartment weakened, causing the tape reels of the GX 365 to slow down. As the speed of the reels decreased, the pitch of the music deepened, resulting in slow-motion, otherworldly vocals. Concurrent with the deepening pitch, the lights in the chandelier dimmed and began to flicker. The change in the flow of current inside my head was palpable. I heard zapping sounds that varied with the flickering of the lights. My thoughts were controlling the intensity of the electrical flow, and before the tape deck shut itself off I quickly adjusted my thought energy to increase the voltage.

There were no verbal thoughts in my mind; the change in the electrical flow had nothing to do with words that I spoke. The electricity changed depending upon feelings that I generated inside my head. When I created a feeling of openness in my head, the electrical flow decreased, so the lights dimmed and the music slowed. The electricity increased when I created a feeling of tightening my brain like I was contracting a muscle. As I did this, the lights became brighter, glowing with an intensity I had never seen before. The reels of the tape machine started spinning faster. They went so fast I thought they might fly right off their spindles. The vocals coming out of the speakers sounded like chipmunks. While merged with the unified field, I felt the vibrations of electrical energy flowing through my body and was able to vary the lights and music up and down at will. As long as I maintained my connection with the unified field, the music and lights continued fluctuating in direct proportion to the variations in my mind.

After several seconds I switched my attention back to the people in the room. As soon as I did that, I was disconnected from the energy field and the lights and music returned to normal. My heart pumped rapidly, I was breathing hard and felt physically exhausted. I quickly rose from my chair, traversed the five steps to the kitchen, and sat down on the floor with my back against the oven door. I was not alone. The new guy, the cop I met that night, followed right behind me. Frantically turning the corner into the kitchen he nearly shouted, "How did you do that?"

Still breathing heavily, I looked into his eyes and said, "I didn't do it alone; all of us were involved. I chose to change the electrical flow in the apartment and our energy combined to make it happen." When I reflected on the process I was able to break down the sequence of steps leading up to the power change. First I chose what I wanted to do, then I generated a laser-like beam of focused energy aimed at fulfilling the choice. While I was building the energy nothing happened. It was only after I released the energy to higher power that we experienced the increases and decreases in the lighting and the speed of the music. I focused only on the final result, making no attempt to understand or interfere with the details of how electricity worked. The universe took care of the details.

Choosing the intention, focusing attention on it, and releasing the focus produced this powerful result while I sat in my chair listening to music. I thought, Good God, if I can do this small thing, I can use the very same process to accomplish anything I choose.

A pebble thrown into a pond generates ripples that radiate out from the pebble. These ripples occur as small waves that impact the movement of everything in the pond. Once the pebble hits the surface of the pond, we cannot control the movement of the rippling water. Every drop of water in the pond is affected and every drop is part of the entire pond. If a fish jumps out of the water it will create additional unpredictable ripples as it splashes back into the water. Those ripples with alter the affect of the ripples created by the pebble. The unified field of thought energy that gives rise to our world is like the pond. Our individual thought energy is like the pebble. When we release our thought energy into the unified field, it causes ripples that would not have occurred had we not generated those thoughts. The ripples of our thoughts affect the entire field and produce experiences in our lives that reflect our thinking. Ripples created by universal entelechy or some other source can alter the affect of the ripples generated by your thoughts, thus producing unpredictable results. It is part of human nature to want to control every aspect and every movement of those ripples. But once the pebble hits the surface of the pond, the ripples move as they move. Ultimate control is an illusion.

My experiences have demonstrated that the most powerful results are produced when we give up the desire for control and completely surrender the focused energy to the unified field. There are too many details involved in achieving complex goals and we can never be in control of all of them. Sometimes the results we produce are not exactly the results we imagine and some goals never happen. This is the nature of reality. Super-consciousness always works for our highest benefit, and whatever the result may be, we have chosen it. We may not consciously choose everything that we experience, but everything that we experience is a choice.

Some choices, like the choice to increase our heart rate when we start running, happen outside of our conscious awareness; they are, nonetheless, our choices.

When a golfer approaches the golf ball for the next shot, he or she always chooses a specific target for that ball. When the golfer begins the backswing, thousands of synapses fire in the brain, sending signals to more than a hundred different muscles throughout the body. No one can consciously control all of the activity involved in generating the swing. All the golfer can do is choose the target, relax, let go, and take the swing. The ball may go directly to the intended target or it may slice off into the rough. Through repeated practice, the golfer gains the faith that his swing will, more often than not, deliver the ball at least close to the chosen destination. That is why the best golf swings happen smoothly and apparently automatically.

I remained on the kitchen floor for a few moments, recovering my composure and thinking through the sequence of events while they were still fresh in my mind. I then stood up, walked into the living room, and sat down in my chair to a rush of questions from my guests. They all saw the changes in lighting and sound that I had just discussed with the security policeman who followed me into the kitchen. Each of them asked the same question: "How did you do that?" I responded with an expanded version of the answer I had given to the cop in the kitchen. I was worn out. After about an hour they all departed and I went to bed.

Chapter 28

A POSSIBLE FUTURE

Early the next afternoon, on the first Saturday in May, 1977, I was in my apartment reading an article about the Middle East in *Time* magazine. The article quoted Anwar Sadat speaking about the possibility of "peace in our area." Sadat's words captured my imagination. I stopped reading, closed my eyes, and relaxed. I thought about what the world would look like if we were all peaceful people. The peaceful thoughts became visual impressions on my eyelids. I opened my eyes and the images on my eyelids continued playing on a large transparent screen that seemed to be suspended a few feet in front of me and slightly above eye level. I saw moving pictures and heard spoken words that underscored the images. I don't remember the exact words that I heard at the beginning, but they sounded like this:

You humans have the opportunity to peacefully and sustainably enjoy the beauty and abundance of life on planet Earth for as long as you choose. Instead, in search of the confused priorities of money and power, you destroy your very source of life. You are killing yourselves in pursuit of an illusion.

The images on the screen changed rapidly, portraying scenes that were all too familiar to me. There were happy children walking to school, husbands and wives kissing in the doorways of little suburban homes, gas guzzling V-8s cruising along new highways, and soldiers killing each other for nothing. The cost of this lifestyle became apparent in scenes of children working in factories and adults taking minerals out of the ground by hand in places far from view of the happy little schoolchildren. Clips of the suburban towns decaying and their automobiles rotting were juxtaposed with shots of dead lakes, fouled oceans, and smoke-filled air. Many specific events played out during the vision; some pertained to me individually but most were important to all humans worldwide.

I saw cash money replaced by a card capable of continuous value replenishment, rendering cash unnecessary. The card was more convenient than cash and ultimately became ubiquitous before being replaced with a small electronic chip implanted under the skin of almost every person in the world. Many were happy to have the chips because they believed the chips kept them safe while giving them the power to pay their mortgages, earn their salaries, and participate in the marketplace like good consumers should.

I experienced this information in an audio/video format. The best way my mind could absorb it was to slow it down and present it to me in images and sound, but the raw data were actually injected into my consciousness very rapidly. A video sequence of the United States invading Iraq seemed to last for two or three hours, but when I looked at my watch only two minutes had passed. The information in the vision indicated that this attack would take place either in 1990 or 1991. It described the entire reasoning

196

process leading to this invasion, making it clear to me that this war, as opposed to the Vietnam conflict, would be popularly supported by the American people and the returning troops would be declared heroes.

I also saw a future "computer on the planet." This was the term that came into my mind on that day to describe what we now know as the World Wide Web. The computer on the planet was the single source of all information about everything that had ever mattered to humans since the beginning of time. More importantly, this planetary computer provided instant access to information about every person, event, and organization on Earth. In 1977, I saw this all-knowing computer as something that would be, for most humans, a wonderful tool that improved life in many ways. Unfortunately, the apparent improvements were only temporary; artificial intelligence deployed in the computer on the planet was ultimately used to exploit individuals by tracking and analyzing all of their everyday movements and habits. The computer on the planet contained the kernel of humanity's brightest and darkest motivations.

The next images displayed on my mind-screen portrayed the decline of the most powerful civilization the world had yet known. This civilization's illusory values were accepted and desired worldwide as the standard of good. Most people wanted things like cars, appliances, tools, and gadgets. Only when earth began to reach the limits of its ability to provide humans with their never-ending wants did people slowly start waking up to the reality that the earth was a finite resource. That is when fear took over and illusory human social structures collapsed. The widely unforeseen speed at which the death of the old paradigm occurred caused incalculable human suffering.

Humans thought they knew things that they did not know. Some of them thought they could live without values and that earth would always supply everything they needed and wanted. As the world's population grew and demand on earth's resources increased, fear of lack led to greed, which led to the acquisition of nearly unlimited wealth by a small number of earth's inhabitants who thought that physical wealth would allow them to escape fear. But only love can replace fear; money cannot do it. Wealth of such magnitude that it could never be spent in a lifetime led to the acquisition of absolute power, which corrupted those who acquired it. Those who most feared for their lives were those with the most to lose. In an effort to alleviate their own fear by controlling their environment, the powerful lured the masses of humanity into believing that they did not have to be responsible for their own lives.

The powerful promised the masses that they would be supported whether they were productive or not. This took the form of financial benefits paid not only to people who really needed them but also to those who had the ability to work and chose not to. The masses of humanity accepted the idea because it was easier than working to support themselves. This financial dependence made the people easier to control and manipulate. When support was ultimately taken away from those humans accustomed to receiving it, they had no other means of support.

I saw in this vision a mad rush of stampeding human flesh running into a huge American supermarket that was completely empty of food except for one loaf of bread on an otherwise bare shelf. I observed as people killed each other with their hands and other crude weapons in an effort to possess even one fragment of one slice of that loaf. I wondered how it could ever be that America's amazing food producing machine, capable of feeding the world's population, could collapse almost in an instant to the degree that food was no longer available anywhere. The visual experience was so appalling that I denied the possibility of its occurring in my lifetime.

General conditions in the U.S. and around the world consisted of widespread starvation, armed gangs, black market economies, and in some places, complete anarchy. I thought, in early May of 1977, Surely this cannot occur in my lifetime. I asked higher power if I could expect to see these things or if these events would happen after my death. The vision was clear in communicating that if humanity remained on its current track, all events would occur in my current lifetime. I grieved for this needless loss of life, freedom, and peace. The genuine tragedy was that humanity did this to itself. The people of the world destroyed themselves. It does not have to go this way. The options are many, the warnings are clear. Humanity can choose love, peace, and a sustainable way of life instead of the short-term satisfaction that can lead to lack and destruction.

The vision went on to portray several attacks perpetrated on interests of the United States, most of them occurring in faraway places. These attacks affected relatively small numbers of Americans overseas; most of us at home paid little attention. In the most serious of these attacks, however, I saw individuals from the

Middle East destroying parts of New York and Washington, DC on the same day. The vision said this attack would occur in 2000 or 2001. In May of 1977 I did not pin it down to September 11, 2001, nor did I see airplanes crashing into the World Trade Center and the Pentagon. The image I saw consisted of Arabs placing dirty nuclear bombs in these cities, detonating them, and killing thousands.

The visual scenes continued unfolding with images and sounds of American troops destroying many human lives throughout the Middle East in a futile effort to prevent a relatively small number of extreme thinkers from ever again damaging the United States. The death and severe wounding of American soldiers in this effort was widely supported by most Americans. These scenes impacted me with a momentary feeling of hopelessness. Why bother if this is what awaits our efforts?

The vision continued to portray events that I had thought about many years before and fully expected to see in my lifetime. Among these was global economic collapse, meaning the complete loss of value of all the world's currencies. It wasn't like the stories I had heard from my parents and grandparents about the Great Depression; it was mass starvation and deprivation. Because of fear, those who had resources kept them for themselves and did not share them with the starving. Instead, they defended their food with weapons. This is an inconceivable nightmare, yet it too was part of the vision that afternoon in Spain. I did not consider this a prophecy or a prediction but a simple extrapolation from historical facts. These were scenes from a potential future, a future subject to change depending upon individual and collective human preference.

In that moment I made a commitment to communicate this information on a grand scale. People needed to know their options so they could make informed decisions for themselves. Given enough individual decisions favoring peace and long-term sustainability, none of these nightmares need ever see the light of day. God does not create a single preordained future. These events were not destined or inevitable. Humans could choose to create a different future.

At that point I became aware of two options, either one of which would result in an improved way of life for humanity. One option prevented nuclear war through the awakening of human consciousness. The other option awakened human consciousness through the waging of nuclear war. Unfortunately, in this vision, even the unimaginably shocking results of the financial collapse failed to awaken us to the need to reform our thinking.

The vision continued with an aerial image of the Mediterranean Sea surrounded by parts of North Africa, Europe, Central Asia, and the Middle East. From this perspective high above the world, I saw the brief flash of a bright pinpoint of light in the Middle East. Another followed about a thousand miles away near the Mediterranean coast. These were the first flashes produced by the detonation of nuclear weapons. The perspective zoomed in to reveal missile exhaust trails rising from other areas around the globe. Bright flashes in several places on both sides of the planet indicated the death of millions. The view suddenly zoomed in again to the individual level and a scene too horrific to put into words. It was unbearable to witness this unspeakable loss of life, but the vision proceeded according to its own pace. This is what we could do to ourselves if we continued along our current path of fear, control, and greed.

The initial explosions, the radiation that blew around the planet, and the dark clouds that blocked the sun took away most of the world's population. Relatively few humans inhabited the post-apocalyptic world. The word apocalypse comes to us from a Greek word meaning "revelation." It is the unveiling of information previously unknown to people who did not want to know. We use that word today to describe the devastation of life as we know it. After the apocalypse, it became clear to most of the survivors that they lacked the resources required to recreate the way of life they had previously known. Once they accepted the implications of this fact they began struggling to survive in their new environment. Whether this nuclear destruction was initiated intentionally or by complete accident no longer mattered. Fear and greed had gotten out of control, eliminating any distinction between haves and have-nots.

In the wake of this horrific destruction, light began to shine on planet earth. As humanity began to accept its collective experience, individuals around the world became filled with the light of love, revealing to them a different way of being. This was not a new way to be, but for most, it was a different way. Realizing that past human behavior clearly did not work, people began seeking a different way to pursue the future. The vision showed people around the world conducting themselves based on their new understanding of the unity of life and the inalienable values of truth, justice, and liberty. The appreciation, acceptance, and integration of the destruction that brought unprecedented loss and pain to the people of the world clarified humanity's path to a new beginning. As individuals outwardly expressed their inner understanding of oneness, they began to flourish in ways that had previously existed only in their dreams.

The tone of the vision shifted with the appearance of a small television set in place of the large screen I had been watching. A distinguished-looking face resembling Jesus appeared on the screen and told me that television would be an excellent medium to communicate the message of peace to the world. The image went on to say that if I chose, I could produce video programming that could help prevent the destructive elements of the vision from occurring. It explained that satellite distribution would allow the images to be broadcast around the world.

Then the small screen also disappeared and the room returned to normal. I sat in my chair, feet on the floor. The parts of the vision portrayed above are only the primary highlights, and there were many more details that I have not described. At that moment I had many questions; I felt somewhat confused and fearful. The question persisted in my mind: Could these things possibly happen in my lifetime? I felt responsible for the knowledge and considered what I could do, if anything, to help turn this around, to help prevent this unprecedented destruction. The vision explained that humanity had options; we could achieve peace without having to suffer the self-annihilation portrayed in the vision.

I thought it might help if everyone in the world understood what I had just seen. The vision told me that television would be a good way to do that, but I knew nothing about television. Meanwhile, I began discussing the content of the vision with nearly everyone I knew and plenty of people I did not know. My intention was to provide a peaceful possibility for the future. The vision illustrated the possible consequences of our present course of action. It also provided an alternative: self-understanding and the proliferation of inner peace from one person to another until enough people experienced their own peace to influence the peace of humanity.

Our essential problems have remained unchanged for thousands of years. Year after year, variations of the same solutions have accomplished nothing to end hunger, clothe and shelter everyone, or end the inhuman ways that we treat each other. My experiences of the past several years had convinced me that individual self-understanding is an especially powerful way to help us rise up from our age-old human struggles. Self-understanding means seeing ourselves as the higher power we truly are. It means literally transforming ourselves from ordinary human beings to the gods that we essentially are. We are eternal, unlimited beings capable of accomplishing anything we choose. Making a choice is critical and following up with action is necessary to fulfill that choice. Before I was able to focus on changing the flow of electricity in our apartment, I had to choose to change it. Without conscious choices our unconscious choices will continue to manifest. If we do not choose consciously, everything in life just shows up. Like a ship without a rudder we will arrive someplace but nobody knows where. I chose something – a targeted goal – I focused single-mindedly on that choice – and it happened.

Most of the experimental choices I had manifested at that time served strictly as learning tools. It was time for me to expand my choices to the larger world, to manifest choices that would make a profound difference in my life and the lives of others. My initial choice, many years ago, was to understand myself – to discover who I really was. After choosing self-understanding I began choosing relatively small short-term goals, like directing the activities of lizards and insects and causing fluctuations in the electrical grid. Short-term projects were necessary at this early stage because I needed instant feedback. Witnessing the instant connection showed me how specific changes in my thought changed my experience of physical reality.

These short-term learning experiences convinced me to invest longer periods of time – years if necessary – in the practice of focusing on one or two long-term goals. The vision I witnessed that day showed me that dangerously frightening things could happen on earth if we humans continued doing what we had always done. The vision also gave me the idea to communicate the message of peace with television programming. That idea seemed so foreign to me that I thought, *How do I go from being an Air Force NCO in Spain to producing television shows?* That would have seemed hopeless had I not already witnessed the incredible changes that I was capable of making. I did not know where to start, but I committed to learn television production and distribution so I could transmit the message of self-understanding around the world.

Chapter 29

FLY AEROBATICS

The most powerful way I knew to contribute to the creation of a peaceful planet was to use the same process I had discovered during my experiments. Communicating the message of the vision, whether by television, newsletters, or speeches, was a step along the way; it was not the ultimate goal. Working to prevent the events shown in the vision was also not the final goal. Attempting to stop those potential outcomes from occurring was resisting them, and working toward the creation of a negative is not effective or possible.

My experiments had shown me that the intended results are most efficiently produced by focusing on the final result as opposed to the steps leading to that result. The goal is self-understanding, which automatically creates the experience of peace within me. My experience of lasting inner peace leads to peace within others and ultimately the peaceful coexistence of human beings on planet earth. Therefore, experiencing peace within ourselves and living together peacefully and sustainably appeared to be the best long-term choice for all of us. Peace within is love within, and fear cannot exist in the presence of love. In the absence of fear, greed disappears. This frees us from the desire to control others, which allows liberty to flourish. Peaceful sustainability is possibly the only choice that will preserve our own individual lives and all of human life on our planet and peace within each of us comes automatically when we understand who we really are. Fulfilling the goal of self-understanding means choosing it, focusing on it, and then surrendering the details of the manifestation process to the universe.

Laser-like focus on the goal increases the energy around that goal, thus causing it to make a quantum leap into our living reality. The experiments taught me to focus on my choices in different ways. Oftentimes I focused on a visual image of the goal, imagining the way I intended the goal to look when it manifested and then focusing on that mental image. Other times I focused on the feelings that I would expect to have upon accomplishing the goal. To do that I generated a feeling of excitement or joy inside myself and then focused my attention on that feeling, causing that feeling to grow stronger and stronger within me. It was most important to focus on the completed goal, paying no attention to any thoughts contradictory to the goal.

When focusing on any object or idea, it is normal to experience extraneous or even defeatist thoughts. Attempting to push those thoughts out or making an effort to ignore them simply strengthens them. When those thoughts interfere with your focus or your clarity, simply notice that they have entered your mind and observe them as they gently drift away on their own. This process, the entire process of enlightenment, and the process of life itself is about ease – not effort.

But there was more to it than choosing a goal and paying attention to it. The first night that the lights dimmed and brightened and the music slowed and sped up, I came to realize that no matter how much I focused, even to the point where I felt like my brains would pop out of my head, nothing happened until I stopped focusing. When I intuitively sensed that I had reached the point of optimal focus, I stopped focusing, and the instant I released my energy everything happened: the lights did something, the little creatures went somewhere, the fire roared or went out, a particular record was played or, whatever the conscious choice might have been at that time, it manifested. Only when all effort and control were released to higher power did the chosen goal become part of my life experience. Release or surrender means releasing control and becoming completely unattached to how or when the result is produced – it does not mean cessation of effort in the sense of giving up. When you surrender, know that the universe will reflect your clear intention into your physical experience in a form that works optimally for you and those around you.

On the Friday following the vision I went to Incirlik, Turkey, and sweltered with the scorpions and giant yellow jumping spiders. I returned to Spain on a hot Friday night in early June and went to bed as soon as I arrived home. I used Saturday morning to write some letters and purchase items in the Base Exchange that I was unable to buy in Turkey. After lunch I sat in the living room looking through the magazines that had accumulated in my mailbox. It was about as hot in Spain as it was in Turkey; our apartment had no air conditioning and no screens on the windows. The only way to get a breeze was to open the windows, which then gave any flying insects or even crawling lizards free access to our home. One wall of the living room had a large window that looked out onto the balcony and the city beyond. The window swung open from left to right, sticking inconveniently into the room when opened. A metal-framed door to the left of the window led from the living room to the small balcony four stories above the street. In Spain the first floor of an apartment building is not counted; our apartment was 306, which meant we lived on the third floor although we were four floors off the ground.

Several friends arrived about two o'clock that afternoon. While talking we failed to notice that a few flies had entered the apartment. Before long many flies, perhaps fifty or more, were buzzing around our heads with everyone swatting futilely, trying to chase them away. The distraction of everyone's arms flailing about made it difficult to conduct a conversation. I sat still and stopped talking so I could tune in more closely to the energy patterns of the unified field throughout the room.

I could see from the appearance of the energy field that swatting at the flies was actually attracting them to us. "I've got an idea," I said. "If you want the flies to leave you alone, stop swatting at them, forget about them; ignore the flies and just get back to the conversation." Nobody said anything; they made their agreement apparent by immediately ceasing their swatting movements and simply tolerating the buzzing of the flies. My friends initially appeared to be forcing themselves to sit still but they soon relaxed. I carried on with the conversation to ensure everyone's focus remained on something more constructive than the flies. The disconnecting of the group energy from the flies was palpable and confirmed by the observable shift in the patterns of the vibrational field. Within seconds of the shift in the energy, the flies stopped buzzing around our heads and flew into the center of the living room, lining up one behind the other in a rotating circle about four feet in diameter. The flies flew around in this circle right in front of our eyes as we each stared in silence, amazed by the spectacle.

The flies remained in formation at eye level in the middle of the room for several revolutions. Then one of the flies suddenly peeled off the circle and flew directly toward the window. The room was silent. Not one of us said a word; I didn't hear a breath. One after the other each fly peeled off the circle and flew in a straight line behind the leader toward the window. I was stunned to see there in front of me a straight line of black flies, one behind the other, flying directly out the window. We continued watching in silent amazement as the last fly cleared the window. Seconds after we intentionally ignored the flies, the entire living room was fly free. My intention to be free of flies was fulfilled and I had made no attempt to predict or control how the intention would be satisfied. The large number of variables and the complex timing involved in fulfilling even the simplest intention makes any attempt to control the details an impractical and inefficient use of time. If we wanted to break down the details of this event, we would have to consider the mind of each one of those flies communicating with some central source that directed them to perform like a highly trained aerobatic team. Such consideration is beyond my ability to comprehend.

When accomplishing our goals by working directly with our inner power we are in effect delegating the details to higher power, which is ultimately us, albeit a part of us of which we are mostly unaware. Any conscious attempt to control how our choice manifests may limit the infinite creativity of our higher self to only those ideas that our relatively limited individual minds are capable of conceiving. For example, if I choose to increase my finances and I decide that it will happen by way of a salary increase from my job, then my thought energy may limit the universe to this single conduit when in reality there are infinite pathways to financial abundance. Our intentions may be fulfilled differently than we imagine. It is also possible that an intention may not be fulfilled at all or that something completely unexpected may occur. Whatever form the fulfillment of an intention may take, it is always in line with our best interests; persist and you will eventually achieve your goal, whether it is self-understanding or tripling your income in three months.

After gathering my thoughts I asked each of my guests to express what he had seen after I suggested ignoring the flies. Each man reported having witnessed the same sequence of events, beginning with the flies entering the apartment and concluding with the flies leaving the apartment in a single line through the window. Nobody could venture a guess about how that had happened. Everyone suspected I had something to do with it because they all knew me well and the flies did not circle up until I offered my suggestion. I told them I had intended that the flies go away and leave us alone but I never thought of the flies forming a circle and peeling off single file out the window.

I understood this phenomenon as a natural product of the singular nature of reality. The flies, and everything in the room and in the universe, were ultimately the same energy; the flies were a manifestation of the unified field, as were my friends and I. When I chose to be free of flies, the entire unified field, the infinity of all of creation, instantly became energized with that intention. I did not communicate my choice directly to the flies' physical sense receptors nor did the flies read my mind. My choice impacted the entire unified field, including the part that manifested in our physical reality as flies. It rippled the energy field with information that shifted the energy of the flies, causing their physical fly manifestations to stay away from the human energy and leave the apartment. Energized with this information, the fly aspect of the unified field followed the flow of the field in the direction of the intention. In this case the flies put on a dramatic display of flying in formation straight out the window. We humans will sometimes create dramatic events to ensure that the information sinks into our consciousness, and an organized formation of flies zooming around the room in a circle then flying out the window in a straight line was a very dramatic event that made a deep impression on my individual consciousness.

The organized action of the flies agitated my guests. "How did that happen?" Craig asked. "Did it even happen, or was it an illusion?" The answer was lengthy and I do not remember the exact words. The explanation went something like this: intention works exactly the same way with the flies as it does in a situation where I might make a choice, for example, to start or sell a business. Energizing the field with my chosen intention shifts the field energy in accordance with that intention. Specific aspects of the field are energized to bring information relative to my intention into the minds of people interested in buying a company, people who I have never met and do not even know to exist. They take actions based on the ideas that occur in their minds, and their thoughts and actions produce results in line with their apparently independent, self-interested intentions. The energy of my chosen intention initiates innumerable activities that ultimately come together to result in the sale of the company, or whatever the intention may be.

I was aware of three particular elements that drove the manifestation of my choice to be fly-free:

1. I chose to be free of flies.

2. I briefly focused thought energy on my chosen intention.

3. I released the thought energy of my choice to higher power.

The unified field is singular and has no parts. In our world of appearances, however, the flies seem separate from the people. This multiplicity is how singular reality presents itself. We are the singularity; the flies are us, but they present to us as separate so we can have objective experiences that will assist us in understanding our true nature. An explanation of how higher power presents itself this way is not necessary – it just does, and the fact that it does is observable. Our ability to speak about the fly part or some other part of the unified field helps us understand that something is actually occurring in the world in response to our thought energy. Attempting to know the details of how our higher self manifests events such as this is completely unnecessary because higher power has provided a way for our limited individual consciousness to communicate with the universal transpersonal consciousness. The time we spend attempting to figure out the details of how the universe manifests the material world could instead be used to further expand our self-understanding, which leads to the fulfillment of all other choices.

Chapter 30

PSYCHIC NAVIGATION

The week following the fly adventure I received a telegram from Richard informing me that he was ready to travel to Spain if I was prepared for a visit. If so, he requested that I wire him part of the transportation funds and confirm a travel date. I knew the name of a bank in Madrid that could transfer funds by wire; however, I still did not know my way around Madrid and I did not know the location of the bank. I decided to approach this dilemma intuitively, as Richard had demonstrated to me when he and I first ventured into Madrid during his previous visit. Two friends, Sandy and Jasmine, were with me when I read the telegram. I discussed my dilemma with them and they volunteered to come along for the ride, even though they knew I had no clue where I was going and didn't know when we would return. We agreed to meet outside their apartment building the following day at ten A.M.

I stopped in front of their building at the moment they walked out the door. Sandy and Jasmine had experienced the results of several of my more dramatic mind experiments and had seen me accurately use the I Ching many times. They were also aware that I always knew the precise time although I had stopped wearing a watch several weeks ago. My arrival at their apartment at exactly ten o'clock that morning was further confirmation of my intuitive time awareness. As soon as they got in the car they asked how I would find our way to the bank without knowing anything about it other than its name. "What time was it when you walked out the door of your building this morning?" I asked.

"I was checking on you, so I looked at my watch as we walked out," Jasmine replied. "It was exactly ten o'clock – the minute hand was straight up on the twelve."

"There you go," I said. "I didn't look at a clock before I left my place and arrived exactly on time. I admit I don't know how any of it works, but I know that it does."

"So, do you know the way to the bank?" Sandy asked.

"Not yet. But I will know it when I need to know it, one step at a time." I explained that, as with all the other apparently impossible things I knew, I would receive directions from the universe straight into my mind at exactly the right time. "Just to make sure I don't miss the instructions, let's please stop talking before we get to the first Madrid exit."

No instructions came into my mind as we whisked passed the first exit for the city. Maybe the bank was located closer to another exit farther up the road. It was too late to do anything now except relax as best I could and know that my inner guide would lead me to the bank. I waited for instructions and just before the second exit for the city I received a clear message to turn off at the exit, and I did. As I approached each intersection, instructions came to my mind, telling me which way to turn. I did not hear a voice but received unmistakable impressions, which I followed without hesitation. About fifteen minutes after leaving the freeway, I pulled the car over to the curb on the right side of the street, and there was the bank. Although I had faith in the system I was surprised at how easy it was. The girls were completely amazed. We went inside and successfully transmitted the wire. The drive back to the apartment was as uneventful as the drive into Madrid. We stopped at a small restaurant in Torrejon and I bought lunch.

This trip was my first attempt at mind navigation. The principles were the same as any other project or goal: I chose to drive directly to and from the bank; I paid attention to that choice, imagining a smooth, calm trip; I let go of the choice and drove the car. There was a definite pattern involved in the manifestation process that slowly became clear. My confidence in the system became stronger every time I saw it work. Since I was a child I had noticed interesting connections between my thoughts and my experiences. In reverse engineering my experiences, I became aware of what I started calling "creative drivers" since these were the elements that drove the creation of my choices. My experiences also told me that these were the same steps that initiated the Big Bang. When I first realized that I was producing results with the power of my mind, I didn't know what was happening. By comparing the results I created with the thoughts and actions immediately preceding them, I became aware of these creative drivers and started using them intentionally.

Richard flew to Madrid and arrived by taxi at the apartment sometime during the second week of June. After he changed his clothes we sat around the living room clarifying the details of our upcoming trip to the States. It was time for me to see Elisa and Frances and Richard had scheduled another business meeting in New York. After a week in Spain, Richard intended to fly to New York for two days and then to Clearwater, Florida to visit with his parents. After clearing customs in New York I would fly directly to Myrtle Beach to be with my family for a week. We would then drive down to Clearwater and meet Richard's mother and father for dinner at their home. After clearing up these details I told Richard about my plans for the Air Force. "The only reason I came back into the Air Force is because I was afraid I would not be able to support my family," I reminded Richard.

"I remember that," said Richard. "Fear is indeed your whole issue."

"Now that I'm planning to get out of the Air Force in two years, I'm feeling that fear again."

"Listen, James, after all that you've learned and accomplished it's hard to believe that you still resist this. Look at me; I've had no visible means of support for years yet my good always comes to me in a way that you haven't experienced yours coming to you because you won't let it," Richard explained. "Yes, I haven't had much because I decided to get away from the material world for a while. But you know my way works because you've seen it – my rent is paid and I always have food and everything else I need. You don't know if it works for you because you won't try it. You've been afraid to take the chance to find out. That's why you've remained in the military – it's a guaranteed income – and that's why you had to experience Vietnam."

Those were difficult words to hear but I knew he was right. "That's true," I said.

"When you know that you are the source of your good, you will always have it in abundant supply, or whatever supply you choose."

"So, if I know that I'll always have what I need, even if I get out of the Air Force, then I will?"

"Yes. Especially if you get out of the Air Force. And you cannot fake knowing."

"But all I know about is weapons – tools of destruction – I get paid for killing people. I don't know anything about making money."

"That's why you're leaving the military. How can you feel good about yourself when you are doing something for a living that you know is unworkable and unsustainable?"

Richard Craig, the lonely man with the combination lock, was here for a big reason. Richard shined a bright light on darkness and gave people something they could not get anywhere else. That caused people to give back to Richard so that he never lacked anything. He departed for New York and I for Myrtle Beach just after the Fourth of July.

While in Myrtle Beach, Frances, Elisa, and I lived in their mother's home while she and her husband George lived in his home with his two daughters. My return to Spain was scheduled for the end of the month but, desiring to remain in Myrtle Beach, I requested cancellation of the remainder of my tour at Torrejon Air Base. In the meantime I made the most of my moments with Elisa and Frances. We played together at home and at the beach, went to the library and read books, and visited amusement parks on the beach. This was what I had been working for: a normal life raising my children in one place. I was willing to do whatever was necessary to achieve it. Richard called from Clearwater about five days after my arrival. I told him we would leave in the morning and be at his parents' home by about six o'clock in the evening for dinner. I bathed Elisa and Frances after dinner, read a bedtime story and they went to sleep.

I woke them early the following morning. After breakfast we left Myrtle Beach and made our way over to Interstate 95 south. Driving with the girls was a beautiful and unprecedented experience for me; they played games in the backseat and I sang songs. We stopped along the way to eat and checked into a motel at about five-thirty in the afternoon. From there we drove directly to the home of Richard's parents, an elegant one-story three-bedroom home in a senior community. Richard introduced us to his parents and his mom led me and the little ones on a short tour of the gracefully appointed home.

Being with Richard in this environment was mind-boggling given where we had met and the boat he lived on in Amsterdam. His hair was now short, his beard trimmed, and he was well dressed. Was this the same person? During dinner his mother and father told us about Richard's youth, his education, and his work in California. They verified everything that Richard had told me in Amsterdam. I had seriously doubted Richard's humanity, thinking he had incarnated just the way he was for the purpose of assisting humans to achieve liberation or enlightenment. In light of the unconditional love he gave to everyone, not to mention the extraordinary powers he displayed, I had seriously considered whether he was something other than a human being. Now I had confirmation that Richard had been born into a family just like the rest of us.

Later that night, Richard told me he would return to Amsterdam as planned. He went on to explain that, based on his successful meetings in New York, he was considering moving to San Francisco to take a job with AT&T. Not knowing when I would see Richard again made it especially difficult to say goodbye the next day. I knew I didn't need Richard but by this time I was feeling dependent upon him. I did not want to go without the energy he brought to every moment and every situation. I wanted more of that and the thought of having to continue on without him was somewhat overwhelming. My little ones were attracted to him too and they looked sad after they hugged him and climbed into the back seat of the car.

Several days after we returned from Clearwater, the Air Force notified me that my tour at Torrejon had been cut short; I would remain in Myrtle Beach until I received permanent assignment orders. That was great news; so far everything was working out according to my intention. I filed another request to be permanently assigned to Myrtle Beach and waited for the Air Force to make a decision. I thought this made sense for the Air Force also because

Myrtle Beach flew the A-7D and I knew the bird well. However, my car and household goods were still in Spain so I called my former roommate Dave who sold my car and returned the money and all my possessions to the States.

I continued my daily meditation practice, losing my individual self in the infinity of the universal one every morning. While waiting for the assignment orders, I lived the dream of being with Elisa and Frances every day. Only eighteen months earlier this was nearly impossible to imagine; now it was my living reality. The family that lived next door to our original Myrtle Beach apartment now lived in the same neighborhood. Their young daughter, Delessie, was Elisa's age and the three girls played together frequently. I quickly became acquainted with Delessie's uncles, Danny and Skip, who visited her on a regular basis.

Instead of continuing the short-term experiments I had created in the past, I focused the creative drivers on larger goals. I had learned a lot from those many experiments with playing cards, electricity, and small animals and had no plans of permanently abandoning them. I chose to use what I had learned to create more meaningful and life-changing events for me, my family, and humanity. I moved on to projects like staying with Elisa and Frances and helping to ensure that we all experienced a peaceful future reality different from that shown in my vision. I also focused on the Air Force assigning me permanently to Myrtle Beach, successfully exiting the Air Force in 1979, and increasing my income.

I became impatient with the Air Force around the time the television news announced the sudden death of Elvis Presley. I should have received new orders before the end of July and it was now past the middle of August. Soon, all the tourists were gone, Myrtle Beach was deserted, and the weather turned cold. Elisa started kindergarten and I was getting nervous. I visited the base personnel office many times and placed many phone calls during the next two months and still received no permanent orders, only excuses and apologies. Halloween came and went and still no assignment. Meditation did little to calm me. When I went to the personnel office in November I was angry and made no effort to hide it. I left with only a promise that I would have orders in my hand by the end of the month.

Chapter 31

FOREVER ONE

A t the end of November I still had no orders. Finally, on December 16 I received my new assignment and, to my disappointment, it was not Myrtle Beach. I was appalled when I read the orders directing me to report to George Air Force Base in Victorville, California no later than Friday, December 30. What happened to the power of my intention? There were few places in the United States that were farther away from my children and they expected me to be there in less than two weeks. I appealed this unfortunate development to no avail; the Air Force wanted me at George for the AGM-65 television-guided missile program.

As I had seen in the past, when events failed to follow my conscious choices something more powerful was always at work. Though I was well aware of this fact, it was difficult for me to accept this assignment. It made no difference to the Air Force whether I accepted it or not; I was going. The most powerful thing I could do about it would be to mentally accept the reality that I was going to California. After spending time in meditation with this new assignment, however, I came to see that I had a more powerful choice: I could go a step beyond acceptance to actually appreciating this unwanted assignment.

This made sense. If all of my life experiences are ultimately chosen and produced by me, then whether I was aware of the process or not, the best thing I could do was appreciate whatever the result might be. Appreciation subsumed acceptance. If I lacked appreciation and acceptance, I would be in a position of mental resistance. So I made a conscious choice to appreciate the need to go to California and to revisit this powerful notion of appreciation sometime down the road.

I made a tentative plan to fly to Ontario, California and then drive, or take a taxi, to Victorville. This extended my time with Elisa and Frances by nearly two weeks. That was good, but I did not like the idea of separating from my daughters again and was not prepared to do so if I could create an alternative. I had no car because I had given my car to Maria as part of our divorce settlement. She had traded it in for a new one, which I had been driving since I arrived in Myrtle Beach in July. If I bought another car I might be able to drive to California with Elisa and Frances. I started shopping for a new car that day.

When Maria and I discussed the details of our divorce in 1976, I laid the groundwork for the revision of our custody agreement so I knew she was open to it. I called her after returning from the Datsun dealership to tell her I wanted to take Elisa and Frances with me to California. Maria was willing to entertain the plan. I asked her to call me back later in the day because if I was driving I had to cement my plan immediately. I called the Myrtle Beach U-Haul office and reserved a trailer just in case I needed it. Late that afternoon Maria called. My idea must have impacted her because she unexpectedly revealed to me the mistake she had made in marrying George. She confessed that she had thought his money would make her happy, soon found that was not the case, and had already filed for divorce.

This was news to me, but I was already dealing with enough input and did not want to discuss her issues with George. Maria said she was okay with me taking the girls to California but she wanted to drive with us in what was now her car. After we arrived she would sell the new car to me and return to Myrtle Beach by air. This could work; perhaps I would not have to be three thousand miles away from my children again. I agreed to her plan, hung up the phone, put jackets on Elisa and Frances, and drove to the U-Haul office to pick up a trailer.

This was Saturday, December 17. I had a lot of boxes to pack and load into the trailer if I wanted to leave by Sunday afternoon. I backed the trailer off the driveway onto the grass close to the front door and left it attached to the car. After preparing our dinner and cleaning up, I began packing things into boxes. I gave the girls their baths and put them to bed with warm pajamas. I went to bed a couple of hours later but did not fall asleep. My mind was filled with lists of things that needed to be done and lists of things that could easily go wrong. I was overwhelmed by the thought of driving my children across the country to California. The car was new and the V-8 fully capable of pulling the trailer so that was not a problem. But what about my job hours, daycare, school, and the other critical details required to raise children? I woke up Sunday morning with Elisa shaking my arm while Frances stood next to her holding a dozen eggs. I did not get enough sleep but my babies were hungry and I had work to do.

After breakfast I completed packing the cardboard boxes, then worked alone loading the trailer while Elisa and Frances played in their rooms. By five-fifteen the sun was down and I was working in the dark. I was frustrated, nervous, and working too fast. I had meant to be on the road already and estimated about another ninety minutes before I would be ready to pick up Maria and eat dinner. With no food in the house we were committed to eating dinner at a restaurant. I packed the girls' Christmas presents into the trailer and went back into the house for another box – a big one to help keep their gifts hidden and in place.

It was about five-thirty when I maneuvered carefully out the door with the large box. It reached to the top of my head, covering my eyes, and I couldn't see where I was going. I walked gingerly down the steps. As I turned right toward the trailer, I caught a glimpse of a patch of green grass in front of the U-Haul. How was that possible? The car was gone! My heart pounded, my brain momentarily shut down, I dropped the box. What happened? I stood there totally confused. Could a car thief have come in here, found my car, and started it that quickly? It wasn't possible. The tongue of the U-Haul was embedded into the lawn, and tire tracks leading out of the community had torn up the grass.

Without another thought I hauled ass, running down the single road leading to the community exit. The roof of Tad's Hardware, a short distance beyond the exit gate, became visible through the trees in the distance. As I drew closer I saw the edges of Tad's parking lot. Under a floodlight with both front doors open was Maria's car. The hood was up, wires strewn all over the ground. A man with his back to me was bent over the engine compartment frantically pulling wires from the engine and tossing them over his shoulder while reaching in for more with two-fisted fury. The man, dressed in a white long-sleeved button-down shirt and dark slacks, heard my footfalls on the pavement. He stood, looked up, and turned around to face me. His eyes opened wide with fear. I was fifty feet away and coming on fast. He moved around to the right side of the car and backed away with his right hand in front of his face, palm out, gesturing to me to stop. He yelled, "Back off, back off," but I continued on. I launched my body into the air and kicked him hard in the face. He fell back to the ground with me standing over him. I wanted to destroy him and it would have been easy. Instead, I lined up for a roundhouse kick, spun around and planted my left foot in his mouth, kicking his teeth out. I stepped back. He recovered in a few minutes, stumbled to his car and drove away.

I recognized him from a photograph; it was George. He apparently wanted to stop me from leaving with Elisa, Frances, and their mother. My initial assessment was that he had succeeded. All the wire bundles from under the dash, all of the ignition wires, and most other wires and vacuum hoses from under the hood were on the ground. No way I was going anywhere without an expert mechanic, a Chrysler mechanic. And in Myrtle Beach, off-season, at almost six on a Sunday night, the streets were already rolled up, everyone was closed for business, and no mechanics of any kind were available.

I had to at least try to find a mechanic. I walked home and called every gas station and auto repair facility in the yellow pages; nobody answered. Desperation overcame me as two state cop cars suddenly wheeled up in the driveway. What were they doing here? I greeted the troopers at the door, stepped outside, and closed the door behind me. One of them instructed me to come with them around the side of the house where their cars were parked. I followed them and when we reached their automobiles they stopped and turned around. They looked very imposing with their uniforms and weapons. "We are here to arrest you for the assault of George Miller," said the trooper on the left. "He's in the hospital. You want to tell us what happened?"

"Definitely, thank you." I was frightened and angry but my words came out clearly. "My two young daughters are in the house. I've been packing our belongings into this little U-Haul trailer here so we can drive to California for my next assignment with the Air Force. I came out to put a box in the trailer and my car was gone. You might've seen it under the light in Tad's parking lot. I found George there ripping all the wires out of it to keep me from leaving. I got upset, kicked him a couple times, and he ran away."

The two troopers looked at each other and then back at me. They stepped closer to the trees and discussed the issue in hushed tones. Meanwhile, my mind was spinning with the nightmare possibilities of what could happen to me. The troopers walked toward me with their thumbs hooked in their belts. The trooper on the left said, "We believe your story."

The trooper on the right spoke his first words of the evening. "Not only that," he said, "we're on your side; we're not going to arrest you tonight."

I let out a long breath; that was the best news I'd heard in months.

"But," the first trooper continued, "if you're not out of here by eight o'clock in the morning, the judge will sign a warrant and more cops will come out here and they will arrest you. If you can make it across the county line before they get here they won't be able to arrest you."

"Thank you officers, I can't begin to tell you how much that means to me," I said. "But I have no idea how to get the car fixed tonight and that's my only way out of here."

At the same time they said, "Good luck."

"Thank you officers, good night." They walked to their cars and drove away.

I did not know what to do for dinner now that I had no transportation. I heated a can of soup, let the girls play for a little while in the bathtub, and put them to bed. Sitting at the kitchen table alone with my thoughts, I thanked God for the miracle that had spared me from jail. With the car in its current condition, there was no way I was driving anywhere by any time tomorrow or maybe even Tuesday. That meant I had less than twelve hours of freedom before the cops came and arrested me at eight o'clock in the morning. First George wrecked my wheels and now he was planning to see me in jail so he could keep my kids. No way had

I come halfway around the world to have anyone keep me away from my babies. But what could I do? At this point, there was not a thing I could do to get that car running, nothing. All I could do was clean up the mess and save the wires, hoses, and tubes.

I called Maria with the update. Clearly shaken by the news, she became emotional. She calmed down after a few minutes and said she would wait to hear from me. That Sunday night I was confronted with a hard reality: *There is nothing you can do.* I was powerless and hated admitting it. I stopped trying to figure it out. Facing the fear of going to jail and not making it to California, of being tried in civilian and military courts, of losing my kids, I had to allow myself to see clearly that, as at all moments of life, going within myself to higher power was the most powerful thing, indeed in this case the only thing, that I could do. It wasn't so easy. My mind was racing with frustration, anger, and fear. What good would it do to meditate when I needed a Chrysler mechanic on a cold December night in Myrtle Beach, South Carolina?

Chapter 32

SECURELY CONNECTED

I could not sit still. I had walked around the living room into the kitchen and back to the living room when I found myself in the silence, leaning with my arms extended and hands pressed against the wall. I easily noticed the sound of my breath as the air passed my nostrils and flowed into my lungs. Two seconds later I heard it flowing back out. I continued breathing slowly and my mind cleared. I started to feel good inside, comfortable, safe. God lives inside of us; the good feeling inside me was God. I touched the power of God within myself. I focused my attention on God, knowing that this is the source of everything in the world. Then I created a vision, a small movie that showed me and the kids happily driving across the country to California. This was the movie that God was manifesting in my living reality.

Somehow, we would make it. I grabbed a flashlight and walked back to the car. It was trashed. Not just any mechanic had the knowledge to get this car going again. Since I saw no way of repairing the car before morning, I resigned myself to having it towed to the Chrysler dealer in Conway as soon as they opened. Wait a minute – if that was the case, I would be in jail before I ever got the thing to the dealer. That was unacceptable. No way would I go to jail. I would fix this car. Remember your vision, remember your focus, I reminded myself. You are driving away this morning; know it, feel it.

As I looked at the car, doubt surrounded me, weighing me down like a five hundred-pound gorilla sitting on my back. I shook my head. I had to face the facts. This car wasn't going anywhere and neither was I, except to Horry County jail. Then the kids would go back to Maria and who knows what would happen to me. My mind was running away with itself. "Wait a minute, what are those lights entering this quiet neighborhood at this time of night?" I wondered out loud. It was about eight-thirty. I didn't recognize the car, but it slowed and stopped in front of me. Someone got out of the car, a tall, gangly guy. When he stood up straight I could see that it was Danny, Delessie's young, long-haired uncle – a wannabe hippy kind of cat, about twenty-two years old.

Danny lived on and off with his older sister, niece, and mother about three doors down from where I lived with Elisa and Frances. He asked me what happened to my ride. I gave him the short version of this horror story. "Oh man," Danny said, "If only Skip was here. He knows this Chrysler mechanic who could fix your car." Skip was Danny's older brother, Delessie's other uncle.

"What?" My spirits immediately picked up. "How do we get hold of Skip? Where does this mechanic live?" I asked anxiously.

"The mechanic lives right across the street from you," Danny replied casually. "But Skip, I don't know where he is, and I think the mechanic is out of town."

In the six months I had lived there, I had never met the person who lived across the street. I hadn't met any of my neighbors other than Danny and Skip, and the only reason I knew them was because their beautiful sister had lived next door to me before I went to Spain and her daughter Delessie played with Frances and Elisa. I was feeling less than positive when I saw another pair of headlights leading a ratty old Gremlin into the community. Jeez, I thought, another car; what is this place already, Grand Central Station? Danny suddenly began jumping up and down, "It's Skip, holy shit, it's Skip; maybe he knows where the guy is."

Sure enough, Skip got out of the car. He didn't live with his sister and Danny, but shared a low-rent apartment on the north end of the beach with some other guy. Danny explained the situation and Skip, nodding his head, understood. I visualized myself speeding down the road out of town.

"Oh yeah, he could fix your car," Skip confirmed. "He's a Chrysler mechanic, works for the dealer in Conway. Lives right across from you. Only thing is, he's on vacation in the Bahamas for another week." No, oh God no, this cannot be, not this close. Why was I creating this frustration for myself? If the only man in the world capable of fixing my car lived right across the street from me but was on vacation, why did I even have to know about it? Why was I standing here with Skip and Danny listening to these useless absurdities?

If my thoughts were creating this reality, I'd better find a way to change those thoughts right now. I needed to settle down and clarify my intention or do something. I saw the vision of Interstate 10 in my mind's eye and then I saw it fade. I felt weak. I looked down at the ground, shaking my head. I took a few breaths to find my center and get a better handle on how screwed I was. No, I am never screwed; we are driving out of here tonight.

"Let's see, Skip," I began slowly, quietly. "What I think you're saying is, the solution to my issue lives across the street." The volume and intensity of my voice increased as I glared into his eyes. "And he could fix my car, but he's in the BAHAMAS? Are you KIDDING ME?"

Skip didn't get a chance to answer because at that moment another set of headlights swung into the community. It was a pickup truck, a light blue Silverado. There were lots of those around the neighborhood so I paid no attention. Skip stared at the truck, moved his head forward, moved it back. "I think it's him," Skip said tentatively, like he was asking a question. "It is, holy shit, that's Fred, that's him." Skip stood there shouting and waving his arms in front of the truck. "He must've come back early!" Once again I thanked God. I was slightly elated, but why would Fred fix my car at eleven o'clock when he'd just come back from vacation and had to work in Conway the next morning – if he could fix my car at all?

Fred had returned early from the Bahamas because the fishing was slow. Now I recognized him and he said he recognized me, too; he had seen me playing with Elisa and Frances outside the house. "The fish weren't biting and I got bored," he said, "so I figured I'd save some money and come back early. Yeah, I'll fix your car." My heart was pumping now – Yes, Lord, I'm getting out of here. "But my tools are in Conway." What? Conway is a half hour away; that's at least an hour round trip – past midnight at best before he even gets started. Fred continued, "I'll get on my way and be back with those tools as soon as I can." I was in a pleasant state of shock. The fish down in the Bahamas were not biting?

You never know what variables might be affected when you go within, to your God self, and create an intention. Here was higher power working in my life like I had never anticipated. The odds were incredibly against me. I was completely out of ideas and realized there was nothing I could do. That was true in the physical world; there was no sense trying to fix the car on my own. I didn't even know the sequence of the ignition wires. Then I breathed consciously and chose to be on the road in time to avoid arrest.

After I released my intention, while my mind was blank, the universe went into action. The energy of my conscious intention diffused into the unified field, connected with God energy, which connected with all of those people, from the cops to Skip, Danny, and Fred the mechanic. I don't know how those details transpired. To produce the result I had visualized, many different variables had to come together, right down to the rare event of the fish not biting in the Bahamas, which had occurred before my car was even damaged. I made a choice and created an intention. I used the universal drivers of creation, as I knew them at the time, to access the power that creates the universe, and that power brought everyone and everything together to get the car fixed, get us out of town, and keep our family together.

Skip told me he had no particular reason for visiting Danny and his sister that night, and he and Danny were also amazed at the situation. This was stranger than a screenplay, wilder than a movie. If I could have consciously imagined a solution to my dilemma that evening, it most certainly would not have been as elegant, or nearly as dramatic, as this. Higher power guided the state troopers away, brought Danny across my path, then Skip, and then Fred. Each one of them not only had to arrive on the scene but had to be motivated from within to take the action he took. Would they have appeared had I not contacted God and focused on my intention? Would Danny and Skip and Fred have driven into the neighborhood that night had George not destroyed the wiring in my car? In reality, these are invalid questions. Now that the men had appeared in the neighborhood and my car was being repaired, there is no way for me to ever know what would have happened if any one of the variables involved had been different.

I was concerned about getting out of town in time to avoid going to jail. Not knowing how long it would take Fred to fix this mess, there was nothing I could do but what I had been doing all night, and that was to trust, to have faith, to know that I would make it across the county line with my children before I was arrested. Even after the car was repaired I still had to pick up Maria. My issues were far from solved, but what had already happened was so powerful that I started to relax. I remembered how I felt that morning on Richard's boat when I read about the prince and the snuffbox and realized that I had nothing to worry about for the rest of my life.

I learned that night that self-understanding was not only about a person realizing him or herself as higher power – as God. It was about individuals intentionally and pragmatically using that realization for the benefit of themselves, their loved ones, and their communities. Self-understanding empowers anyone who chooses it to consciously create the rest of their lives in line with their preferences. Higher power is always available to each of us for this co-creative process.

Skip, Danny, and I pushed the car into position in Fred's driveway. The U-Haul was loaded and everything was ready to go as soon as the car repair was complete. It was close to midnight when Fred returned from Conway, took his tools from the back of his pickup truck, positioned two drop lights over the engine compartment of the car, and began working. Sleep would have been a great thing but I was too nervous and wanted to stay with Fred so that he wouldn't feel alone.

He had it running in just over four hours. To me, this man had accomplished the impossible and the sound of the smoothly running engine was a miracle. Looking up at the night sky, I felt so tiny. I was humbled by the power I had just witnessed. I had an intention, I focused on that intention, I let go of it. And now there I was, filled with gratitude, my car running smoothly. Fred brought me back to the world when he said, "It's running now but you better stop at a Chrysler dealer as soon as you can so they can make sure everything is proper; I don't know if it will hold all the way to California." I thought about Fred's drive to Conway, his Herculean efforts in the middle of the night, and his obligation to be at his job in a few hours. I wondered what had inspired him to go to that extent to help me, a complete stranger who he would never see again.

"Fred," I said, "Thank you so very much for helping me. Please accept some cash to help show my appreciation." I had two hundred dollars in my hand but Fred refused it without ever looking at it.

"I'm happy to help you. You can thank me by helping somebody else someday when you get a chance. Have the car checked as soon as you can and drive carefully." I hugged Skip and Danny, thanking them for being there when I needed them most. I hooked the trailer to the car, put my little ones in the backseat, locked the door, and drove away.

Chapter 33

LIVING CONSCIOUSNESS

The eastern horizon glowed faintly red as I parked the car in front of the motel office at 6:55 in the morning. It was a mom and pop place a few miles outside of St. George, safe from the arrest the state police had warned me of just twelve hours earlier. The previous night seemed like a year ago and Myrtle Beach could have been a thousand miles away. I relaxed my brain for a few seconds but then immediately began mentally questioning how the rest of the trip might go. I had so many doubts. I thought about all the things that can go wrong on a trip across the country. I worried about where we would live; I thought about Maria going back to Myrtle Beach after the events of last night; I was as concerned about where we would eat, sleep, and find gas as if we were headed off into Siberia.

Lying there in the motel bed, unwinding from the tension of the night, I reviewed the amazing highlights of the past few hours. Why would I doubt my next experience? I came up with all kinds of reasons to have doubt and fear but none of them made sense anymore. The complex events that came together to get me out of town in time to avoid arrest did not happen by accident or coincidence. Somehow God, working with my intention, made that happen, and that same power would help me to successfully drive my family across the United States.

After a few hours of sleep, we loaded our suitcases into the trunk, Elisa and Frances climbed into the back seat, and we continued south toward Interstate 10. Sitting behind the wheel, warm in the heated car, I left last night's events in the past. The moment was perfect.

We arrived in El Paso late in the afternoon on December 24, 1977 and checked into the Holiday Inn. It was emotionally difficult to be on the road on Christmas Eve, always one of the most important days of the year. After dinner, a bath, and some Christmas stories Elisa and Frances went to bed. I went outside and quietly carried our small Christmas tree and their gifts into the room. They were very surprised and so happy when they woke in the morning to see that Santa Claus had found them even in the middle of the United States. When I went to Spain without them, I might have thought this scenario impossible, but now here we were, celebrating Christmas together in the Holiday Inn just off US 10 in El Paso, Texas. It may not have been the best of all possible worlds, but it was an awesome accomplishment given the many less desirable alternatives.

We enjoyed a traditional Christmas dinner that evening. Early the next morning our westbound journey continued. We spent two nights in motels, then as day became night on December 29 we turned onto Interstate 15 and headed up the Cajon Pass to Victorville. We checked into the Green Tree Inn, the first motel I saw as we exited the freeway in Victorville. This was the most expensive motel in town but it was not a showplace. After everybody got settled I drove a couple of miles down Seventh Street and brought dinner back to the Green Tree.

The next morning I reported to the squadron administrative office to begin in-processing at George Air Force Base. The administrative clerk told me that the wing commander wanted to see me as soon as I came in, and promptly walked me to the colonel's office door; I opened it, walked in, and reported. The colonel told me to take a seat as he opened a file on his desk. He lifted out a single sheet of white paper with typing on one side. "Sergeant Wilhelm, I have a report here from the Myrtle Beach police department. It says they have a warrant for your arrest and I am to detain you here. What do you have to say for yourself?"

"I am sorry, sir, that your valuable time is taken up by a matter as trivial as this. This man destroyed my car in an effort to keep me from leaving Myrtle Beach with my family. After he destroyed my car I defended myself and he ran away."

"I see. Please bring me a letter describing the events and I will send it to Myrtle Beach. You won't hear about this again."

"Sir, I will have a letter in your hands tomorrow and I appreciate your help very much."

After completing inbound processing on the base, I returned to the Green Tree Inn. We packed up and moved out of the Green

Tree and into temporary family quarters on base. This small apartment was far more comfortable than the Green Tree and about one-third the cost. Later that evening I asked Maria when she planned to return to Myrtle Beach. She told me she had spoken with George while I was meeting with the commander and if I was agreeable she would not return to Myrtle Beach but would live with me until she found a place of her own. My real preference was to create a great relationship with Maria and continue living together in Victorville as if we had never divorced. We both knew that this was not in the cards so I agreed with her plan, asking only that she find employment to help share the expenses and give me notice before moving out. She said she would begin looking for a job right away and would keep me informed about her progress in finding an apartment.

I got nervous again the following day when I discovered how expensive housing was in Victorville. I looked at a few shabby apartments that I wouldn't live in, and even they were priced above our budget. I searched all available resources every day with no results. Five days later I woke up sweating at three o'clock in the morning. We had just enough money to pay our hotel bill and put a deposit down on a place to live – if we found a reasonably priced place that day. If we stayed in the base quarters any longer we would not have the money to put down on a home or apartment. These thoughts kept me awake for two more hours so I got myself out of bed.

I had already called every rental place I could find. I called every ad in all the newspapers, I read the cards on the coin laundry bulletin boards, and more than once I had called everyone on the housing list supplied by the base personnel office. Thinking I had exhausted all options, I once again realized that following my breath to my higher self was the most important thing I could do. But I didn't want to. I was running out of time. I didn't want to sit still. I wanted to stay in action, I wanted to drive from place to place, I wanted to place phone calls and find a place to live right now. It was too early in the day for any of that so after a few minutes of running around inside my brain, I sat down, centered my mind, and paid attention to the stillness of my higher self. When I opened my eyes again, the sun was up.

I walked outside and purchased the daily newspaper from the machine, opened it to the real estate section, and noticed a new advertisement for a house for rent. The ad, placed by a husband and wife, stated that they would rent only to a family with children. I called them and after ensuring we were a family with children they asked us to come out to their residence along Highway 18 in Apple Valley. We drove to their beautiful home where we met the couple; they were a very attractive and energetic pair at least eighty years of age. They knew they were asking an incredibly low rate for their home in Victorville. They did it, they said, because they enjoyed helping younger people with children.

They asked many questions then ultimately agreed to rent their Victorville home to us. It was in a beautiful part of town on a half-acre lot, and I was filled with gratitude and praised God for this miracle. Just a few hours ago I was soaked in sweat wondering what we would do. I thought about how much time I had wasted in fruitless worrying. When I woke up at three o'clock that morning, I was free to choose my state of mind. I spent hours worrying about things that never occurred before I realized I could choose a different way to be. That's when I began following my breath, and that is when I centered myself and calmed down. Not only is that a good feeling, but that very state of being allows for the manifestation of the home to live in, the car to drive, the money to spend, and knowledge of self. Our state of mind is always a choice: sad or happy, ill or well, fast or slow, hot or cold.

I came to like Victorville and the work was good at George Air Force Base. I was part of the AGM-65 development program, which flew G model F-4s modified specifically for a TV guided missile. I planted a big vegetable garden in the backyard and the little ones helped me keep the weeds out. In early April of 1978 Maria experienced intense pain that was diagnosed as an ovarian cyst. I drove her to St. Mary's Hospital in Apple Valley where they admitted her for surgery. After recovering at home for three weeks Maria resumed work. About a week later she stopped me in the driveway on my way to work. She said, "I thought I could give you more notice, but next Saturday I'm moving to Trona with Elisa and Frances."

"What? There's no work in Trona; when did you get this idea?"

"I know there's no work there; we're moving in with John, a security guard at the casino." This was too much news with too little notice. Surely this relationship did not begin when she went back to work last week. Two choices came up in my face like giant billboards on a desert road. One said, "Freak out!" The other said, "Go with it."

I resigned myself to single status and purchased a new 1978 Kawasaki 650SR motorcycle. I stayed in the house for two months and then drove out to Apple Valley to return the keys to our gracious and sad landlords. Facing them was difficult. We had lived in the house only eight months. I thought it strange when the old lady told me that in January she had known right away that Maria would be leaving. I moved into the barracks to save money.

Several months after I arrived at George Air Force Base a good friend from Spain, John Walther, arrived. He and I had known each other almost our entire time in Spain. John was assigned to a different squadron with F-4Es so we didn't see each other much while working. When we were not at work we were together. In October of 1978 I drove my motorcycle to his house, and while I was there he told me about two women who had moved in right next door to him. I mentally filed this information away for future use. He also told me that the property manager had a beautiful blond daughter. The family was from Great Britain, John said, and the beautiful daughter was recently divorced from an Air Force guy. John had become attracted to her after seeing her walk her infant daughter past his kitchen window in a stroller. Just then she came around the corner with her little girl in the stroller. She was beautiful. John said he intended to ask her out.

About a week later, while waxing my motorcycle in the shade of John's driveway, one of those young ladies he had mentioned walked by with a little girl about three or four years old, and said, "Nice motorcycle."

I smiled and said, "Thank you, maybe one day we'll take a ride on it." I was unaware of the relationship between the woman and the little girl but assumed they were mother and daughter. That night I knocked on her door and she invited me in. No child was present but the second woman, her roommate, was. I introduced myself and discovered that the person who commented on my bike was Patti and the other was Wyota – an interesting name with which I was previously unfamiliar. We had a lot of laughs, Patti told me I was "advanced," and I laughed some more. I asked her what she thought about God. She said her relationship with God was her most important relationship. "I was raised a Christian but I don't go to church anymore. I have my own ideas about God," she said.

I left after about an hour. Patti and I continued seeing each other intermittently, during which time I discovered that the little girl was Patti's niece, Shawnecie. I was happy to see that Patti's mom Darlene was very cautious about her daughter's new relationship. Patti's dad Marty looked me in the eyes and shook my hand. He accepted me right away and, given some time, so did. Darlene. Their acceptance meant a lot. Patti and I started seeing each other more regularly and we celebrated my thirty-first birthday together on November 19, 1978. She became part of my circle of friends and I became part of her family.

Chapter 34

PRIMING THE SYSTEM

As the holiday season approached, John and I planned a small holiday party at his house. On Saturday night, December 16, about twelve male and female friends, including Patti, gathered in John's small home to celebrate Christmas 1978. John and I had put out plenty of food but we had forgotten a dip for the vegetables and potato chips.

When someone asked if we had any dip for the potato chips we realized we needed a solution. John had packets of dry onion soup mix that could be mixed with sour cream to make dip, but we lacked the sour cream. In spite of the cold weather and late hour we drove his little Triumph Spitfire to a nearby Circle K convenience store in search of sour cream. We parked the car in the empty lot, entered the store, and passed the clerk on our right as we turned left toward the refrigerator section. The left end of the back wall was lined with several refrigerated cabinets with glass doors; to the right of those were similar cabinets where the frozen foods were kept. John and I walked to the dairy section and looked for sour cream. We found several containers of cottage cheese, which were the same size and shape as the sour cream containers but with a different color scheme, making it easy to distinguish cottage cheese from sour cream.

We thought the sour cream might be in the same section as the cottage cheese, but we didn't see any. The Circle K was our only possibility at that time of night so we were highly motivated to find the sour cream there. We thoroughly searched every one of the refrigerator and freezer cabinets in the store and finding no sour cream, we walked to the counter and asked the clerk. The clerk was a young man, maybe twenty-two years old, tall and thin with short-cropped red hair. I told him we were looking for sour cream and that we had discovered containers of cottage cheese, "But we can't find any sour cream; would you mind helping us please?"

I had an idea. If the clerk confirmed the store had no sour cream I would immediately initiate the universal creative drivers with the intention to create sour cream right there. I had never created a physical object out of nothing or changed one thing into another but past experience told me that anything was possible. Asking the clerk to help was my way of ensuring there were no hidden containers of sour cream that John and I may have over-looked. My request also brought the clerk into the experiment as a witness in addition to John. To prevent clouding the witnesses' expectations, I gave no advance briefing about what I was intend-ing to accomplish. The clerk searched each of the cabinets while John and I waited by the refrigerator where we had found the yellow-labeled container of Breakstone's Cottage Cheese. After the clerk searched every refrigerator and freezer cabinet in the store he looked at me and said, "I'm sorry sir, but we don't have any sour cream."

I wanted to be absolutely sure that he was certain and that John heard the clerk confirm that there was no sour cream in the store. I asked him, "Did you look everywhere? Are you certain there is no sour cream in the store?"

"Yes, I searched everywhere. There is no sour cream."

I looked at John. "Did you see any sour cream?" John had witnessed several outrageous events in Spain and I could see from his face that he suspected I was getting ready to do something out of the ordinary.

John shrugged his shoulders, shook his head and said, "No." Now I had confirmation; everyone agreed there was no sour cream anywhere in the entire store. Without hesitation, I opened the glass door with my right hand, reached in with my left hand, wrapped my fingers around the container with the yellow lettering that said "cottage cheese," and removed it from the refrigerator cabinet. I held that container in front of us for all to see. The package said "sour cream" and the lettering was deep blue. John's eyelids peeled back. The clerk narrowed his eyebrows in suspicion and said nothing.

I didn't know if I could even speak at that point. My heart pounded rapidly. I stood without moving for several seconds. To ensure the container was filled with sour cream, I opened the lid to confirm that yes, most certainly, the sour cream container was filled with sour cream. Although my body appeared to be standing still I felt like every bit of it was shaking. A huge smile spread across my face. Some people would have called it a miracle, others a trick. I wasn't sure what to call this experience except an extraordinary demonstration of the singular nature of reality. This was the result of a relationship between intentional human thinking, God, and what we call physical reality.

I have been asked many times over the years to produce miracles on demand. There was a time when I did it because I thought it might help people understand that God was real and know what they were capable of themselves. It didn't matter what I did, I never convinced anyone of anything; most of us are too locked into our conditioned belief systems. So I stopped doing that and explained my reasons. A few times, however, I have demonstrated a miracle by raising my right hand in front of my face and rotating it from left to right, saying something like, "There's your miracle." When people denied the miraculous quality of the hand movement by saying it was completely ordinary, I asked them to explain how it happened. Where does the thought come from to raise my arm and how does that thought translate into a particular movement of my wrist? Perhaps a neurologist could accurately answer the second question; most of us, however, would have great difficulty explaining where the thought came from and how it initiated the action. Not one person I have asked has ever attempted to answer either one of those questions. They all have simply remained silent.

In spite of their inability to explain it, nobody thought that raising my arm and rotating my wrist constituted a miracle. Why not? The thought energy that turns my hand is the same as the thought energy that transforms one substance into another. My intention was to bring home sour cream for our guests, not to bring attention to myself or cause a miracle. I had assumed that the store would have sour cream, which we would pay for and leave. At first they had no sour cream. Three people, John, the clerk, and me, the only people in the store, each searched the store for sour cream. I watched the clerk do the same thing I did when he moved the containers of cottage cheese, looking behind each one to see if one of them had concealed a container of sour cream. None did, and there were no other similar containers in the store. Then I grabbed a container of cottage cheese and removed a container of sour cream, so we paid for it and left. That is how simple it is.

If John and I had not looked behind everything in the refrigerator cabinets to see if any sour cream was hiding in the back, I might have forever doubted the result. We may have rationalized that the container I grabbed had been there all along and we had simply missed it. I eliminated this possibility by first conducting a thorough search with John and then introducing the totally neutral clerk into the experiment. It was the clerk, someone who did not know us at all, who confirmed that the product we were seeking was not in the store. After the transformation, the clerk also joined John and me in confirming that I held a container of sour cream in my hands. John and I walked out of the store with the sour cream, drove back to John's place, mixed up the chip dip, and our guests loved it.

As time passed Patti and I grew closer and fell in love. On April 1, 1979 we moved into a three-bedroom home in Victorville; I was still in the Air Force and scheduled to be discharged in

December, shortly before Christmas. When school closed for the summer Elisa and Frances came to live with us while their mother entered the hospital for more surgery. This was a breakthrough for me and my family, bringing me a step closer to my daughters on a full-time basis. After recovering from her surgery, Maria returned to Trona. Elisa and Frances stayed with us for the entire summer vacation. They did not return to school in Trona. During the summer Maria had moved to Ft. Worth to be near her mother and sisters. It was difficult when Maria called and asked me to send our daughters to Ft. Worth, but I sadly maintained my agreement and put them on a plane.

"I'm not happy about letting Elisa and Frances go back with Maria," I said to Patti while driving back from LAX. Patti was still shedding some tears and said nothing. "I'll talk to their mother and to Elisa and Frances to see if we can make a different arrangement," I said. "I will arrange with Maria that they will live with us except for vacations with her."

"That will be great," Patti replied.

"It will happen," I assured her. "It's like everything else: we make a choice, we focus, we surrender it to the universe and it happens."

"Have you been writing anymore about those creative drivers?" Patti asked.

"Oh yeah, I call the paper, Priming the System. It explains the creative drivers and how they can be used to create our lives as we choose them."

"Where did you get that title, Priming the System?"

"Well, it's like a water pump, you have to prime it before it will pump any water," I began. "Priming the system means preparing a system to function in accordance with its intended purpose. The first two creative drivers accomplish this. When you choose and then focus on your choice you prepare the system to function but it doesn't yet do any work. The third driver, surrender, activates the system – which is higher power. When you surrender your choice to higher power you set it free and it is only in releasing your choice freely from your control that higher power manifests it in your physical reality."

"I like that explanation!" Patti looked excited and her answer helped reassure me.

I completed Priming the System that summer. The paper explained how God initiated the creation of the universe and how those same principles used by God motivate the creation of all human ideas, things, and experiences. I had at that time identified three such energetic forces and called them universal creative drivers:

1. Choose

2. Focus

3. Surrender

We all use these principles to create our world whether we are aware of them or not. Awareness of the creative drivers, however, makes it possible for us to consciously create our lives in any way we choose. The creative drivers are the motive engines of creation which, beginning in 1958, I had slowly distinguished by reverse-engineering the process of creation. The creative drivers did not pop into my mind one day; I did not suddenly wake up with them and begin experimenting with them. It was the other way around in that after I generated a reality shift, I looked back on everything I had done that might in any way have contributed to that shift. By recognizing patterns, I was then able to repeat the patterns until I discovered the pattern that most accurately and most rapidly produced the chosen result.

My practice of reverse engineering was simple:

- Think something or do something.

- Observe what happens.

- If anything happens, examine every thought, action, and variable leading up to the moment of the happening.

- If a connection between a thought and the happening is detected make a note of it.

- Clarify the connection between my thoughts and the corresponding happening.

- Practice that thinking in the next experiment.

I didn't plan this approach either; it also was reverse-engineered by looking back at what I had been thinking and doing. I paid attention to what I was thinking while I was doing things. When I noticed something unexpected happen I looked back at what I was thinking at the moment it happened. If I distinguished a connection between my thinking and what had happened, I repeated that kind of thinking in the future to see if I noticed another connection.

Over a long period of time many of these notable connections regarding relatively insignificant things added up. The accumulated data revealed patterns that assured me that my thought energy and the world were more than connected, they were the same thing. I could only speak for myself at the time but soon realized that this is how the world works for everyone, all the time. Our thoughts, apparently ephemeral and non-substantive, are as real as a block of concrete. The thought is the same substance as the concrete, both made of the same energy that everything else in the universe is made of.

We constantly radiate our thought energy throughout the universe, creating and recreating the world around us in accordance with our deepest, even unconscious intentions. Thought energy, passed through the filter of our conditioned belief systems, is creating our world right now; it creates our reality whether we are aware of it or not. Self-understanding brings our unconscious intentions into our conscious awareness, thus allowing us to more accurately steer our ship of life to our chosen destination. Choosing self-understanding and practicing the creative drivers with self-understanding as the focus brought my previously unconscious choices into conscious awareness. With my choices clearly in front of me I could navigate my life, creating it with intention and experiencing what had once existed only as a dream.

My paper, Priming the System, also explained the fact that there are no guarantees in the universe. More than our conscious and unconscious thoughts are involved in the manifestation process. Everything that comes to us is also affected by transpersonal entelechy. That means the larger force, God consciousness, contributes to everything we experience and everything we experience is always designed for our highest good. This is why I learned to appreciate everything I experienced, even if I could not see the good of it at that time. Each of us is an eternal being, part of and one with infinite reality. The experiences of this life on earth come from and are part of the eternal oneness that we are. Though we may not see the good of all of our experiences in the moment they occur, we will see that good at some point. We live forever so it may be that the benefit of what we learn while on earth will come into our awareness after we leave these bodies behind, thus advancing the development of our eternal essence. Whenever we grow to accept the changes that constantly and inevitably come into our lives, we positively impact the lives of all sentient beings everywhere.

I made some copies of Priming the System and distributed them to selected friends and relatives. Everyone who consistently practiced the creative drivers achieved results, some within a day or two and some within weeks or several months. Several who continued practicing have attributed their successful lives to their practice of the universal creative drivers.

Chapter 35

VISUALIZE THE DREAM

Richard had been living in San Francisco for about twelve months when I drove up to visit him with my brother Gerry, a Marine at El Toro Naval Air Station. Gerry was the fourth child born in our family of five boys and four girls. About six hours after leaving Gerry's apartment in Anaheim we were in San Francisco sitting in Richard's sparsely furnished apartment. He had acquired a position at the telephone company and was writing another screenplay. Richard said he intended to stay in the United States for about a year, after which he would return to London. Gerry and I stayed that night in a hotel and in the morning we returned to Richard's apartment, where we discussed my imminent discharge from the Air Force.

Although I displayed complete confidence, I was nervous about leaving the Air Force after so many years and Richard knew this. He helped increase my confidence by reminding me of some of the things we had done together in Amsterdam and Spain. He said, "Remember, go directly for the snuffbox and you will accomplish anything you choose." I did not want to leave San Francisco. I had a bad feeling that I would never see Richard again. But it was time to go. We walked downstairs. Richard and I hugged. Gerry and I got into the Super Beetle. I looked back as we pulled away from the curb. There stood Richard with his red flannel shirt, his red hair and beard, his arm raised, hand waving.

The morning of December 21, 1979 dawned clear, blue and cold. Christmas was four days away; Elisa and Frances would be there in two days. I drove to George Air Force Base while listening to the Moody Blues. I parked at the base personnel office and waited inside while the clerk typed up my DD form 214 and other discharge papers. A few minutes later I signed the document that honorably discharged me from the United States Air Force. My feelings oscillated between sadness and joy. With the stroke of a pen I left behind a long familiar way of life and opened the doorway to a new beginning.

I looked for work and found none. I remained unemployed and knew I had to return to basics to generate additional income. That meant a shift in perspective, which I facilitated by choosing specific intentions for income, housing, education, and all areas of life. I wrote my goals on pieces of paper and taped them to the walls and mirrors throughout the house so I would see them wherever I went. I paid attention to my source, God, and to the goals I had declared, not the doubts I had about them. I also composed several affirmation statements that I repeated to myself throughout the day. When doubts arose or I had thoughts that were counter to my goals, I shifted my mind energy to thoughts that were in line with the goal. For example, if a thought suddenly entered my mind that said, "You will never achieve that goal," I simply noticed the thought without attaching myself to it or creating a story around it. Observing the thought without becoming attached to it allowed it to move on. While the thought drifted out of my consciousness I focused on God and mentally repeated an affirmation designed to support the manifestation of the intention.

Because the most important and powerful work happens within us, I focused my thought energy on God, the creator of everything that exists. God is everything and you are God, therefore you are the abundance of all things. You are the energy of infinite wealth and by focusing on your supply within, you manifest your wealth in the world of appearances. Your wealth is not money; your wealth is love and you are love. When you focus on the cause of your wealth, which is the energy of the higher power within you, your good comes forth effortlessly. Your higher power knows your needs and desires and is continuously in action to provide them to you in abundance.

As I turned my attention on God within me I appreciated my life exactly as it was. I recognized myself as the source of my abundant wealth. In understanding myself I came to understand money as the energy that it is, just like everything else in the universe is energy. We are each the source of all our good. The people in our lives who write us checks and give us cash are merely conduits for a spendable form of value that we already are. All transactions exchange energy. When we give our energy in our unique way, the person to whom we give it then balances the exchange by giving us energy in the form of money or any other form we choose. It is important to remember that the third creative driver, surrender, means allowing the universe to deliver our choice to us in its way and according to its schedule. If you choose to increase your income, do not limit the universe by attempting to decide how that increase will take place. If you choose a new job, do not attempt to figure out how to get the new job. Allow the universe to create your choice in its own way. The way of the universe will always be more powerful and effective than anything your limited ego mind may imagine.

During the past year I had managed to maintain income close to my Air Force level. But as winter turned to spring in 1981 I still had found no consistent and meaningful work. The incredible power I had previously witnessed in my life now seemed unavailable to me. I was not meeting my goals and felt powerless. Patti and I were expecting a new baby in November. My small income and savings had dried up and by March 1981 we were nearly out of money and out of ideas. Something about me was blocking the flow of my good. Then I remembered the words of God toward the end of my vision in 1977: "Everyone who sticks with me will be all right."

I got an idea to visit the Victorville unemployment office again; perhaps they had some new listings. I had already been interviewed there, but when the idea popped into my mind to go there I could not ignore it. When I arrived at the unemployment office the clerk told me I could apply for a position that had recently become available with the Santa Fe Railroad in Barstow. I followed the instructions the clerk gave me and successfully submitted my application to the Atchison, Topeka and Santa Fe Railway Company. Since more than three hundred people applied for that position, I suspected I had little chance of winning the job. This thought was out of line with acquiring the position, so I quickly released it and focused on receiving an offer for the job.

Focusing on God as the source of all my needs and desires, I chose to be hired for this position with the Santa Fe Railroad. I then focused briefly on the excitement and happiness that I could expect to feel when learning I had won the job and surrendered the outcome of the choice to higher power. This meant that I gave up thinking about the details involved with producing the result; I stopped trying to control the outcome, how it looked, or how it would be delivered. I followed this routine each day and repeated it at various times throughout the day. Sometimes I doubted that practicing the three creative drivers of self-understanding could result in a job. But when I mentally reviewed some of the things that had occurred during the past ten years I could not doubt my approach. When I felt like quitting I released that thought like a helium balloon drifting away on the wind. I maintained the mental discipline necessary to stay on track by keeping a journal, making lists of the intended results, and reading over the previous day's entry and list of choices every day.

The human resources person in charge of hiring for this position called me back for two additional interviews. After the third round of interviews, which took a few weeks, the gentleman from the Santa Fe notified me that I had been selected for the position. I expressed to God within me and to the man who made the decision my deep appreciation for this opportunity. After offering the position to me in person he said the same thing that Fred, the Chrysler mechanic who repaired my car that night in Myrtle

Beach, had said. "When you have a chance to help someone else, help them." Several days later I began work as a perishable traffic inspector for the Santa Fe Railway.

Chapter 36

PRAGMATIC MYSTICISM

Inspecting perishable traffic consisted of recording the temperature and operational status of refrigerated railroad cars and truck trailers on flat cars on their way through Barstow yard, the biggest switching yard on the Santa Fe. We shipped huge quantities of potatoes, melons, fruits, vegetables, and frozen meats and it was my job to ensure that these food products departed Barstow yard at the proper temperature and with a running refrigerator unit that held enough fuel to reach its destination. The line of refrigerated cars entering and leaving the yard appeared endless. There were no breaks during the night. I climbed into the refrigerator compartments of one freight car after another, restarting engines that had stalled and refueling tanks that were empty. The intense workload was good news, because I perceived it meant job security.

Toward the beginning of August I heard that most of the Barstow traffic inspectors would soon be laid off. The end of summer would bring a huge reduction in the perishable traffic coming out of the San Joaquin Valley, reducing the need for perishable traffic inspectors. By the end of the week I was the only perishable traffic inspector remaining in the yard other than the supervisor. On what I expected would be my last night on the job my boss told me that because of the quality of my work he had a position available for me in Bakersfield if I wanted it. I could not pass on this opportunity and agreed I would report to the Bakersfield freight office on Monday morning.

I strapped my bag to the back of my motorcycle on Sunday, kissed Patti and my children, and rode out of Victorville toward Boron. This part of the drive was straight, flat desert. The desert was redeemed, however, when I reached the Tehachapi foothills, wound my way through the Tehachapi Pass and then down the mountain and into the flats toward Bakersfield. I drove home every weekend until I found a beautiful apartment in southwest Bakersfield. In September 1981 Patti, Elisa, Frances, Fritz the cat and I moved to Bakersfield. Ian was born in November 1981 and Alethea was born in September 1983.

In 1983 I rode my motorcycle out to California State University Bakersfield and enrolled with about forty-eight credits that they accepted from St. Norbert. I majored in philosophy and religious studies with a minor in television production. After seventeen years out of college, the prospect of being a full-time student again was harrowing. Scheduling classes around the fifty or sixty hours I worked at the Santa Fe each week was also a challenge. I made a choice to attend all my classes, not miss work, and graduate with a 4.00 average. I seldom missed a class in the four years at Cal State. Even when my eyes were bandaged for a week after laser surgery to correct a detached retina, I did not miss class: my mother came from San Diego and walked me by the hand to each of my classes for the entire week. Patti and our little ones sacrificed as well – they seldom saw me for four years. The study of philosophy helped me understand how my thought fit in with the history of the world's great philosophers. I also benefited from the freedom to research and write papers about God and the practical functioning of the universe.

Patti and I worked together for twelve months researching a notion we called the pre-creation state. This was our way to explicate man's true nature as it has existed since even before the Big Bang. We spent many hours at the library and many more at home prompting each other to go deeper within ourselves to answer specific questions about the nature of God and the universe. The interwoven tapestry that is the unified field gave us a glimpse of the singularity that existed prior to the Big Bang and its subsequent development into stars, planets, and human life. Our effort resulted in a twelve thousand-word paper that clarified our discoveries and explained the pragmatic connection between humans and God. The process of researching and writing this document increased my understanding about the work I had been engaged in since I was child. I saw clearly that everything I had done was part of an intention and a progression of thought that began before the creation of the universe. The natural progression of this intention led me to the next action step – the fulfillment of the choice I made in Spain to become a television producer.

Patti is a California native who loves everything about living in California. All of us loved California. We took many family camping trips in some of the greatest mountain and coastal areas in the United States. Our children were well educated; we had a beautiful home and a good standard of living. In spite of the fact that I worked many hours and spent many more at Cal State Bakersfield, we took vacations and shared a lot of great times together. Then, in the mid-1980s, our two eldest children stopped playing outside and feared going to bed at night. The media had begun reporting on a serial killer and rapist named Richard Ramirez, who had murdered some women in Los Angeles. The intense publicity on the television news and in newspapers disturbed Elisa and Frances to the point that they had trouble sleeping. Patti and I also experienced increased anxiety, especially when news reports announced that Ramirez, known as the Night Stalker, was thought to be moving north.

The Night Stalker killed in different ways, often climbing through the windows of homes while his victims slept. He then woke them from their sleep and murdered them. Elisa and Frances told us their dreams were invaded by images of the Night Stalker coming through their window to kill them. They checked every closet in the house and shined flashlights underneath their beds before they went to bed every night. When I arrived home from work at around quarter of midnight on the last Friday night in August 1985, Patti and I talked about what we could do to help our family get back to normal. We decided it was our responsibility to our family and to our community to do something about the Night Stalker. What happens in the mind is much more powerful than our efforts in the world, so we devised a plan based on the creative drivers and decided to put it into action in the morning.

On Saturday morning, August 31, 1985, Elisa and Frances came to me in the kitchen where I was preparing breakfast for the family. Elisa said, "I'm mad because today is Saturday and Frances and I want to go outside and play but we can't because we're afraid of the Night Stalker." Frances, who was nervous and fearful about a lot of things anyway, was especially afraid. I went into the laundry room to retrieve Patti so she could talk to Elisa and Frances while I finished cooking breakfast.

Patti said, "Don't worry, girls, your dad and I have a plan to catch the Night Stalker and we're going to do it right after breakfast."

"You and Dad can catch the Night Stalker?" Frances asked.

"We won't catch him ourselves with our own hands, but we'll make sure he gets caught this morning," Patti explained while stroking Frances's hair.

"But while you and Dad are doing your plan," Elisa said sadly, "Frances and I will be afraid." I suggested that after breakfast Elisa should read a story to Frances, Ian, and Ali until their mom and I completed our mission. This satisfied them. After breakfast, Patti and I walked into our bedroom and closed the door.

The first step is choosing, so we chose to see Richard Ramirez constrained immediately, no matter how it happened. We created our intention by putting that choice into simple words: "Richard Ramirez is now unable to harm anyone ever again." We agreed that this described the desired result without restricting the universe by stating any particular method of restraint, whether dead or alive, in jail, or having fallen off a cliff. We declared this statement out loud together. We then sat still and breathed quietly, focusing our thought energy on God, the source of everything. We then focused on the words of the intention and visualized Ramirez safely stopped from harming others right that moment. We continued this process for about three minutes. I focused with ease and peace. When I perceived that I had focused sufficiently on the intention I then relaxed my mind, stopped focusing, and released the outcome to higher power. I opened my eyes and about that time Patty opened hers. We then left the room and spoke with Elisa and Frances about what we had done while Ian and Ali played with toys.

Patti and I hung the laundry to dry in the backyard and cleaned the house. About an hour later I walked into the backyard with another basket of laundry. I heard Elisa and Frances shrieking inside the house. My first reaction was fear but then I realized they were shrieking in joy. They came running excitedly to the backyard, Elisa announcing, "They caught the Night Stalker, they caught the Night Stalker!"

Frances shouted behind her, "People caught the night stalker and beat him up!" I dropped the basket of laundry and asked Elisa how they knew the Night Stalker had been captured. She grabbed my hand and pulled me toward the family room, where Patti and I saw the television news broadcast confirming that indeed, Richard Ramirez – the Night Stalker – had been captured by people in Los Angeles who lived in the neighborhood where he was hunting for his next victim. They recognized him, jumped him, and held him until police arrived and threw him in jail. Patti and I practiced the three creative drivers together and the energy we directed rippled the unified field in a way that it most likely would not have rippled without our action. The difference in particle wave interactions triggered by the focused thought energy of our intention initiated a chain of events that showed up as a difference in the physical world. In this case, that difference occurred as the apprehension of a serial killer.

Patti and I could not be absolutely certain about our direct role in the capture of Ramirez. In discussing it, however, we had to face the fact that Ramirez committed many murders, about thirteen or fourteen, over a period of fourteen months and was never apprehended. Patti and I had decided late on Friday night that we would do something to help stop this person. On Saturday morning, we acted in the most powerful way we knew. Within minutes of our actions the man was in jail, and about an hour after Patti and I completed our ceremony, the news of the Night Stalker's capture was reported on television. Given our personal history, our intention to see this man captured, and our choice to focus our mind energy on his apprehension, it would be ludicrous for us to deny our role in this result. There is value in the capture of a serial murderer, but the overarching value of this experience was that it was delivered through the process of self-understanding. The exercise of writing Priming the System helped me learn how to apply the creative drivers to my pursuit of self-understanding. The process of self-understanding taught me about peace. Coming from peace clarified my choices and strengthened my focus. In this case the result was the capture of the Night Stalker.

Chapter 37

UNCONSCIOUS CHOICES

Though my individual consciousness played a powerful role in the experiences I had created over the years, it could not, by itself, make any of them happen. Because my higher power, that is, my transpersonal consciousness, also impacts the outcome of my conscious choices it only made sense that I turn my life over to higher power. This required consciously releasing my effort to control everything that happened. It was a slow and ongoing process and it continues. When I allowed my life events to unfold in their own way – in God's way – I experienced outcomes far more enjoyable than outcomes forced into existence by my personal ego.

Priming the creative process of the universe with the energy of my intention triggered the manifestation process but did not control it. We can plant a rosebush but we cannot force a rosebud to produce a flower nor can we cut the bud open to see the rose inside. The beauty of the rose unfolds in its own time. We cannot cause the chrysalis to produce a butterfly nor can we cut it open to see the butterfly inside. The caterpillar transforms into the butterfly and flies away only when it is ready. I found it most powerful to guide my direction with intention while allowing my peace to follow its own course. The more I let go of control, the more amazing the results in my life became.

Our family was on a peaceful course in a new home and a secure income in October of 1986 when Carl, my friend from Spain, and his wife Sharon visited Patti and me in Bakersfield. Carl had returned to his childhood home in Niles, Ohio after departing Spain and receiving a discharge from the Air Force in the spring of 1977. In Niles, he found a job and met Sharon, who he married in 1978. I was part of the wedding party. In 1985 Carl and Sharon moved to Boca Raton, Florida where Carl began producing a local television program about tennis. He was working on making a business out of it when he came to Bakersfield. Carl knew about my education and training in television production and thought his tennis show might offer a pathway to my TV programming vision. He also needed help turning his programming idea into a business. He asked if I was interested in moving to Florida for a piece of the company and an opportunity. Inspired by this discussion and by my vision of 1977, I flew to Boca Raton in January 1987 on an exploratory trip. When I returned home Patti and I considered the potential and the risk but made no decision at that time. I graduated from Cal State Bakersfield in 1987 with a 3.8 average, a degree in philosophy and religious studies, and a minor in television production. Shortly after I graduated, Patti and I made the choice to move our family to Florida.

Several days after making the decision I went into the trainmaster's office at the railroad yard and resigned my position with the Atchison, Topeka and Santa Fe Railway Company. It was very difficult. Patti and I rented a large truck, filled it with everything we owned, and set out with our four beautiful children across the country to Florida. We left before dawn on July 5, 1987; Patti drove our new Plymouth Voyager and I drove the rented truck. I was frightened; we were homeless at that moment, planning to live in motels for about fourteen days before arriving in Florida. We had a small pewter statue of a wizard holding a crystal ball high in the air with one hand. As she drove down the street away from our home, Patti raised the wizard for me to see and then placed it on the dashboard of the Voyager to guide us across the country to our new home and new careers. Ian rode with me that morning; Ali was only three years old and she, Elisa, and Frances were in our Voyager with Patti.

While driving toward Victorville to say goodbye to Patti's family, I reflected on the sequence of events from 1977 to 1987. Viewed over time, the pattern of the power of intention was obvious. Looking back, I had the impression that I was literally following a preplanned script that I had written and was continuing to write. With the power of focused thought energy, Patti and I had created from nothing a solid foundation for our family of four children. Elisa and Frances had lived with us permanently for several years since we gained full custody from Maria. We lived in a beautiful new home in California about forty minutes from the Sequoia National Forest, where we camped out during the summer. We picnicked on the banks of the Kern River, a wild environment fifteen minutes from our home. I earned more than three times the median income for our family size and worked for one of the greatest companies in the country. We were not looking for a way out of California. Patti was born in California; we both loved California, and would probably have never left had it not been for the vision that took place that day in Spain in May of 1977.

It was intention that drove the journey to Florida and it was the vision that inspired the intention. After experiencing that vision in 1977 I asked myself, "How do I get from the Air Force here in Spain to producing Emmy award-winning television programs that will positively impact viewers around the world?" I did not know how. I did not try to figure out how; I followed the opportunities that my focused attention presented to me. Nothing happened by magic or miracle. Practicing the three creative drivers with my focus on the peace of self-understanding helped clarify my goals and presented action steps, most often one at a time. Following the action steps and persevering in the face of apparent defeat nearly always manifested my intentions and goals. I also manifested goals that I was not aware I had. Some of these life experiences were extremely difficult to endure; it was these, however, that created my greatest opportunities for understanding, and with time I came to appreciate them all.

Patti and I, with Elisa, Frances, Ian, and Ali, arrived in Delray Beach, Florida in a heavy thunderstorm at about nine PM on July 17, 1987. After breathing California air for so many years I didn't know the meaning of the word humidity. I jumped out of the truck and breathing the wet air felt like inhaling a solid substance. My first thought was to turn around and go back to Bakersfield. But this was now home and it would soon become much more difficult. We moved into an apartment that sucked in comparison to the beautiful homes we had always had in California. Nothing in Florida was advancement, everything was a decline; nothing was as wonderful, everything was worse. I was angry, upset, and full of complaints.

This did not resemble my vision at all. Everything I attempted to accomplish was more difficult and more time-consuming than I had naively anticipated in California. I faced harsh reality when Carl told me that there would be no ownership in the company for me and my salary would not be as we had discussed. I was now earning less than a third of my income in California, which I would have understood had I owned part of the company. I received another major surprise when the entire small staff departed for the 1987 U.S. Open in New York City, leaving me behind alone to "run the company." I discovered during this short time that the position was not a fit for me. In a tight financial position right after the move, however, I continued working for the company with a plan to make my escape as soon as I could come up with another idea.

The stress I was feeling manifested itself in 1988 as episodes of irregular heartbeat. From out of nowhere my peacefully beating heart would suddenly begin beating in a very uncomfortable way that was diagnosed as ventricular tachycardia. Rhythmic heartbeat would generally restore itself within minutes, but sometimes I had to submerge my head in a sink full of ice water to convert it back to normal. My cardiologist prescribed more medication and told me that stress could be causing the condition. Finally, with my health and other considerations in mind, I typed my resignation and presented it to Carl at 3:17 one Friday afternoon in August 1989. It was a sad departure for both of us that temporarily impacted our friendship.

I was without health insurance for the first time in my life when, about six weeks later, my heart began beating severely out of rhythm. Nothing I did, including submerging my face in a sink full of ice water, coughing, altering my breathing patterns, and meditating, converted the rhythm back to normal. Patti drove me to the emergency room at Bethesda Hospital in Boynton Beach, where I was admitted immediately and given intravenous drugs to regulate my heartbeat. This procedure had worked in the past but this time it had no effect. A little while later some doctors came in and injected me with another drug that didn't work. My heart continued beating wildly. I certainly didn't feel any better when the doctor told me that this could kill me quicker than a heart attack. I lay in fear of instant death until about two o'clock in the morning when two nurses came into my room. They had one more drug they wanted to try. The nurses warned me that if this drug did not work they would have to apply electrical paddles to my chest in an attempt to shock my heart back into rhythm. That scared me and stressed me out even more.

One nurse stationed herself out at the nurse's station to watch the heart monitor while the other slowly pushed the drug into the intravenous tube attached to the needle in my arm. The nurses communicated using a speaker, which I could hear, so that the nurse watching the monitor could tell the nurse injecting the drugs whether my heartbeat changed. Nothing happened as I watched the nurse slowly push the plunger on the syringe. My fear increased. Then through the fear I suddenly remembered what to do. With my heart beating wildly, I closed my eyes, observed my breath, and allowed all the frightening thoughts that were speeding around my head to drift away. I imagined my heart beating normally while I said, "God, please convert my heartbeat now." In that instant my heartbeat returned to normal. I felt it first and then heard the nurse at the monitoring station tell the nurse with the needle in her hand, "His heart just converted."

Chapter 38

RIDE THE WAVE

Lying in the hospital bed, my head reeling, I felt like I had just come back from the brink of death. I gave thanks for my breath and was still on edge over the ordeal. I trembled at the possibility of the electrical paddles being pressed against my chest and then expressed gratitude by saying simply, "Thank you God." I was exhausted from a day and night of fear but my mind would not stop. I took a deep breath, closed my eyes, and saw an image of my heart beating in perfect harmony. As I observed my breath my perception shifted into the world of the very tiny. I effortlessly merged with the nonmaterial energy of God, the energy that precedes, imbues, and subsumes all of time and space.

This nonmaterial energy is God's primordial thought energy. Everything in existence, everything we can know, including our individual thoughts, arises from this nonmaterial energy, which is not a thing and is not a concept; it has no name and no words can describe it. We call it the universe; we call it God. We give it many names but none can portray the depth of the Mysterium

Tremendum et Fascinans. Whatever we choose to call it, this un-namable nothing moves eternally toward self-awareness. We are this unnamable nothing, we are the universe; it is you and I who are on this timeless journey toward self-awareness. This physical creation exists only to serve as God's means – our means – of self-understanding. Consider that God brought forth this incredible creation of billions of galaxies, each containing billions of stars and planets, only to answer the question, "Who am I?" If that is the sole purpose of this infinite creation, then it makes wonderful sense for us humans to follow God in our individual pursuit of self-understanding. It is in understanding our true nature that we discover the answer to the question, "Who am I?"

It is through our life experiences and the practice of the creative drivers that we constantly expand our understanding of ourselves. As God peers out from your eyes and sees itself in me, it simultaneously looks through my eyes to see another aspect of itself in you. This process goes on forever. There is no destination and the journey never ends. After we understand everything there is to know about ourselves in this universe, we will imagine and create other ways of discovering even more. So seek not the destination; there is no time or place in the future when or where you can expect to arrive. Seek instead the peace and joy of being fully present in this moment. For guidance along your path, follow the crumbs you left behind the last time you traveled this way. The universal creative drivers are these crumbs.

I had not been happy since moving to Florida and knew I had created my unhappiness. Somewhere inside of me I had chosen to experience unhappiness, so I invented a complicated situation that

I could be unhappy with and blame somebody else for – at least for a little while. I knew I created everything in my experience but that did not stop me from complaining about it and blaming someone else for it. The worst part was that I could not or would not accept that I had intentionally chosen to give up what I had slowly built during my eleven years in California. I lived in Florida for two years, angry, disappointed, and upset with myself, resulting in my heart attacking itself. All this happened without my noticing it until I was compelled to do something about my heartbeat.

This is why self-understanding is so important. If I understood who I really was and what I was affecting when I started disparaging myself and thinking of myself as a failure, I might have been able to heal myself more gently and with less fear. Something in my inner being healed in that moment in the hospital, that moment of peaceful serenity when my heartbeat converted. That inner healing manifested itself in the elimination of the life-threatening symptoms my heart displayed. I saw something about myself; I did not like what I saw and I resisted it. I wanted to deny it, but having seen it I knew I had to accept it. When I did, it disappeared and set me free.

When we become aware that our purpose on earth is the discovery of our true nature, we understand that everything we experience is intended to contribute to this discovery. Nothing comes into our lives by accident or coincidence. I played a part in the creation of the erratic heartbeat, the stress, and the fear that put me in the hospital. I had ignored the good in my life and complained about everything else. Focusing on my complaints necessarily produced the undesirable results about which I had been complaining.

Through this crisis, however, I was able to discover the gold of self-understanding. It was a difficult experience to go through, and looking back upon it while lying in the hospital bed, I appreciated every detail of it. We all have something to appreciate in life, no matter how our life's circumstances appear. If we are breathing we have reason for appreciation and in appreciation we accept and integrate reality. The reality of our lives is what is happening right now and we cause no transformation when we regret the past or wish the present could be different. Soon after this episode I took a cardiac stress test and the doctor told me I was "as fit as an astronaut." Several years after that I was taken off the heart medication and never took it again. When we feel the sense of appreciation, no matter the problems, no matter the difficulties, we will, at that point of acceptance, begin the powerful process of transforming our lives.

My full recovery from the tachycardia situation was a major turning point. I created a one-day workshop based on the creative drivers, which I presented on Saturdays at venues from West Palm Beach to Miami. The workshops were an opportunity to give the creative drivers to many people at the same time. I received valuable feedback from the people attending the workshops who told me how the creative drivers had positively impacted their personal and business lives. The workshop imparted the wisdom and techniques that help people know their inner peace and create anything they choose for themselves. I closed each workshop with the message that personal peace was the most important result of self-understanding. I told the participants that when they departed the workshop with peace in their minds and hearts, others would notice it, want it, and then peace would spread around the planet one person at a time. Teaching these workshops also helped maintain my focus on abundant living. I received great gifts from teaching these workshops.

In May of 1993 Carl introduced me to Scott and Ron, two of the three partners of a well-known company called Five Star Productions, rated by the South Florida Business Journal as the largest television production company in south Florida.

People I knew from the TV business had good things to say about the quality of the work produced at Five Star. After three conversations at the Five Star offices, Scott and Ron asked me to manage the production department. I called a few days later and accepted the position; we agreed I would start on August 5. On Wednesday, August 4, 1993, the last day before starting my new position, I went to the beach with my youngest daughter Alethea, then nine years old, her friend Emily, Emily's dad, and Emily's cousin who was visiting from France. We went to an area of Delray Beach without lifeguards. The wind was blowing and the surf was rough. The waves were breaking on the sandbar far out from the beach. Alethea brought her boogie board and I told her to stay in the shallow water where the remnants of the waves washed up on shore. I walked into the less than knee-deep water with the three girls, about thirty-five feet inland from the crashing waves. Ali and her friends held on to the boogie board in the shallow water and floated in front of me while Emily's dad stood farther back on the dry sand.

I looked over my shoulder at the beach for Emily's father. That took less than a second, and when I turned around the girls were being pulled rapidly out toward deeper water and into the surf. I ran in after them to grab the board. Ali's friends jumped off the board and swam the short distance back toward shore, but for some reason Ali clung to the board as the rip current pulled her into deeper water. The water was nearly over my head when I caught up with her seconds later. My heart pounding, thinking of nothing other than getting Ali onto the beach, I grabbed the boogie board with Ali on it and threw it on top of a breaking wave.

The wave carried Ali and the boogie board toward shore and she landed safely on the sand while the incredible pull of the ocean sucked me into deeper water like a little fish circling in a flushing toilet bowl. Before I knew it I was in deep water with waves from all directions breaking over my head.

I'm not a good swimmer and, exerting all my power, I made no headway toward shore. I was caught in a rip current and did not realize it. After going underwater two or three times, completely exhausted and out of breath, I realized I could die out there that day. I thought, Oh no, not with Ali watching me, not the day before starting my new job. Just then a wave crashed over me, pushed me underwater and held me there. I struggled to get my head above water and was choking and breathing hard when I broke the surface gasping for air. After that I went into a state of complete panic, my mind totally scattered and helpless.

A few seconds later the panic suddenly disappeared and I realized I had to do something to save my life. Looking back toward the beach I saw Emily's father standing there looking at me. I waved my arm and yelled but he made no effort to find help. I had already tried to swim back in and could not. I was focused in the moment and all my fear was gone. I calmly asked God to send me a wave that would carry me toward the shore. Just then I noticed a large swell building in the distance. It came toward me; I paddled toward shore and caught the crest of the wave, but the wave folded on itself in an explosion of white foam far short of the beach. Still in deep water, I was immediately swept back out but did not panic. I maintained my focus and asked for an even bigger wave, one that would carry me close enough to shore that I could make it to safety by myself. I said, "Thank you God for a huge wave that will carry me to shore." Again I saw a large swell building in the distance and as it approached I began to paddle. I caught it and it began to curl over as I rode the top of the wave. It finally broke, landing me in water just over my head. After a few strokes, my toes touched bottom. By clawing my toes into the bottom and stroking at the same time I slowly made my way toward the beach and collapsed onto the sand. Ali grabbed hold of me, weeping. I thanked God for life.

We can look at almost any situation in our lives and try to figure out what would have happened if we had made a different choice at that time. It is forever impossible to know the answer. That is why I had to develop the mental discipline and clean logic that permitted me some degree of objectivity in my observations. It is possible that those waves would have carried me to shore no matter what I thought about. However, if I chose something and it manifested, then it was totally inappropriate and illegitimate for me to attempt to convince myself that the result would have been the same no matter what I did. I refused to tell myself that everything that occurred was just a coincidence or that nothing mattered because it was all predestined. I really don't want to know what might have happened had I not called forth those waves. All I know now is that I did call, the waves came, and I'm alive.

Chapter 39

LOVE OF SELF

I awoke the next morning frightened by the memory of how close I had come to death. My right shoulder was in extreme pain from having thrown Ali and the boogie board onto the wave that carried her to shore. I thought about different ways I could have handled the situation, quickly let go of that unproductive thinking, and focused on the appreciation I felt for being alive on the first day of my new job.

Before preparing for work I began my normal meditation practice. As I began consciously following my breath I was impacted with the awareness of how rare the experience of being in a human body is. Each of us is here for only a brief moment and that moment can end without notice at any time. Don Juan Matus once told Carlos Castaneda that death rides on our shoulders at all times and takes us in a flash without warning. The knowledge that our earthly lives will one day end makes each moment rare and precious. We can go through life unaware of the value of the present moment and possibly miss the beauty of our entire time on earth, or we can greatly increase the value of every second of our lives by appreciating each moment exactly as it is.

As I rode the vibration of meditation deeper into myself, I lost any awareness of thought and merged with the unity of creation, as I did nearly every time I meditated. This union connected me to my original self as it did when I first experienced it when I was thirteen. Since I had become more accustomed to the experience over the years, it no longer shook my system as it did in 1961. Sixty minutes later I opened my eyes and was ready to function normally in the world. After a shower and breakfast I drove from my home in Delray Beach to the company's headquarters on Federal Highway in Boca Raton. I met with Scott and he introduced me to the production department employees. I then went to my office to begin analyzing the company's production situation.

From the beginning I approached Five Star with the intention of growing with it and making a career out of it. The company had many good things going for it. I was proud of the programs we produced, especially Parenting in the 90s, Today's Environment, and Today's Health. We received many complimentary viewer calls and letters each week. Quality production values, solid content, and customer service were important to me and they were to the Five Star partners also. What I did not and could not have known at the outset was the underlying reason I came to Five Star. I quickly learned that this good job was not about the job; it was really about the close relationships I formed with two of the owners, Patty and Ron. Ron and I discovered that we had several common interests, the foremost being the power of thought. Ron was a practitioner of the Silva Mind Control System and he sponsored several workshops, which I attended, that taught the system. Ron was also a pilot and he inspired me to pursue my long-time desire to learn to fly. Because this relationship was deep, I was grieved in February of 1995 when Ron resigned his position with Five Star. After Ron's departure, Five Star was no longer the same for me.

A few weeks after Ron left I created an intention to develop a new path to create another production company. I focused on generating an idea good enough to support that – a unique programming idea that would attract and maintain strong viewership. After dinner that night I saw an article in Forbes Magazine that included a reference to a web site. I don't remember the web address but the familiar format, http://www.xxxxxx.com, started me thinking that night about the World Wide Web. I had been using CompuServe for email and Internet research since the early 1980s. My first 300 baud modem in 1984 transformed my computer from a powerful office tool to a worldwide communications system. The Internet was a useful research and news gathering tool with cool news groups and bulletin boards, but I did not see it as a business opportunity in 1984. That night in 1995, however, the "www" in that magazine article flipped on a light bulb in my brain. I quickly learned more about the web, stirring my excitement about the future of television and opportunities in web development and hosting.

This was a time-critical idea. I wanted to be the first production company to launch a show about the Internet. I decided to leave Five Star, reasoning that sponsorship dollars would be available because television was an excellent vehicle for companies needing exposure for their new websites. The program I envisioned would be the first to fill this need. I predicted big viewer numbers because most people knew nothing about the web; they would watch the show because they wanted to learn about the Internet and how to get the most out of it. I had seen a show called CNet, but that was nothing like what I had envisioned for the show I tentatively named *.com*. The timing was right for this program and I did not want to miss the opportunity.

I called Ron and visited him in his office during my lunch break to discuss the Internet and television programming ideas. Ron liked both ideas, especially the web development idea. We shook hands and began our business together. I submitted my resignation to Scott the following morning and told him I would stay as long as needed to make the transition. He cut me loose on the spot.

Ron and I named our new web design and hosting business CyberOne, and the television production company was TV Innovations, Inc., doing business as TV Interactive (TVI). We sublet office space in Boca Raton from one of Ron's stockbrokers. Ron and I occupied a single room with two desks, two phones, two pads and pens, and one computer with a VGA monitor and a modem. In another room, Ron had two salesmen attempting in vain to sell sponsorships for a golf program; one of those salesmen was my old friend Carl. They had made no sales for the golf show so we shut it down and Patrick and Carl became CyberOne salesmen.

Three days after resigning from Five Star I woke up at two o'clock in the morning, confronted with fear. I thought about our four children and all the expenses: their private school, our home mortgage, and everything else. I suddenly had no income and if I failed to make something work soon ... No more of that thinking. Breathe, focus on your breath, and let those thoughts move on.

That morning I went to the new office and Ron and I got to work. We knew nothing about making websites or hosting them. Instead of taking time to learn more about the business, we sent out five thousand direct mail pieces inviting company presidents, owners, and officers to free seminars about the Internet. We created a slide presentation, rented a large hotel meeting room, and packed it with local business executives anxious to learn about web sites and email. The weekly seminars explained why every company needed a web presence. Ron and I presented the seminar and at the conclusion our salespeople patrolled the room answering questions, creating appointments, and closing business. I was amazed at the high number of self-proclaimed savvy businesspeople who chose not to create web sites in 1995 because they thought the Internet was "just a fad" and would fade away in a year. A standout on the other end of the spectrum was Southwest Airlines – hip enough to be the first to begin using electronic ticketing and boarding passes in 1995.

Necessity forced us to learn the technicalities of the business quickly. We also needed people. Unfortunately, web designers, UNIX programmers, and other necessary technical people were in short supply. We moved to 3600 square feet of office space in Ft. Lauderdale, hired five more salespeople, and found the technical people we needed.

Installing a high-speed Internet connection was a huge effort at that time. First the phone company ran fiber underneath the railroad tracks and across the road to our office building. That took several weeks. Running the cable through the entire building required another couple of weeks. Meanwhile, I was developing marketing tools and teaching salespeople to sell the products we were developing. After the employees went home at night I worked on the *.com* TV concept. I was a television producer and did not want to miss the opportunity to introduce the first television program aimed at marketing corporate web sites and helping consumers navigate the Internet. Regardless of how great the show was, however, we needed someone who knew how to sell it. Ron and I gave this a lot of thought because the best person we knew for the job, Patty, already had one.

One night in September 1995, after everyone else had left the building, Ron took a seat in my office and told me that Patty had quit Five Star. My eyes popped open and my brain clicked like a key in a lock. Patty had been selling television since 1985 and was the best person for TV Interactive. Ron contacted her and made arrangements to meet. We discussed our ideas during dinner at Houston's in Boca Raton. Patty was the potential key to TVI's marketing success, so I don't know why we did this, but we told her it would cost her $35,000 for a position with the company. Ron pulled out a couple of spreadsheets we had created to justify the investment and Patty laughed as she said, "I'm not paying you so I can become part of this company." The spreadsheets went back in the pocket and that was the end of the investment idea.

Chapter 40

FOCUSED INTENTION

Patty soon joined TV Interactive and CyberOne as a major shareholder and vice president of sales and marketing. She managed and trained two sales teams: one sold web sites and the other team sold the television program *.com*. After several months of diligent and focused effort Patty closed our first *.com* sponsorship with Kodak. Within five months *.com* sales exceeded CyberOne web sales ten to one. After much debate we ceased the web business to focus all of our energy on our core skill. We redesigned our small office space to accommodate more salespeople; the place pulsed with excitement as the growth rate continued increasing.

To help our people improve their skills and stay inspired, we purchased a library of motivational audio CDs and videotapes and made them available to staff. We also created a structured weekly class focused on Napoleon Hill's *Think and Grow Rich*. Everyone in the company read the same chapter each week; we began every Wednesday morning by reviewing that chapter together. I trained our employees in the principles and application of the three creative drivers, which they used in their personal and professional lives. While sales increased every month, we also developed production efficiencies that made the company more profitable.

Before long our 3600 square feet of space housed thirty-six employees, two edit suites, a small shoot studio, a graphics room, two sales rooms supporting twelve salespeople, and two private offices. With *.com* running smoothly, we developed another television program for our lineup and named it *Healthy Solutions*. Our sales proposition for the show was focused directly on the big pharmaceutical companies. We filled their need for a targeted media outlet and were rewarded with immediate and consistently increasing sales.

I chose and focused on personal goals as well. As a result Patti and I moved our family from Delray Beach into a new home in Boca Raton. Ron and I became partners in an airplane and Patty arranged for all three of us to become members of the Boca Raton Resort and Club. Patti and I knew we were blessed. We expressed our appreciation in many ways, including sharing our blessings with individuals and charitable groups. TV Interactive was a success; the company won many awards for the shows we produced and I became an Emmy-winning television producer. As with everything that has ever been created by any of us, it all started as a thought in my mind. The energy of the thought rippled through the unified field. The ripples in the unified field manifested as focused points of energy. The focused energy took the form of changes in the world that beneficially affected individuals' experiences.

By spring of 1997 the office was severely overcrowded; it was our biggest constraint. The broadcast schedules for both *.com* and *Healthy Solutions* were filled four months in advance; sales continued increasing and we did not want to turn away business. Our limited space prevented us from hiring the people needed to take advantage of the increased demand for TV Interactive programming. We had several other programming ideas in mind and needed space to build the sales force, increase the production team, and build a soundstage. We explored expansion options, looked at several buildings, and decided instead to move to a new building in the Florida Atlantic University Research and Development Park. Before beginning construction we hired a feng shui consultant. Patty and Ron and I stood with the consultant on the ground where the building would soon exist. While walking the ground, we visualized the location of each department and organized the structure of the office in accordance with the energy. Ron created the floor plan. The state soon approved our business plan and construction started early in 1998.

Within two months after we moved to the new facility at the end of 1998, our sales had doubled. The first huge surge in sales came in like a tsunami, causing me to look at the schedule and scratch my head. This was a great problem to have. Where would I find the people and resources needed to make all this happen? The same place I had found the resources that had brought us this far. I knew of only one way to handle all the complicated details involved in producing the high-quality television programming for which TV Interactive was known, and I followed the same pattern every time. Whether shooting the program hosts on complicated sets in Hollywood, locating high-end lighting grips in South Florida, closing national and international distribution deals, or creating and meeting monthly sales goals, everything came together as a result of thought energy focused in accordance with the universal creative drivers.

Having tightly organized the business around processes, I was now working only nine or ten hours each day instead of fifteen. This allowed me to be with my family every day, wake up earlier, and resume my thirty-year practice of devoting one hour each morning to observing my breath and being within myself. Before beginning the meditation practice I typically thought about appreciation. I said silently, "Thank you God for this new day, for my life, and everything in it." I thanked the God self within me, knowing that I was ultimately thanking myself since I was responsible for the experiences of my life. The meditation practice consisted mostly of watching my breath move in and out of my body. After completing my morning meditation I remained seated for a few minutes to focus on my intentions.

Focusing attention on my intentions produced ideas about what I could do in the world to manifest those intentions. Sometimes new action ideas occurred to me within minutes of the focusing meditation and sometimes days went by before anything occurred. When an idea came to mind, I acted on it. The process was the same whether I was moving electrons around, changing cottage cheese into sour cream, or moving from a $200,000 home to a one million dollar home. I gave thanks to the creative source for the action ideas that occurred to me and for the energy, health, and resources to accomplish them.

From the day nearly twenty years ago when I sequenced the creative drivers, I had consistently expanded their application from short-term projects with little or no risk to more meaningful, longer-term projects with potentially greater personal risk and reward. As I achieved goals, I experienced gratitude and satisfaction. My greatest reward was my ability to be with my children and to help provide them with opportunities for their personal growth.

As my inner satisfaction increased, I experienced commensurate levels of dissatisfaction. When my television programs reached financial and critical success and my personal financial situation improved, some of my responsibilities at TV Interactive began to seem mundane. I made excuses to leave the office and sometimes flew our plane in the middle of the day. Flying was hard to resist because the hangar was visible across the runway from my office window. My thoughts often wandered to my vision of May 1977. Several events from that vision had already occurred in the world; I had no doubt that the balance of the events would also occur if all of us citizens of planet earth continued doing what we had always done. In December 1998 I listed some critical events from the 1977 vision that had already happened:

- The United States attacked Iraq in January 1991. In 1977 I had correctly identified the reason given by the U.S. for this invasion, its support by the American people, and its commencement date in 1990 or 1991.

- Failing to pursue available alternative energy sources like solar, wind, and other natural resources in the early 1970s, the U.S. allowed itself to become dependent upon and enslaved by imported energy.

- Clean water was in short supply in 1977 and had become a dangerously scarce resource in many parts of the world long before 1998.

- Rechargeable plastic cards were largely used in place of cash.

- CDs were invented and made available less than ten years after the vision showed them to me.

- Women held positions of corporate and political power.

- I had produced and distributed award-winning television programs that made a positive difference for people around the world.

Given the events from the vision that had already occurred, we could also expect to experience the events that had not yet occurred. It was clear to me in 1977 that all of the events portrayed in the vision were revealed for the benefit of human peace. The vision provided both a warning and a solution, which was made available on the same day that the vision occurred. The solution is available to us now and has been available in many forms, all over the world, for thousands of years. We have the choice to pay attention to it now and find peace within ourselves now. Or we can choose to wait until this same solution is revealed through the events depicted in the vision.

The solution lies in our personal choices. Every one of us on earth has both light and dark within us. Each of us has a choice in this matter. We can choose to focus on our own darkness or we can choose to shine the light within us brightly across the planet. Every choice that we make for ourselves impacts our individual lives and the lives of others in the world. Indeed, every choice we make impacts the entire universe. Although parts of the vision had already occurred by 1998, the events that had not occurred could be altered or avoided if we so chose. Making the choice is enough, but when we choose to understand ourselves, we begin to find ways to live together peacefully and sustainably. If we choose peace we will have peace. Our future is not written in stone and is known by no one, including God.

In addition to saying that it was possible to live peacefully and sustainably, the vision provided a way to experience it. Moving the entire self-destructive history of humanity toward the deep transformation revealed in the vision is like the transformation that takes place when a caterpillar becomes a butterfly. A caterpillar is a rather unattractive earthbound insect that slowly crawls around eating leaves all day. The post-transformation caterpillar – the butterfly – bears no resemblance to its former caterpillar self. The butterfly is a colorful winged beauty capable of transcending the bonds of gravity and flying wherever it chooses. The butterfly does not chew coarse leaves; it floats on warm breezes from one colorful flower to another, drinking the sweet nectar of life. This same transformative power lives within each of us. Within you and only within you is a star too bright to be contained in the heavens. Within you exists the beauty of the stars and the power to create the stars. Your access to that power depends only upon your choice.

Knowing a tested and proven way to help individuals understand and transform themselves, I chose to make the universal creative drivers available to everyone. Sitting in my office thinking about that 1977 vision motivated me to tell as many people as possible about self-understanding. I had been doing it on a part-time basis for thirty years and now chose to make it a full-time commitment. This huge leap would fulfill my dream of sharing what I knew about self-understanding, and the level of satisfaction I had achieved with TVI pushed me to another level of possibility. But this was a long-range plan; I had no thoughts of leaving TV Interactive. I began focusing thought energy on this long-range plan. I said goodnight to the late-shift editors and drove home.

Chapter 41

APPRECIATION

The first thing I thought about when I arrived home that evening was appreciation. I appreciated my breath, and of course my beautiful family, home, business, and the other great things in my life. Those were easy to appreciate. It required more time and self-reflection to appreciate the painful circumstances, especially the thoughts, decisions, and actions for which I derided myself. When I realized that the thought energy in our minds is made of love, and love drives all of creation, I learned to stop judging myself. All of our thoughts produce results that work to benefit us regardless of our personal judgment or opinion about them. We do not make mistakes; we sometimes take side trips in order to learn something about ourselves that we could not learn if our goals had manifested exactly as we envisioned them in our ego-based conscious minds.

Nothing we create in our lives can be said to be bad or good; these words are relative value judgments. What is true is that some of our actions work for us and some do not; it is up to each of us to choose which actions we prefer. Twelve hundred years ago a peasant farmed a plot in the Chinese countryside. The food he grew fed his family and earned some extra money to carry them through to the next harvest. The farmer was unable to bring in the harvest alone and depended upon his fifteen-year-old son to help farm the land. In his sixteenth year, the farmer's son was working in the field when he fell and broke his leg. This was a disaster for the family: it was time to harvest the crops and the son was unable to work. Much of the food was now liable to rot in the field and be eaten by animals. This was a very bad situation for the family.

About three weeks after the son's accident, war broke out in the western provinces. When the army came through the villages to conscript all men over fourteen, the boy could not go because of his broken leg. With his father and all the local men now gone to war, the women had to find a way to gather enough food to eat. Fortunately for the family, their son had recovered from his broken leg several weeks after the men and boys of the village had been forced into battle. He harvested the remaining crops and continued farming the land that fed his mother, his two sisters, and some of his neighbors. When the war finally ended, bad news preceded the return of the militia. Many of the men and boys from the village had been killed, including the father of the family. The boy's family gave thanks for the good fortune of the broken leg.

Appreciation subsumes acceptance, so expressing a deep sense of appreciation for all experiences, including the most painful and difficult, meant that I accepted everything in my life exactly as it looked in that moment. Acceptance removed resistance, released me from the past, and opened me to possibility. Acceptance of circumstances is acceptance of self. It was self-understanding that helped me experience self-acceptance. I often failed to notice when I was resisting something. Sometimes the resistance showed up in an important action that I never got around to handling or an undesirable result that I could not accept. At that point, instead of realizing I was resisting the flow of energy I made up excuses for the undesirable results I created. I said to myself that I simply did not like it or didn't want to do it. Through the practice of self-understanding, I finally realized that when I resisted something I ensured its continued existence. Resistance is recalcitrance and "recalcitrant" means "immovable;" before moving past an undesirable, seemingly unacceptable condition, I had to consciously choose the present condition and appreciate it no matter what it was. With acceptance, I released resistance, which relieved the pressure on the situation, allowed its energy to dissipate, and thus dispelled the undesirable circumstance.

I knew I created, and thus chose, all of my experiences even if I was unaware of having done so. I would not consciously cause myself pain, so when I found myself in an undesirable situation I knew I had chosen it unconsciously. This realization allowed me to choose that situation again – consciously this time. Consciously choosing the undesirable situations that seemed to just show up in my life removed any resistance I may have built up around them. Releasing the resistance allowed me to create something new.

If I was breathing, I had something to appreciate. My good friend Richard Hey told me, "What you resist persists." If I am not accepting and appreciating, then I may be unconsciously resisting, thus maintaining the very experience that I want to transform and transcend. I made it a practice to accept and appreciate all of life's conditions exactly as they looked in the moment, no matter what my opinion of them may have been. That meant that appreciation was as important as any of the other universal creative drivers. That night, while thinking over my life, I made a note to make appreciation the first of the creative drivers.

With the addition of appreciation and one other element that I had previously overlooked – perseverance – the creative drivers were complete. Perseverance, the desire to keep going and never quit, has moved life forward since its beginning. Had our ancestors not persisted in the face of harsh living conditions, we would not be here now. Had Thomas Edison not persisted through fourteen thousand attempts, we might not have electric light today. Perseverance is important because we will most likely not experience the result of a newly chosen intention the very first day that we declare it and write it down; therefore we must persevere in pursuit of our intention. If we persevere we will succeed.

Buddha said there are only two ways we can fail to reach liberation: one is to not begin and the other is to quit along the way.

It was 1999; the gift of the five universal creative drivers that constitute the process of self-understanding was delivered complete:

1. Appreciate: Give thanks for what you have right now. Say the words "I appreciate . . ." and then name what you are thinking of and appreciating. Mentally review and appreciate all the things you have in your life now and everything that has occurred in the past that stands out for you. If you find yourself blocked by circumstances or people that you

think you cannot appreciate or value, remember that you have chosen those circumstances and they are in your life to benefit you by helping you grow and transform. Continue looking for the benefit in those situations each day until you find yourself accepting and appreciating whoever or whatever they may be.

2. Choose what you intend to create for your life. Choose self-understanding, peace, money, a new job, a relationship, being in two places at one time, or anything you imagine that you need or desire. Say the words "I choose . . ." and then name what you are choosing.

3. Focus on your choice. Pay attention to your choice. Ignore any thoughts or ideas that are contrary to the manifestation of your choice. When thoughts arise that attempt to tell you that your choice will never happen or create negative "what if" scenarios, simply notice that you are having these thoughts and allow them to move on without force. Practice forming a mental picture of your choice and generate within you the feelings you will experience when you manifest this choice in your life.

4. Surrender your choice to your higher power or whatever name you use to define the creative energy of the universe that lives within you. After focusing your energy on your choice, release your focus and let the energy go freely into the universe. Take a deep breath and stop trying to control the outcome or the delivery method of what you have chosen. Do not think that your choice will manifest in any preconceived way. Suspend thinking about your choice until the next time you practice the creative drivers.

5. Persevere: Never quit; repeat creative drivers one through four until your choice manifests as your living reality.

When eternal being, God, became aware that it was alone and did not know who or what it was, it expressed its desire in the form of the question: "Who am I?" The asking of that question, the urge to know, initiated the process that created everything that exists. God's intention to know his own – our own – identity took the form of all created universes everywhere. The five universal creative drivers are part of the structure of the universe we live in. They are available to all human beings for use in the realization of their personal dreams. You are the higher power that created this universe and now you have the power to create whatever you choose by using the five universal creative drivers.

I started unconsciously using the universal creative drivers long before I became aware of them. My conscious practice of the creative drivers started around the time I wrote Priming the System. The practice of the creative drivers every morning and throughout the day helped me feel peaceful and carried me to the next level of my ability, where I can contribute to others who are interested in transformation.

After completing my meditation and gym workout one morning in early spring of 1999, I drove to TV Interactive as usual. I entered through the rear production entrance and went directly to my office. Shortly after my arrival Patty called me and asked if I would join her and Ron in her office. I walked over to Patty's office and we exchanged normal morning greetings. With that out of the way, we got down to the reason for the impromptu meeting. Patty told me that her friends, a husband and wife who I knew, had recently sold their lighting company. "They used a business broker called the Geneva Group," Patty said. Ron nodded in agreement and Patty continued. "They helped them find a buyer and negotiate the deal. They did very well financially and now they do whatever they want."

"Patty just told me about it," Ron explained, "and we think it could be a good thing for us."

"What do you think about the idea of selling the company?" Patty asked. "Ron likes the idea so we called you in to talk about it together."

"It could be a good possibility for us; I'm certainly open to talking with the Geneva Group," I responded. Once again I was impressed with the power of thought energy focused on a choice. This meeting was no accident. I had been focusing on my long-term intention for five months and did not expect results this soon. Patty's sudden idea to sell our company fit with my intention to break away from TVI and talk about the peace of self-understanding and the creative drivers full time. I was humbled by the awe-inspiring power that we are. This is what happens when we touch the power within us and express it in the choices we make. I thought, God, thank you, I love you. Yes, I thanked God and I thanked higher power. I understood there was no God separate from me who heard this expression of gratitude, but that does not mean that my words had no effect. My thoughts of gratitude rippled the unified field, which is what some humans call God, with the energy of gratitude and appreciation. Everything in the unified field, the whole of creation including me, was affected by these vibrations.

"I think we should call the Geneva Group and make an appointment," Ron said excitedly. I always admired Ron's willingness to take immediate action. We had agreed in the beginning that unless all three of us agreed on something we would not go forward with it. We reaffirmed that policy before contacting the Geneva Group, agreeing that we would not sell TVI unless all of us concurred and that any one of us could stop the process at any time. Ron called the Geneva Group later that day.

That Friday, three Geneva representatives flew to Boca Raton from Tampa. We ate lunch at Max's in Mizner Park and discussed the basics of the Geneva process. After lunch we returned to the office where the three representatives explained their fee structure and how they would market our company to synergistic businesses around the world. We negotiated a retainer and wrote them a check. After three months of meetings, conference calls, research, development, and marketing on the part of the Geneva Group, we had appointments to meet with representatives from four U.S. based communication companies and one British investment firm. As usual, I practiced the five creative drivers every morning as part of my normal meditation practice.

The Geneva team scheduled and organized the meetings so that the five visits were spaced out over four weeks with the British firm scheduled last. Each visit began with an introductory meeting in the conference room. We then took the visiting representatives on a complete tour of our facilities while answering their questions and introducing them to key employees along the way. Several days after the fourth domestic company had taken the tour, three representatives from the British investment organization visited TV Interactive. These men were dressed elegantly. They looked, spoke, and behaved like I imagined British royalty would. They liked TV Interactive a lot. Before they departed we set a date for a follow-up meeting to further discuss the opportunity with other members of their company.

Chapter 42

LIVING THE CHOICE

Our meetings with the five interested companies proved to us that the marketplace had a serious interest in TV Interactive; selling our company was a real possibility. My intention to communicate the message of peace and self-understanding remained the same. How the universe fulfilled my intention was not my concern. I did not think about where I would find the time and money or how I would handle travel logistics. Because of the self-understanding I had gained, I relaxed and forgot about all those details. That is why I was not surprised that day when Patty and Ron first asked me if I had an interest in selling the company. I knew that conversation flowed out of my intention and that intention also resulted in five suitors courting TV Interactive.

I continued focusing on broadening the reach of the message of peace. I paused at various times throughout the day to appreciate life and review the creative drivers. I gave thanks for my life exactly as it occurred at the moment; I then repeated my choice, briefly focused on it, and let it go many times each day. Only a few moments were required to take some breaths and relax while repeating the words and focusing my attention on them. When I was at home or alone in my office I focused for extended periods and with deeper concentration and visualization. I took advantage of every opportunity, even red traffic lights, to appreciate life, to choose, focus, and surrender throughout the day.

The day after our meeting with the British company, Patty, Ron and I went to lunch at J. Alexander's to discuss and agree upon our minimum selling price. Since we would soon be receiving offers from at least one of our visitors we wanted to make sure that we had a general agreement about the numbers. Ron opened the conversation by asking if I had a selling price in mind. I had been thinking about this.

I looked first at Ron and then at Patti before responding. "I would be willing to sell TV Interactive for nothing less than twenty million dollars. Any deal will be part cash and part stock, so it will have to be at least ten million in cash and ten million in stock." Without further discussion Ron and Patty agreed that we would sell TV Interactive for no less than ten million in cash and ten million in stock.

In August of 1999 the Geneva Group presented the five interested companies with a deadline for their offers on TV Interactive. We soon received four written offers from the American organizations. One company offered only three million dollars. The others went up from there, with offers of five million, seven million, and nine million dollars. Each of these proposals consisted of different proportions of cash and stock. Even the highest offer was far from our required twenty million, so we rejected each of these offers and gave them no further thought.

The following day the offer from the British company arrived. They proposed to purchase TV Interactive for twenty million dollars with ten million dollars in cash and ten million in stock in the new company. This was the direct outcome of priming the universe with the power of the five universal creative drivers, and of my many experiments conducted over forty years and applied to this goal. The numbers we stated were met and the intention I had created to communicate the power of peace and self-understanding on a full-time basis had been fulfilled. We accepted the British offer and received a letter of intent in late October 1999.

Many hurdles had yet to be crossed, including two weeks of intense due diligence by one of the world's top five accounting firms. Five or six accountants ran around our office every day for two weeks interviewing me, Ron, and Patty, looking through production records, and picking apart every number entered in the books since the day we started the company. Our bookkeeping was impeccable because we had worked with a large accounting firm experienced with mergers and acquisitions.

The Bank of Scotland and Barclays Bank performed additional due diligence because they were providing part of the financing to the purchasers of TVI. That process required us to meet with teams from each bank. Three representatives from Barclays arrived sometime in the second quarter of 2000 and stayed with us for three days. Their visit was an intense process of group meetings, individual interviews, and shadowing each of us individually wherever we went. We flew to England to meet with the Bank of Scotland. While there, we also visited the headquarters of the British team in Halifax, England.

I continued focusing on closing this deal by practicing the creative drivers throughout the course of each day. I first thought of how much I appreciated exactly what life looked like at that moment. Appreciating what I have means that I fully accept the present condition of my life. Simply taking a few seconds to consciously appreciate my life brought immediate relaxation. I then repeated my choice to devote full-time attention to disseminating the message of inner peace and world peace. After that I focused on this choice by visualizing the workshops and speeches I planned to present. I reinforced this picture by feeling what I expected to feel on the day the sale closed. I then relaxed and released my focused energy to the universe. After releasing the energy of the choice I simply forgot about it and continued with my normal daily business until I thought about reviewing the process again. Inspired and energized by this intention, I persevered.

One Friday during the summer of 2000, just as we were all getting ready to go home, Patty entered Ron's office where he and I had been relaxing in anticipation of the weekend. She announced that she had changed her mind – she no longer wanted to sell TVI – the deal was off. Ron and I wanted to know what had caused this sudden change and Patty explained herself. I didn't have to understand it; I had agreed, as had we all, that one person could stop the sale. Ron and I agreed to call the British team on Monday morning to inform them that we had chosen to retain ownership. I was surprised, especially given that Patty had initiated the idea from the start. However, in spite of Patty's statement and my sincere agreement, I had no doubt we would sell TVI as planned. I went home that weekend and continued working with the universal creative drivers to create my intention. I maintained single-minded focus throughout the weekend, never doubting that we would continue with the sale.

I walked into Ron's office at 8:50 Monday morning in advance of our nine o'clock meeting. Patty was already there, seated in front of Ron's desk in her usual chair. She turned to me, smiling, and announced that she had changed her mind over the weekend and was prepared to sell the company. We continued running the company and building the business while Geneva informed us of progress. In the middle of October we received a phone call from our Geneva representative informing us that the closing date was set for November 13, my son's birthday.

On November 13, 2000 I entered the TV Interactive conference room with seven attorneys. The Brits had hired a team of attorneys from Chicago and ours were from New York. I entered the conference room and read the documents. I signed everything and then Ron and Patty entered and signed their documents. The sale of TV Interactive was complete.

Two days later, on the agreed-upon day for our receipt of funds, I called my bank. The wire had not yet arrived. A few minutes later I called again; in that instant everything changed. Two wires, one from each bank, had arrived as agreed. I walked through the sliding door to our backyard pool area and looked up at the clear, bright, blue sky and said out loud: "Thank you God. I will never worry about money again." I did not make the commitment to "never worry about money again" because I thought I would never run out of the money I had just earned. I made that statement because I knew I was the source of everything in my life and, no matter what happened, my needs and desires would always be fulfilled.

Chapter 43

FULFILLMENT

Beginning with pure thought in the form of a conscious choice, Ron, Patty, and I created something that very few ever accomplish. Knowing that this power was available to everyone, I remained focused on my intention to share the five creative drivers on a broader scale. This was the most powerful and efficient way I knew to give people the opportunity to know peace and realize their wildest dreams.

To me, the sale of TV Interactive was the biggest example yet of the connection between thought energy and my experience in the world. I traced my thoughts back to that first day in Spain when I received the idea to use television to distribute programming that made a positive difference for people. From that day twenty-five years ago, my life slowly took shape around that idea and that idea was made manifest in the world. But it did not start in Spain. I was transported back in time to that day when I first named the playing cards as I lifted them from the deck and they showed up as I had named them. I did not know it at the time, but the creative drivers were alive on that day. I chose to name a card, I focused on the card, I relaxed, and the name of the card came into my mind.

I learned it was possible to execute impromptu "miracles" in the space of seconds. It was also possible to create and manifest powerful transformation over longer periods of time. I don't know the details of how these things happen. I do know that the something/nothing that many call God has always existed and it is present within each of us right now. It vibrates always within every person and everything. That is why we are able to use our thought energy to change our lives. We are this energy and our thoughts are the world. When we shift the way we think, life shifts accordingly.

I am empowered by the knowledge and at peace in the understanding that I alone am accountable for everything in my life. The knowledge that I create my world frees me from wondering whether some imaginary being will choose to answer my prayers. I am not subject to whim or to fate but to the power of my own inner being. That power is the same power that many of us call God.

The creative drivers make the peace that I experienced available to all of us. This peace of self-understanding can lead to peace among nations by removing the fear of imminent destruction, starvation, or deprivation from the minds and hearts of all the world's people. This lofty goal begins very simply with individual self-understanding. Between now and the day when billions of us around the earth find a way to live together, each of us must continue living now. The creative power to live in accordance with our conscious choice is available to each of us, and we have been given five simple universal creative drivers to help make it happen.

When I returned to the office the following day, everything was different yet it was all the same. Ron and I were connected to the new owners by three-year employment agreements with lucrative salaries. The generous salary deposited in my bank account every other week was a strong incentive to remain with TVI. We operated the company and sold our products as we had in the past. Bob, the new CEO, arrived from England at the end of November to begin operating the company. Ron had second thoughts and left TVI in April 2001. Bob was off-site most of the time so responsibility for the day-to-day operations fell solely to me. I continued focusing on my intention and the next five months passed without incident.

On my daughter Frances' twenty-eighth birthday I stopped at the Boca airport after my workout at the Athletic Club. It was a beautiful Tuesday morning and I did not want to miss the opportunity for a flight to Pahokee for touch and go landings. The time of day was ideal for the approaches over Lake Okeechobee. I greased the Bonanza onto the runway several times and headed back to town at about 8:40. After landing about 9:05, I backed the A-36 into the hangar with the tractor and in less than two minutes was in my parking space at the rear of the TVI building. I entered through the back entrance directly into the production area. Strangely, I was the only one in the room.

The large, normally busy production room was silent except for the voice of the newscaster on the television. I looked up at the TV in time to see a plane crash into the World Trade Center. I thought it must have been a confused Cessna pilot lost in the New York airspace. After entering my office and tuning my monitor to

CNN I got the story and slipped out of my chair onto my knees. To my horror I realized that this was one of the final segments of the 1977 vision: New York and Washington D.C. were just attacked by Arab terrorists on the same day. Twenty-four years earlier, in May 1977, I declared this would occur in 2000 or 2001 and most everyone who heard my message told me the same thing: "Come on, Jim, Arab terrorists will never attack the United States."

TV Interactive was not productive on September 11, 2001. I called Frances. She was distraught about this unprecedented disaster; the fact that it occurred on her birthday really affected her. I sent the TVI people home and sat there switching mentally from May 1977 to September 11, 2001. Who am I? What am I supposed to do? Why did this happen? I thought about Patti, my wife. I was nervous because she was not in Florida. A week earlier she had flown to New Mexico for a Shamanic Journey workshop. The attacks grounded nearly all aircraft and Patti was stranded out west. I gathered up Ian and Ali and drove home.

I went to bed that night comfortable in the knowledge that Ian and Ali were safely in their rooms upstairs. Patti was far away, stranded and concerned about when she would be able to fly home, as was I. Certainly no one knew what might happen next; I knew only that I felt overwhelmingly driven to share self-understanding and the five universal creative drivers. I had feelings of failure because 9/11 happened. I knew it in advance, spoke the message of the vision to hundreds and hundreds of people since 1977, and was unable to make a difference. Perhaps I had not worked hard enough; maybe I had not communicated with enough people.

I reflected on my commitment to communicate peace and then thought about how much money I received for being at TV Interactive each day. I was hesitant to give up those dollars, knowing that my next phase was going to be financed totally out of my own funds. As did so many Americans that night, I went to bed with a lot on my mind. Should I stay with guaranteed money for two more years of my time at TVI or leave with possibly no income while working full-time in accordance with the vision? The events of September 11, 2001 were horrific in and of themselves. Having foreseen these events caused me to think that my responsibility was to devote my efforts to creating peace in the world, one person at a time.

I was reminded of how I felt in Vietnam when I realized I could no longer make my living by killing people. I clearly had access to information and I was responsible to act on that knowledge. I could not simply keep it to myself and go about my business as usual. When I woke up the next morning I knew what I had to do. In the face of the September 11th disaster, I could no longer collect my paycheck for what I was doing at TV Interactive. I felt the light shining within me and I was passionate about letting it out. I left TVI on November 30, 2001. It was a sad day, a surreal one, for me and for the few remaining employees who had been with the company through most of its life. I already had a new office from which to operate the next phase. I wanted to take the weekend off and begin anew on Monday. That afternoon Patti and I flew the Bonanza to Marco Island for a weekend on the Gulf of Mexico.

On Monday I drove to my new office in Delray Beach to commence the next phase of the journey. Sitting at my new desk, I immersed myself in the first creative driver, appreciation. I appreciated and gave thanks for everything. This was where I chose to be; this was where I could make the biggest difference. In 1977 I had a vision that inspired me to make the effort to accomplish the things that put me in this seat behind this desk. I trusted that vision to take me to the next level of making a difference in the world. Most of the events in the vision had already occurred; several had not.

Nothing in that vision was fated or guaranteed to occur. Thoughts in people's minds all around the world caused decisions to be made and actions taken that contributed, along with other variables, to creating the world as it was on that day in December 2001. If enough of us transformed our own thought, we would transform the way the world worked in the future. I chose to contribute thoughts and actions that I believed could help create a world full of people who felt peaceful inside.

The first product I created was a two-day personal development workshop. The workshop helped produce transformational breakthroughs in the lives of the participants by giving them the tools of self-understanding and the pathway to it – namely, the practice of the five universal creative drivers. We produced the workshop in many cities in south Florida and in New York. Each workshop concluded with the same message to the participants: "You now know what peace feels like. Your experience of peace radiates from you like a beacon. People who come in contact with you will feel the peace you have found and will want to experience it for themselves. As your peace passes from person to person and they pass it along to others, the entire human population will become peaceful. We will find ways to work together and will create a sustainable and workable way of life for humanity."

When I was thirteen I was so excited about what I had discovered that I wanted to tell the world about it. I was excited because I knew that if other people experienced it they would be excited too. While looking for a connection between human and God, I found an unexpected truth that I wanted everyone to know: there is no connection between human and God because God and human are one; we are more than connected to God, we are identical with God. In the beginning was nothing and nothing called out to the darkness, "Who am I?" It was we who asked that primordial question, and in the asking we initiated the creation of everything that was, is now, or ever will be. It is this creation that reveals to us our true nature and in so doing reveals to us the true nature of God.

On the path to self-understanding, I trusted something that I could not see, hear, or touch. It led me within myself and showed me how to appreciate myself just as I was. The answer to the question, "Who am I?" was there within me all the time, and the answer is, "I am God." I learned that we are all God – the singularity of being – and we can all trust ourselves to fulfill all of our choices without judgment. Only we are accountable for making the choices and for carrying out the actions necessary to realize them. Most importantly, this answer told me that each of us can know peace within ourselves right now. In knowing peace, we can share it with each other, and in sharing it, we can live together peacefully and abundantly.

I continued speaking to people about self-understanding, and the more I spoke the more I understood. As the number of listeners increased, so did the number of questions I was asked. Among the hundreds of different questions, a long-familiar one kept recurring; it was that question first asked many years ago. And when I was asked, "Are you God?" I could only answer, "I am God and so are you."

FOR MORE INFORMATION

To learn more about manifestation, inner peace, *The Five Universal Creative Drivers*, and how you can use them in your life, please visit www.jamescwilhelm.com or www.clearpurposepress.com and download our free eighty page eBook, *Five Steps to Lasting Inner Peace*.

Also available on the web sites are several meditation CDs, a DVD about the Creative Drivers, and additional books designed to help you reach a state of peaceful openness from which to transform your world, experience lasting inner peace, and manifest your dreams.

Also please visit us on Facebook at www.facebook.com/iamgodandsoareyou and follow @jameswilhelm on Twitter for new information on enlightenment, peace, and transformation.

Contact Jim with any questions or comments by email: james@jamescwilhelm.com

CPSIA information can be obtained at www.ICGtesting.com
Printed in the USA
BVOW01s2152231013

334533BV00001B/18/P